FIRST PRINCIPLES OF THE REFORMATION

OR

THE 95 THESES AND THE THREE PRIMARY WORKS OF DR. MARTIN LUTHER

EDITED BY HENRY WACE
AND C. A. BUCHHEIM

A Digireads.com Book
Digireads.com Publishing

First Principles of the Reformation (95 Theses and Other Works)
By Martin Luther
Edited by Henry Wace and C. A. Buchheim
ISBN 10: 1-4209-4300-6
ISBN 13: 978-1-4209-4300-9

Please visit *www.digireads.com*

CONTENTS

ADVERTISEMENT

The purpose and plan of this publication, which has been prompted by the celebration of the fourth centenary of Luther's birth, is explained in the Introductory Essay. Here it is only necessary to state that, of the works of Luther contained in it, the "Address to the Nobility of the German Nation," which was written in German, has been translated by Professor Buchheim, from the text given in the Erlangen, or Frankfort, Edition. The translation of this work offered very great difficulties, as it was written in Luther's earliest German style, before the language had been improved, and rendered comparatively definite, by his translation of the Bible. Dr. Buchheim has endeavoured to make it as literal as was compatible with the genius of the English language, and with the necessity of modifying, now and then, some obscure or obsolete expression; and he has offered a few annotations. He desires, at the same time, to express his great obligations to Dr. Wace, who carefully compared his translation with the original work, and whose suggestions have been of great service to him. The Theses, and the two Treatises, "On Christian Liberty," and "On the Babylonish Captivity of the Church," have been translated from the original Latin Text, as given in the Frankfort Edition, by the Rev. R. S. Grignon, to whose generous assistance and accurate scholarship the editors feel greatly indebted.

INTRODUCTORY ESSAYS

I. ON THE PRIMARY PRINCIPLES of LUTHER'S LIFE AND TEACHING

By Dr. WACE

The present publication is offered as a contribution to the due celebration in this country of the fourth Centenary of Luther's birth. Much has been written about him, and the general history of his life and work is being sketched by able pens. But no adequate attempt has yet been made to let him speak for himself to Englishmen by his greatest and most characteristic writings. The three works which, together with the 95 Theses, are included in this volume, are well known in Germany as the *Drei Grosse Reformations-Schriften*, or "The Three Great Reformation Treatises" of Luther; but they seem never yet to have been brought in this character before the English public. The Treatise on Christian Liberty has indeed been previously translated, though not of late years. But from an examination of the catalogue in the British Museum, it would appear that no English translation is accessible, even if any has yet been published, of the Address to the German Nobility or of the Treatise on the Babylonish Captivity of the Church. Yet, as is well understood in Germany, it is in these that the whole genius of the Reformer appears in its most complete and energetic form. They are bound together in the closest dramatic unity. They were all three produced in the latter half of the critical year 1520, when nearly three years' controversy, since the publication of the Theses, on Oct. 31 1517, had convinced Luther of the falseness of the Court of Rome, and the hollowness of its claims; and they were immediately followed by the bull of excommunication in the winter of the same year, and the summons to the Diet of Worms in 1521. Luther felt, as he says at the commencement of his Address to the German Nobility, that "the time for silence had passed, and the time for speech had come." He evidently apprehended that reconciliation between himself and the Court of Rome was impossible; and he appears to have made up his mind to clear his conscience, whatever the cost. Accordingly in these three works he spoke out with a full heart, and with the consciousness that his life was in his hand, the convictions which had been forced on him by the conduct of the Papacy and of the Papal theologians.

Those convictions had been slowly, and even reluctantly, admitted; but they had gradually accumulated in intense force in Luther's mind and conscience; and when "the time for speech had come" they burst forth in a kind of volcanic eruption. Their maturity is proved by the completeness and thoroughness with which the questions at issue are treated. An insight into the deepest theological principles is combined with the keenest apprehension of practical details. In the Treatise on Christian Liberty we have the most vivid of all embodiments of that life of Faith to which the Reformer recalled the Church and which was the mainspring of the Reformation. In the Appeal to the German Nobility he first asserted those rights of the laity, and of the temporal power, without the admission of which no reformation would have been practicable, and he then denounced with burning moral indignation the numerous and intolerable abuses which were upheld by Roman authority. In the third Treatise, on the Babylonish Captivity of the Church, he applied the same cardinal principles to the elaborate Sacramental system of the Church of Rome, sweeping away by means of them the superstitions with which the original institutions of Christ had been overlaid, and thus releasing men's consciences from a vast network of ceremonial bondage. The rest of the Reformation, it is not too much to say, was but the application of the principles vindicated in these three works. They were applied in different countries with varying wisdom and moderation; but nothing essential was added to them. Luther's genius—if a higher word be not justifiable—brought forth at one birth, "with hands and feet," to use his own image, and in full energy, the vital ideas by which Europe was to be regenerated. He was no mere negative controversialist, attacking particular errors in detail. His characteristic was the masculine grasp with which he seized essential and eternal truths, and by their central light dispersed the darkness in which men were groping.

It occurred therefore to my colleague and myself that a permanent service might perhaps be rendered to Luther's name, and towards a due appreciation of the principles of the Reformation, if these short but pregnant Treatises were made more accessible to the English public; and although they might well be left to speak for themselves, there may perhaps be some readers to whom a few explanatory observations on Luther's position, theologically and politically, will not be unacceptable. My colleague, in the Essay which follows this, has dealt with the political course of the Reformation during his career; and in the present remarks an endeavour will simply be made to indicate the nature and the bearings of the central principles of the Reformer's life and work, as exhibited in the accompanying translations.

It is by no mere accident of controversy that the Ninty-five Theses mark the starting-point of Luther's career as a reformer. The subject with which they dealt was not only in close connection with the centre of Christian truth, but it touched the characteristic thought of the Middle Ages. From the beginning to the end, those ages had been a stern school of moral and religious discipline, under what was universally regarded as the divine authority of the Church. St. Anselm, with his intense apprehension of the divine righteousness, and of its inexorable demands, is at once the noblest and truest type of the great school of thought of which he was the founder. The special mission of the Church since the days of Gregory the Great had been to tame the fierce energies of the new barbarian world, and to bring the wild passions of the Teutonic races under the control of the Christian law. It was the task to which the necessities of the hour seemed to summon the Church, and she roused herself to the effort with magnificent devotion. Monks and Schoolmen performed prodigies of self-denial and self-sacrifice, in order to realise in themselves, and to impose as far as possible on the world at large, the laws of perfection which the Church held before their vision. The glorious cathedrals which arose in the best period of the Middle Ages are but the visible types of those splendid structures of ideal virtues, which a monk like St. Bernard, or a Schoolman like St. Thomas Aquinas, piled up by laborious thought and painful asceticism. Such men felt themselves at all times surrounded by a spiritual world, at once more glorious in its beauty and more awful in its terrors, than either the pleasures or the miseries of this world could adequately represent. The great poet of the Middle Ages affords perhaps the most vivid representation of their character in this respect. The horrible images of the *Inferno*, the keen sufferings of purification in the *Purgatorio*, form the terrible foreground behind which the *Paradiso* rises. Those visions of terror and dread and suffering had stamped themselves on the imagination of the medieval world, and lay at the root of the power with which the Church overshadowed it. In their origin they embodied a profound and noble truth. It was a high and divine conception that the moral and spiritual world with which we are encompassed has greater heights and lower depths than are generally apprehended in the visible experience of this life; and Dante has been felt to be in an unique degree the poet of righteousness. But it is evident, at the same time, what a terrible temptation was placed in the hands of a hierarchy who were believed, in whatever degree, to wield power over these spiritual realities. It was too easy to apply them, like the instruments of physical torture with which the age was familiar, to extort submission from tender consciences, or to make a bargain with selfish hearts. But in substance the menaces of the Church appealed to deep convictions of the human conscience, and the mass of men were not prepared to defy them.

Now it was into this world of spiritual terrors that Luther was born, and he was in an eminent degree the legitimate child of the Middle Ages. The turning-point in his history is that the awful visions of which we have spoken, the dread of the Divine judgments, brought home to him by one of the solemn accidents of life, checked him in a career which promised all worldly prosperity, and drove him into a monastery. There, as he tells us, he was driven almost frantic by his vivid realization of the demands of the Divine righteousness on the one hand, and of his own incapacity to satisfy them on the other. With the intense reality characteristic of his nature he took in desperate earnest all that the traditional teaching and example of the Middle Ages had taught him of the unbending necessities of Divine justice. But for the very reason that he accepted those necessities with such earnestness, he did but realize the more completely the hopelessness of his struggles to bring himself into conformity with them. It was not because he was out of sympathy with St. Anselm or St. Bernard or Dante, that he burst the bonds of the system they represented; but, on the contrary, because he entered even more deeply than they into the very truths they asserted. Nothing was more certain to him than that Divine justice is inexorable; no conviction was more deeply fixed in his heart than that righteousness is the supreme law of human life. But the more he realized the truth, the more terrible he found it, for it seemed to shut him up in a cruel prison, against the bars of which he beat himself in vain. In one of his most characteristic passages, in the Introduction to his Latin Works, he describes how he was repelled and appalled by the statement of St. Paul respecting the Gospel, that 'therein is the righteousness, or justice, of God revealed.' For, he says, 'however irreprehensible a life I had lived as a monk, I felt myself before God a sinner, with a most restless conscience, and I could not be confident that He was appeased by my satisfaction. I could not, therefore, love—nay, I hated—a God who was just and punished sinners; and if not with silent blasphemy, certainly with vehement murmuring, I was indignant against God. As if, I said, it were not enough that sinners, miserable and eternally ruined by original sin, should be crushed with all kind of calamity by the law of the Decalogue, but God by the Gospel must needs add grief to grief, and by the Gospel itself must inflict still further on us His justice and anger. I raged with this savage and disturbed conscience, and I knocked importunately at Paul in that place, with burning thirst to know what St. Paul could mean.' Such an experience is not a mere revolt against the Middle Ages. In great measure it is but the full realization of their truest teaching. It is Dante intensified, and carried to the inevitable development of his principles.

But if this be the case, what it meant was that the Middle Ages had brought men to a deadlock. They had led men up to a gate so strait that no human soul could pass through it. In the struggle, men had devised the most elaborate forms of self-torture, and had made the most heroic sacrifices, and in the very desperation of their efforts they had anticipated the more vivid insight and experience of Luther. The effort, in fact, had been too much for human nature, and the end of it had been that the Church had condescended to human weakness. The most obvious and easy way out of the difficulty was to modify, by virtue of some dispensing authority, the extreme requirements of Divine justice, and by a variety of half-unconscious, half-acknowledged devices, to lessen the severity of the strait gate and of the narrow way. Such a power, as has been said, was an enormous temptation to unscrupulous Churchmen, and at length it led to the hideous abuses of such preaching of indulgences as that of Tetzel. In this form the matter came before Luther in his office as parish priest and confessor; and it will be apparent from the Theses that what first revolts him is the violation involved of the deepest principles which the Church of his day had taught him. He had learned from it the inexorable character of the Divine law, the necessity and blessedness of the Divine discipline of punishment and suffering; he had learned, as his first Thesis declares, that the law of Christian life is that of lifelong penitence; and he denounced Tetzel's teaching as false to the Church herself, in full confidence that he would be supported by his ecclesiastical superiors. When he found that he was not—when, to his surprise and consternation, he found that the Papal theologians of the day, under the direct patronage of the Pope and the bishops, were ready to support the most flagrant evasions of the very principles on which their power had originally been based—then at length, though most reluctantly, he turned against them, and directed against the corrupted Church of the close of the Middle Ages the very principles he had learned from its best representatives and from its noblest institutions.

Luther, in the course of his spiritual struggles, had found the true deliverance from what we have ventured to call that deadlock to which the grand vision of Divine righteousness had led him. He realised that the strait gate was impassable by any human virtue; but he had found the solution in the promise of a supernatural deliverance which was offered to faith. To quote again his words in the preface to his Latin works already referred to: 'At length by the mercy of God, meditating days and nights, I observed the connection of the words namely "therein is the righteousness of God revealed from faith to faith, as it is written: The just shall live by faith." Then I began to understand the justice of God to be that by which the just man lives by the gift of God, namely, by faith, and that the meaning was that the Gospel reveals that justice of God by which He justifies us beggars through faith, as it is written: "The just shall live by faith." Here I felt myself absolutely born again; the gates of heaven were opened, and I had entered paradise itself. From thenceforward the face of the whole Scriptures appeared changed to me. I ran through the Scriptures, as my memory would serve me, and observed the same analogy in other words—as, the work of God, that is, the work which God works in us; the strength of God, that with which He makes us strong; the wisdom of God, that with which He makes us wise; the power of God, the salvation of God, the glory of God. And now, as much as I had formerly hated that word, the Justice of God, so much did I now love it and extol it as the sweetest of words to me; and thus that place in Paul was to me truly the gate of paradise.' In other words, Luther had realised that the Gospel, while reasserting the inexorable nature of the moral law, and deepening its demands, had revealed a supernatural and divine means of satisfying and fulfilling it. All barriers had thus been removed between God and man, and men had been placed in the position of children living by Faith on His grace and bounty. He offers to bestow upon them the very righteousness He requires from them, if they will but accept it at His hands as a free gift. Their true position is no longer that of mere subjects living under a law which they must obey at their peril. They may, indeed, by their own act remain in that condition, with all its terrible consequences. But God invites them to regard Him as their Father, to live in the light of His countenance, and to receive from Him the daily food of their souls. The most intimate personal relation is thus established between Himself and them; and the righteousness which they could never acquire by their own efforts He is ready to create in them if they will but live with Him in faith and trust. That faith, indeed, must needs be the beginning, and the most essential condition, of this Divine life. Faith is the first condition of all fellowship between persons; and if a man is to live in personal fellowship with God, he must trust Him absolutely, believe His promises, and rest his whole existence, here and hereafter, upon His word. But let a man do this, and then God's law ceases to be like a flaming sword, turning every way, with too fierce an edge for human hearts to bear. It assumes the benignant glow of a revelation of perfect righteousness which God Himself will bestow on all who ask it at His hands.

This belief is essentially bound up with a distinction on which great stress is laid in the Theses. It touches a point at once of the highest theological import, and of the simplest practical experience. This is the distinction between guilt and punishment; or, in other words, between personal forgiveness, and the remission of the consequences of sins. In our mutual relations, a son may be forgiven by his father, a wrongdoer by the person whom he has injured, and yet it may neither be possible nor desirable that the offender should be at once released from the consequences of his offence. But for all generous hearts, the personal forgiveness is infinitely more precious than the remission of the penalty, and Luther had learned from the Scriptures to regard our relation to God in a similar light. He realized that he must live, here and hereafter, in personal relationship to God; and the forgiveness of God, the removal from him, in God's sight, of the imputation and the brand of guilt, his reception into God's unclouded favour—this was the supreme necessity of his spiritual existence. If this were assured to him, not only had he no fear of punishment, but he could welcome it, whatever its severity, as part of the discipline of the divine and loving hand to which he had trusted himself. His deepest indignation, consequently, was aroused by preaching which, under official sanction, urged men to buy indulgence from punishment, of whatever kind, as practically the greatest spiritual benefit they could obtain; and he devoted his whole energy to assert the supreme blessing of that remission from guilt, of which the preachers of indulgences said practically nothing. It is this remission of guilt, this personal forgiveness, which is the essential element in the justification of which he spoke. It involves of course salvation from the final ruin and doom which sin, and the moral corruption of our nature, would naturally entail; but its chief virtue does not consist in deliverance from punishment, nor does it in any way derogate from the truth that "we must all appear before the judgment seat of Christ, that every one may receive the things done in his body, according to that he hath done, whether it be good or bad." What it taught men was to accept all God's judgements and discipline in perfect peace of soul, as being assured of His love and favour.

No divine, in fact, has ever dwelt with more intense conviction on the blessedness of the discipline of suffering and of the Cross. The closing Theses express his deepest feelings in this respect, and a passage in one of his letters, written before the controversy about Indulgences had arisen, affords a most interesting illustration of the manner in which the principles he came forward to assert had grown out of his personal experience. "Away," he says, in the 92nd and 93rd Theses, "with all those prophets who say to the people of Christ, 'Peace, peace,' and there is no peace. Blessed be all those prophets who say to the people of Christ, 'The Cross, the Cross,' and there is no Cross." These somewhat enigmatic expressions are at once explained in the letter referred to, written to a Prior of the Augustinian order, on the 22nd of June, 1516.[1] He says:—

"You are seeking and craving for peace, but in the wrong order. For you are seeking it as the world giveth, not as Christ giveth. Know you not that God is 'wonderful among His saints,' for this reason, that He establishes His peace in the midst of no peace, that is, of all temptations and afflictions.' It is said 'Thou shalt dwell in the midst of thine enemies.' The man who possesses peace is not the man whom no one disturbs—that is the peace of the world; he is the man whom all men and all things disturb, but who bears all patiently, and with joy. You are saying with Israel, 'Peace, peace,' and there is no peace. Learn to say rather with Christ: 'The Cross, the Cross,' and there is no Cross. For the Cross at once ceases to be the Cross as soon as you have joyfully exclaimed, in the language of the hymn,

> "'Blessed Cross, above all other,
> One and only noble tree.'"

One other extract of the same import it may be well to quote from these early letters, as it is similarly the germ of one of the noblest passages in Luther's subsequent explanation of the Ninety-five Theses.[2] The letter was addressed to a brother Augustinian on the 15th of April, 1516. Luther says:—

"The cross of Christ has been divided throughout the whole world, and every one meets with his own portion of it. Do not you therefore reject it, but rather accept it as the most holy relic, to be kept, not in a gold or silver chest, but in a golden heart, that is, a heart imbued with gentle charity. For if, by contact with the flesh and blood of Christ, the wood of the Cross received such consecration that its relics are deemed supremely precious, how much more should injuries, persecutions, sufferings and the hatred of men,

[1] *Letters*, edited by De Wette, i. 27.
[2] It is a pleasure to be able to refer for this passage to the first volume of the new Critical Edition of Luther's works, just published in Germany, page 613, line 21. This magnificent edition, prepared under the patronage of the German Emperor, is the best of all contributions to the present Commemoration. It must supersede all other editions, and it ought to find a place in all considerable libraries in England. A translation of the passage in question will be found in the Bampton Lectures of the present writer, p. 186.

whether of the just or of the unjust, be regarded as the most sacred of all relics—relics which, not by the mere touch of His flesh, but by the charity of His most bitterly tried heart and of His divine will, were embraced, kissed, blessed, and abundantly consecrated; for thus was a curse transformed into a blessing, and injury into justice, and passion into glory, and the Cross into joy."[3]

The few letters, in fact, in our possession, written by Luther before he came forward in 1517, are sufficient to afford the most vivid proof both of the mature thought and experience in which his convictions were rooted, and of their being prompted, not by the spirit of reckless confidence to which they have sometimes been ignorantly ascribed, but by the deepest sympathy with the lessons of the Cross. The purport of his characteristic doctrine of justification by faith was not to give men the assurance of immunity from suffering and sorrow, as the consequence of sin, but to give them peace of conscience and joy of heart in the midst of such punishments. What it proclaimed was that, if men would but believe it, they could at any moment grasp God's forgiveness, and live henceforth in the assured happiness of His personal favour and love. Of this blessing His promise was the only possible warrant, and like all other promises, it could only be accepted by Faith. Every man is invited to believe it, since it is offered to all for Christ's sake; but by the nature of the case, none can enjoy it who do not believe it.

The ground, however, on which this promise was based affords another striking illustration of the way in which Luther's teaching was connected with that of the Middle Age. Together with that keen apprehension of the divine judgments and of human sin just mentioned, the awful vision of our Lord's sufferings and of His atonement overshadowed the whole thought of those times. St. Anselm, in *the Cur Deus Homo*, had aroused deeper meditation on this subject than had before been bestowed upon it; and in this, as in other matters, he is the type of the grand school of thought which he founded. As in his mind, so throughout the Middle Age, in proportion to the apprehension of the terrible nature of the Divine justice, is the prominence given to the sacrificial means for averting the Divine wrath. The innumerable Masses of the later Middle Ages were so many confessions of the deep-felt need of atonement; and formal as they ultimately became, they were in intention so many cries for forgiveness from the terrorstruck consciences of sinful men and women. Luther was a true child of the Church in his deep apprehension of the same need, and it was precisely because he realised it with exceptional truth and depth that he was forced to seek some deeper satisfaction than the offering of Masses could afford. He reasserted the truth that the need had been met and answered once for all by the Sacrifice on the Cross; and by proclaiming the sufficiency of that one eternal offering he swept away all the "Sacrifices of Masses," while at the same time he provided the answer to the craving to which they testified. The doctrine of the Atonement, as asserted at the Reformation, is the true answer to that cry of the human conscience which the Church of the preceding age had vainly endeavoured to satisfy. The Sacrament, of which the Mass was a perversion, was thus restored to its true character on a pledge and an instrument of blessings bestowed by God, instead of a propitiatory offering on the part of men. The Cross of Christ, the favourite symbol of the mediæval Church, was thus held aloft by the Reformer in still deeper reality, as the central symbol of the Church's message, and as the one adequate ground for the faith to which he called men.

Now the view of the Christian life involved in this principle of Justification by Faith found its most complete and beautiful expression in the Treatise "On Christian Liberty,"

---

[3] *Letters*, edited by De Wette, i. p. 19.

translated in this volume; and a brief notice of the teaching of that treatise will best serve to explain the connection between Luther's cardinal doctrine and the other principles which he asserted. As is explained at the close of the introductory letter to Leo X. (p. 101), he designed it as a kind of peaceoffering to the Pope, and as a declaration of the sole objects he had at heart, and to which he desired to devote his life. "It is a small matter," he says, "if you look to its bulk, but unless I mistake, it is a summary of the Christian life in small compass, if you apprehend its meaning." In fact, it presents the most complete view of Luther's theology, alike in its principles and in its practice, almost entirely disembarrassed of the controversial elements by which, under the inevitable pressure of circumstances, his other works, and especially those of a later date, were disturbed. Perhaps the only part of his works to compare with it in this respect is the precious collection of his House-postills, or Exposition of the Gospels for the Sundays of the Christian Year. They were delivered within his domestic circle, and recorded by two of his pupils, and though but imperfectly reported, they are treasures of Evangelical exposition, exhibiting in a rare degree the exquisitely childlike character of the Reformer's faith, and marked by all the simplicity and the poetry of feeling by which his mind was distinguished. It is by such works as these, and not simply by his controversial treatises or commentaries, that Luther must be judged, if we wish either to understand his inner character, or to comprehend the vast personal influence he exerted. But in its essence, the Gospel which he preached, the substance of what he had learned from the temptations, the prayers, the meditations—*tentationes, orationes, meditationes*—of his life as a monk, is sufficiently embodied in the short Treatise on Christian Liberty.

The argument of the Treatise is summed up, with the antithetical force so often characteristic of great genius, in the two propositions laid down at the outset. "A Christian man is the most free lord of all and subject to none: A Christian man is the most dutiful servant of all, and subject to every one." The first of these propositions expresses the practical result of the doctrine of Justification by Faith. The Christian is in possession of a promise of God, which in itself, and in the assurance it involves, is a greater blessing to him than all other privileges or enjoyments whatever. Everything sinks into insignificance compared with this word and Gospel. "Let us," he says, "hold it for certain and firmly established that the soul can do without everything except the word of God, without which none of its wants are provided for. But, having the word, it is rich and wants for nothing, since it is the word of life, of truth, of light, of peace, of justification, of salvation, of joy, of liberty, of wisdom, of virtue, of grace, of glory, and of every good thing." If it be asked, "What is this word?" he answers that the Apostle Paul explains it, namely that "it is the Gospel of God, concerning His Son, incarnate, suffering, risen, and glorified through the Spirit, the Sanctifier. To preach Christ is to feed the soul, to justify it, to set it free, and to save it, if it believes the preaching . . . For the word of God cannot be received and honoured by any works, but by Faith alone." This is the cardinal point around which not merely Luther's theology, but his whole life turns. God had descended into the world, spoken to him by His Son, His Apostles, the Scriptures, and the voice of the Church, and promised him forgiveness in the present, and final deliverance from his evil in the future, if he would but trust Him. The mere possession of such a promise outweighed in Luther's view all other considerations whatever, and absolute faith was due to it. No higher offence could be offered to God than to reject or doubt His promise, and at the same time no higher honour could be rendered Him than to believe it. The importance and value of the virtue of Faith is thus determined entirely by the promise on which it rests. These "promises of God are words of holiness, truth, righteousness, liberty, and peace, and are full of universal goodness, and the soul which cleaves to them with a firm faith is so united to them, nay, thoroughly absorbed by them, that it not only partakes in, but is penetrated and saturated by all their virtue. For if the touch of Christ was health, how much more does that most tender spiritual touch, nay, absorption of the word, communicate to the soul all that belongs to the word? In this way, therefore, the soul through faith alone, without works, is by the word of God justified, sanctified, endued with truth, peace, and liberty, and filled full with every good thing, and is truly made the child of God . . . As is the word, such is the soul made by it; just as iron exposed to fire glows like fire on account of its union with the fire." Moreover, just as it is faith which unites husband and wife, so faith in Christ unites the soul to Him in indissoluble union. For "if a true marriage, nay, by far the most perfect of all marriages, is accomplished between them—for human marriages are but feeble types of this one great marriage—then it follows that all they have becomes theirs in common, as well good things as evil things; so that whatsoever Christ possesses, the believing soul may take to itself and boast of as its own, and whatever belongs to the soul, Christ claims as his . . . Thus the believing soul, by the pledge of its faith in Christ, becomes free from all sin, fearless of death, safe from hell, and endowed with the eternal righteousness, life and salvation of its husband Christ."

It is essential to dwell upon these passages, since, the force of the Reformer's great doctrine cannot possibly be apprehended as long as he is supposed to attribute the efficacy of which he speaks to any inherent quality in the human heart itself. It is the word and promise of God which is the creative force. But this summons a man into a sphere above this world, bids him rest upon the divine love which speaks to him, and places him on the eternal foundation of a direct covenant with God Himself in Christ. As in the Theses, so in this Treatise, Luther reiterates that it in no way implies exemption from the discipline of suffering. "Yea," he says, "the more of a Christian any man is, to so many the more evils, sufferings, and deaths is he subject; as we see in the first place in Christ the first-born and in all His holy brethren." The power of which he speaks is a spiritual one "which rules in the midst of enemies, in the midst of distresses. It is nothing else than that strength is made perfect in my weakness, and that I can turn all things to the profit of my salvation; so that even the cross and death are compelled to serve me and to work together for my salvation." "It is a lofty and eminent dignity, a true and Almighty dominion, a spiritual empire in which there is nothing so good, nothing so bad, as not to work together for my good, if only I believe."

If we compare this language with those conceptions of spiritual terror by which Luther had been driven into a monastery, and under which, like so many in his age, he had groaned and struggled in despair, we can appreciate the immense deliverance which he had experienced. The Divine promise had lifted him "out of darkness and out of the shadow of death, and had broken his bonds in sunder." It is this which is the source of the undaunted and joyful faith which marks the whole of the Reformer's public career. "Whose heart," he exclaims, "would not rejoice in its inmost core at hearing these things? Whose heart, on receiving so great a consolation, would not become sweet with the love of Christ: a love to which it can never attain by any laws or works? Who can injure such a heart, or make it afraid? If the consciousness of sin, or the horror of death rush in upon it, it is prepared to hope in the Lord, and is fearless of these evils and undisturbed, until it shall look down upon its enemies." Such a conviction, uttered in such burning language, lifted the same cloud of darkness and fear from the hearts of the common people of that day, and was welcomed as good tidings of great joy by multitudes of burdened and terror-stricken hearts. Nothing is more characteristic of Luther's preaching, and of the Reformers who follow him, than the sense they display that they have before them souls "weary and heavy-laden." Their language presupposes the prevalence of that atmosphere of spiritual apprehension and gloom already described, and their grand aim is to lead men out of it into the joy and peace and liberty of the Gospel. The consequence is that a new confidence, hope and energy is infused into the moral and spiritual world of that day. The tone of unbounded joy and hope which marks the earliest Christian literature, particularly in the Apostolic Fathers, re-appears in such a Treatise as we are considering, and in the whole religious thought of the Reformers; and it would almost seem as if the long agony of the Middle Ages had but enhanced the joy of the final deliverance.

It is unnecessary, for our present purpose, to dwell long upon the second point of the Treatise, in which Luther illustrates his second proposition that "a Christian man is the most dutiful servant of all and subject to every one." It will be enough to observe that Luther is just as earnest in insisting upon the application of faith in the duties of charity and self-discipline as upon the primary importance of faith itself. The spirit of faith, he says, "applies itself with cheerfulness and zeal" to restrain and repress the impulses of the lower nature. "Here works begin; here a man must not take his ease; here he must give heed to exercise his body by fastings, watchings, labour, and other reasonable discipline, so that it may be subdued to the spirit, and obey and conform itself to the inner man and to faith." Similarly, he will give himself up to the service of others, and it is partly with a view to rendering them such service that he will discipline his body and keep it in due energy and soundness. He starts from the belief that God, without merit on his part, has of his pure and free mercy bestowed on him, an unworthy creature, all the riches of justification and salvation in Christ, so that he is no longer in want of anything except of faith to believe that this is so. For such a Father, then, who has overwhelmed him with these inestimable riches of His, must he not freely, cheerfully, and from voluntary zeal, do all that he knows will be pleasing to Him and acceptable in His sight? "I will, therefore," he says, "give myself as a sort of Christ to my neighbour, as Christ has given Himself to me; and will do nothing in this life except what I see will be needful, advantageous and wholesome for my neighbour, since by faith I abound in all good things in Christ." These practical considerations will afford the measure by which a man determines the discipline to which he subjects himself, and the ceremonies which he observes. They will not be observed for their own sake, but as means to an end, and therefore will never be practised in excess, as though there were some merit in the performance of them. They are like the scaffoldings of builders, valuable only as a temporary assistance, in the construction of the building itself. "We do not condemn works and ceremonies; nay, we set the highest value on them. We only condemn that opinion of works which regards them as constituting true righteousness." In asserting these principles, Luther was certainly putting the axe to the root of the portentous growth of ascetic and ceremonial observances which prevailed in his day, and which were too generally regarded as of the very essence of religion. He enabled men, as it were, to look on such ceremonies from the outside, as a thing external to them, and to reduce or rearrange them with a simple view to practical usefulness. But no more earnest exhortations to due self-discipline, and to true charity, could well be found than are contained in the second part of the *De Libertate*.

It will be evident, however, what a powerful instrument of reformation was placed in men's hands by the principles of this Treatise. Every Christian man, by virtue of the promise of Christ, was proclaimed free, so far as the eternal necessities of his soul were concerned, from all external and human conditions whatever. Nothing, indeed, was further from Luther's intention or inclination than the overthrow of existing order, or the disparagement of any existing authority which could be reasonably justified. His letter to Pope Leo, prefixed to the Treatise we have been considering, shows that while denouncing unsparingly the abuses of the Court of Rome, he was sincere in his deference to the See of Rome itself. But the principle of justification enabled him to proclaim that if that See or any existing Church authority, misused its power, and refused to reform abuses, then, in the last resort, the soul of man could do without it. In that day at all events—and perhaps in our own to a greater extent than is sometimes supposed—this conviction supplied the fulcrum which was essential for any effectual reforming movement. As is observed by the Church historian Gieseler, in his admirable account of the early history of the Reformation, the Papacy had ever found its strongest support in the people at large. In spite of all the discontent and disgust provoked by the corruption of the Church and the clergy, an enormous though indefinite authority was still popularly attributed to the Pope and the ecclesiastical hierarchy. The Pope was believed to be in some sense or other the supreme administrator of spiritual powers which were effectual in the next world as well as in the present; and consequently when any controversy with the Church came to a crisis, men shrank from direct defiance of the Papal authority. They did not feel that they had any firm ground on which they could stand if they incurred its formal condemnation; and thus it always had at its command, in the strongest possible sense, the *ultima ratio* of rulers. The convictions to which Luther had been led at once annihilated these pretensions. "One thing and one alone," he declared, "is necessary for life, justification and Christian liberty, and that is, the most holy word of God, the Gospel of Christ." As we have seen, he proclaimed it "for certain, and firmly established, that the soul can do without everything except the word of God." It is the mission of the Christian ministry, in its administration of the Word and Sacraments, to convey this Gospel to the soul, and to arouse a corresponding faith. But the promise is not annexed indissolubly to that administration, and the only invariable rule of salvation is that "the just shall live by faith." By this principle, that vague fear of the spiritual powers of the hierarchy was removed, and men were endowed with real Christian liberty.

But the principle went still further; for it vindicated for the laity the possession of spiritual faculties and powers the same in kind as those of the clergy. All Christian men are admitted to the privilege of priesthood, and are "worthy to appear before God to pray for others, and to teach one another mutually the things which are of God." In case of necessity, as is universally recognized, Baptism can be validly administered by lay hands, and English Divines, of the most unimpeachable authority on the subject, have similarly recognized that the valid administration of the Holy Communion is not dependent on the ordination of the minister by Episcopal authority.[4] Luther urges accordingly that all Christians possess virtually the capacities which, as a matter of order, are commonly restricted to the clergy. Whether that restriction is properly dependent upon regular devolution from Apostolic authority, or whether the ministerial commission can be sufficiently conferred by appointment from the Christian community or congregation as a whole, becomes on this principle a secondary point. Luther pronounced with the utmost decision in favour of the latter alternative; but the essential element of his teaching is independent of this question. By whatever right the exercise of the ministry may be restricted to a particular body of men, what he asserted was that the functions of the

---

See, for instance, Bp. Cosin's *Works, Appendix*, vol. i., 31, in *the Library of Anglo-Catholic Theology*.

clergy are simply ministerial, and that they do but exercise, on behalf of all, powers which all virtually possess. This principle Luther proceeded to assert in the first of the Treatises translated in this volume, the "Address to the Christian Nobility of the German Nation respecting the Reformation of the Christian Estate." This Treatise is perhaps the one which appealed most widely and directly to the German nation at large. Luther completed it at the very moment when the Bull of excommunication against him was being prepared, and it contributed, perhaps more than anything, to paralyze the influence of that Bull with the mass of the people and their lay leaders. It appeared in August, 1520, and by the 18th of that month more than four thousand copies had been already dispersed—a prodigious circulation, considering the state of literature at that day. The reader, however, will not be surprised at this popularity of the Treatise when he sees with what astonishing vigour, frankness, humour, good sense, and at the same time intense moral indignation, Luther denounces in it the corruptions of the Church, and the injuries inflicted by the Court of Rome on the German people. So tremendous an indictment, sustained with such intense and concentrated force, could hardly be paralleled in literature. The truth of the charges alleged in it could be amply sustained by reference to Erasmus's works alone, particularly to the *Encomium Moriæ*; but Erasmus lacked alike the moral energy necessary to rouse the action of the laity, and the spiritual insight necessary to justify that action. Luther possessed both; and it was the combination of the two which rendered him so mighty a force. It is this perhaps which essentially distinguishes him from previous reformers. They attacked particular errors and abuses, and deserve unbounded honour for the protests they raised, and Wycliff in particular merits the homage of Englishmen as one of the chief motive powers in the first reforming movement. But they did not assert, at least with sufficient clearness, the central principle without which all reform was impracticable—that of the equal rights of laity and clergy, and of the soul's independence of all human power, by virtue of the truth of Justification by Faith. Luther's doctrine of Christian liberty was the emancipation alike of individuals and of the laity at large. It vindicated for the whole lay estate, and for all ranks and conditions of lay life, a spiritual dignity, and a place in the spiritual life of the Church. It restored a sense of independent responsibility to all natural authorities; and it reasserted the sacredness of all natural relations. Practically, even if not theoretically, the Roman system had disparaged the ordinary relations of life as compared with the so-called "religious" or ecclesiastical. Luther, by placing all men and women on the same spiritual standing ground, swept away any such privileges; and gave men as clear a conscience, and as great a sense of spiritual dignity, in the ordinary duties of marriage, of fatherhood, and in the common offices of life, as in any ecclesiastical order.

The "Address to the Nobility of the German Nation" exhibits these principles, and their application to the practical problems of the day, in the most vigorous and popular form; and if some expressions appear too sweeping and violent, due allowance must be made for the necessity which Luther must have felt of appealing with the utmost breadth and force to the popular mind. But it remains to consider a further aspect of these principles which is illustrated by the third Treatise translated in this volume—that on the "Babylonish Captivity of the Church." Luther, as has been seen, was appealing to laity and clergy alike, on the ground of their spiritual freedom, to abolish the abuses of the Roman Church. But it became at once a momentous question by what principles the exercise of that liberty was to be guided, and within what limits it was to be exerted. In a very short time fanatics sprung up, who claimed to exercise such liberty without any restrictions at all, and who refused to recognize any standard but that of their own supposed inspiration. But the service which Luther rendered in repelling such abuses of his great doctrine was only second to that of establishing the doctrine itself. The rule of faith and practice on which he insisted was indeed necessarily involved in his primary principle. Faith, as has been seen, was with him no abstract quality, but was simply a response to the word and promise of God. That word, accordingly, in its various forms, was in Luther's mind the sole creative power of the Christian life. In the form of a simple promise, it is the basis of justification and of our whole spiritual existence; and similarly in its more general form, as recorded in the Holy Scriptures, it contains all truths, alike of belief and of practice, which are essential to salvation here and hereafter. The word of God, in whatever form, whether a simple promise, or a promise embodied in a Sacrament, or a series of revelations made by God's Spirit to the soul of man, as recorded in the Bible, is the grand reality which, in Luther's view, dwarfed all other realities on earth. It must needs do so, if it be a reality at all; but no one has ever grasped this truth with such intense insight as Luther. Consequently, in his view, the Anabaptist, who held himself emancipated from the authority of God's word on the one side, was as grievously in error as the Romanist on the other, who superseded its authority by that of the Church; and in applying his great principle and working out the Reformation, Luther's task consisted in upholding the due authority of the Scriptures against the extremes on both sides.

Now in the Treatise on the Babylonish Captivity of the Church he applies this rule, in connection with his main principle, to the elaborate sacramental system of the Church of Rome. Of the seven sacraments recognised by that church, he recognizes, strictly speaking, only two, Baptism and the Lord's Supper; and the connection of this conclusion with the central truth he was asserting is a point of deep interest. Here, too, the one consideration which overpowers every other in his view is the supreme import of a promise or word of God. But there are two institutions under the Gospel which are distinguished from all others by a visible sign, instituted by Christ Himself, as a pledge of the Divine promise. A sign so instituted, and with such a purpose, constituted a peculiarly precious form of those Divine promises which are the life of the soul; and for the same reason that the Divine word and the Divine promise are supreme in all other instances, so must these be supreme and unique among ceremonies. The distinction, by which the two Sarcaments acknowledged by the Reformed Churches are separated from the remaining five of the Roman Church, is thus no question of names but of things. It was a question whether a ceremony instituted by Christ's own command, and embodying His own promise in a visible pledge, could for a moment be put on the same level with ceremonies, however edifying, which had been established solely by the authority or custom of the Church. It was of the essence of Luther's teaching to assert a paramount distinction between these classes of ceremonies and to elevate the two Divine pledges of forgiveness and spiritual life to a height immeasurably superior to all other institutions. He hesitates, indeed, whether to allow an exception in favour of Absolution, as conveying undoubtedly a direct promise from Christ; but he finally decides against it, on the ground that it is without any visible and divinely appointed sign, and is after all only an application of the Sacrament of Baptism.

If, moreover, the force of his argument on this subject is to be apprehended, due attention must be paid to the efficacy which he thus attributes to the two Sacraments. The cardinal point on which he insists in respect to them is that they are direct pledges from God, through Christ, and thus contain the whole virtue of the most solemn Divine promises. They are, as it were, the sign and seal of those promises. They are messages from God, not mere acts of devotion on the part of man. In Baptism the point of importance is not that men dedicate themselves or their children to Him, but that He, through His minister, gives them a promise and a pledge of His forgiveness, and of His Fatherly good will. Similarly in the Holy Communion the most important point is not the offering made on the part of man, but the promise and assurance of communion with the Body and Blood of Christ, made on the part of God. It is this which constitutes the radical distinction between the Lutheran and the so-called Zwinglian view of the Sacraments. Under the latter view they are ceremonies which embody and arouse due feelings on the part of men. On the former principle, they are ceremonies which embody direct messages and promises from God.

It may be worth while to observe in passing the position which Luther assumes towards the doctrine of Transubstantiation. What he is concerned to maintain is that there is a Real Presence in the Sacrament. All he is concerned to deny is that Transubstantiation is the necessary explanation of that Presence. In other words, it is not necessary to believe in Transubstantiation in order to believe in the Real Presence. There seems a clear distinction between this view and the formal doctrine of Consubstantiation as afterwards elaborated by Lutheran divines; and Luther's caution, at least in this Treatise, in dealing with so difficult a point, is eminently characteristic of the real moderation with which he formed his views, as distinguished from the energy with which he asserted them. Another interesting point in this Treatise is the urgency with which he protests against the artificial restraints upon the freedom of marriage which had been imposed by the Roman See. It would have been too much to expect that in applying, single-handed, to so difficult a subject as marriage, the rule of rejecting every restriction not expressly declared in the Scriptures, Luther should have avoided mistakes. But they are at least insignificant in comparison with the value of the principle he asserted, that all questions of the marriage relation should be subjected to the authority of Holy Scripture alone. That principle provided, by its inherent force, a remedy for any errors in particulars which Luther or any individual divine might commit. The Roman principle, on the contrary, admitted of the most scandalous and unlimited elasticity; and of all the charges brought by Roman controversialists against Luther's conduct, none is marked by such effrontery as their accusations on this point. While there are few dispensations which their Church is not prepared, for what it considers due causes, to allow, Luther recalled men's consciences to the Divine law on the subject. He reasserted the true dignity and sanctity of the marriage relation, and established the rule of Holy Scripture as the standard for its due control.

Such are the main truths asserted in the Treatises translated in this volume, and it is but recognising an historical fact to designate them "First Principles of the Reformation." From them, and by means of them, the whole of the subsequent movement was worked out. They were applied in different countries in different ways; and we are justly proud in this country of the wisdom and moderation exhibited by our Reformers. But it ought never to be forgotten that for the assertion of the principles themselves, we, like the rest of Europe, are indebted to the genius and the courage of Luther. All of those principles—Justification by Faith, Christian Liberty, the spiritual rights and powers of the Laity, the true character of the Sacraments, the supremacy of the Holy Scriptures as the supreme standard of belief and practice—were asserted by the Reformer, as the Treatises in this volume bear testimony, almost simultaneously, in the latter half of the year 1520. At the time he asserted them, the Roman Church was still in full power; and the year after he had to face the whole authority of the Papacy and of the Empire, and to decide whether, at the risk of a fate like that of Huss, he would stand by these truths. These were the truths—the cardinal principles of the whole subsequent Reformation, which he was called on to abandon at Worms; and his refusal to act against his conscience at once translated them into vivid action and reality. It was one thing for Englishmen, several decades after 1520, to apply these principles with the wisdom and moderation of which we are proud. It was another thing to be the Horatius of that vital struggle. These grand facts speak for themselves, and need only to be understood in order to justify the unprecedented honours now being paid to the Reformer's memory.

It may not, however, be out of place to dwell in conclusion upon one essential characteristic of the Reformer's position, which is in danger at the present day of being disregarded. The general effect of this teaching upon the condition of the world is evident. It restored to the people at large, to rulers and to ruled, to clergy and laity alike, complete independence of the existing ecclesiastical system, within the limits of the revelation contained in the Holy Scriptures. In a word, in Luther's own phrase, it established Christian Liberty. But the qualification is emphatic, and it would be wholly to misunderstand Luther if it were disregarded. Attempts are made at the present day to represent him as a pioneer of absolute liberty, and to treat it as a mere accident of his teaching and his system that he stopped short where he did. But on the contrary, the limitation is of the very essence of his teaching, because that teaching is based on the supremacy and sufficiency of the Divine word and the Divine promise. If there were no such word and promise, no such Divine revelation, and no living God to bring it home to men's hearts, and to enforce His own laws, Luther felt that his protest against existing authority, usurped and tyrannical as it might be, would have been perilous in the extreme. But when men shrank from the boldness of his proclamation, and urged that he was overthrowing the foundations of Society, his reply was that he was recalling them to the true foundations of Society, and that God, if they would have faith in Him, would protect His own word and will. The very essence of his teaching is summed up in the lines of his great Psalm:

> "Das Wort sie sollen lassen stahn,
> Und kein Dank dazu haben,
>   Er ist bei uns wohl auf dem Plan
>   Mit seinem Geist und Gaben."

Luther believed that God had laid down the laws which were essential to the due guidance of human nature, that he had prescribed sufficiently the limits within which that nature might range, and had indicated the trees of which it could not safely eat. To erect any rules beyond these as of general obligation, to restrict the free play of nature by any other limitations, he treated as an unjust violation of liberty, which would provoke a dangerous reaction. But let men be brought face to face with God, and with His reasonable and merciful laws, let them be taught that He is their Father, that all His restrictions are for their benefit, all His punishments for their reformation, all His restraints on liberty for their ultimate good, and you have then established an authority which cannot be shaken, and under which human nature may be safely left to develop. In this faith, but in this alone, he let loose men's natural instincts, he taught men that married life, and lay life, and all lawful occupations, were holy and divine, provided they were carried on in faith and in obedience to God's will. The result was a burst of new life wherever the Reformation was adopted, alike in national energies, in literature, in all social developments, and in natural science. But while we prize and celebrate the liberty thus won, let us beware of forgetting, or allowing others to forget, that it is essentially a Christian Liberty, and that no other Liberty is really free. Luther's whole work, and his whole power, lay in his recognition of our personal relation to God, and of a direct revelation, promise, and command, given to us by God. Any influences, under whatever colour, which tend to obscure the reality of that revelation, which would substitute for it any mere natural laws or forces, are undoing Luther's work, and contradicting his most essential principles. If he was a great Reformer, it was because he was a great divine; if he was a friend of the people, it was because he was the friend of God.

II. THE POLITICAL COURSE of the REFORMATION IN GERMANY

(1517–1546.)

By PROFESSOR BUCHHEIM.

I.

There is hardly any instance on record in the annals of history of a single peaceful event having exercised such a lasting and baneful influence on the destinies of a nation, as the coronation of Charles the Great at Rome towards the close of the eighth century. By placing the Imperial crown on the head of the then most powerful ruler in Christendom, Pope Leo III. symbolically established a spiritual supremacy over the whole Christian world, but more especially over Germany proper. It is true it was alleged that the new Cæsar was to be considered the secular head of the Christian world by the side of the spiritual head, but as it was the latter who crowned the former, it was evident that the sovereign pontiff arrogated to himself superior authority over the sovereign monarch.

Another disadvantage which resulted from that coronation was the peculiar nature of the newly created dignity, which became manifest by the designation, applied to Germany, of the "Holy *Roman* Empire of the *German* nation." This self-contradictory title was intended to convey the notion that the German Emperors were—through transmission from the Greeks—the heirs and successors of the Roman Cæsars. They were not to be German sovereigns of the *German* monarchy, but *Roman* Emperors of the *German Empire.*[5]

It is true the ancient German institution of royalty was not actually abolished, but it was so much eclipsed by the more pompous, though recent dignity, that in the course of time its former existence was almost entirely forgotten, or at least looked upon with contempt; so much so, that a German sovereign of the fourteenth century—Henry VII.— considered it an insult to be addressed as "King of Germany," instead of as "King of the Romans." Even the German Electoral Princes claimed to exercise the function of "Roman Senators." The foreign stamp thus imprinted upon Germany at the time when she had only just begun to emerge from a state of barbarism had, therefore, a most pernicious influence on the Germans, diverting as it did the free development of their national character from its natural course. Thus it may be truly said, that on Christmas Eve of the year 799, Germany was conquered a second time, if not by the Romans, still by Rome.

---

[5] Cp. pp. 82–85, in this volume.

It was not long before the conflict between the two principal elements in the government of the world—the secular and the clerical—broke out in the two-headed Empire. This antagonism became manifest even under Charles the Great himself, in spite of the splendour of his reign, and the firmness and circumspection of his government. The encroachments of the clergy soon showed in what sense they understood the division of power. It was the practical application of the old fable about the lion's share. Everything was to be done for the clergy, but without it nothing. This ambitious aim revealed itself more openly and effectively under the descendants of Charles the Great, the internal dissensions of whose reigns greatly facilitated the victory of the clerical order in their interference in secular matters.

Under the powerful rule of Henry I. (919–936), surnamed "The Fowler," or more appropriately "the founder of the *German Empire*," and also under the still more splendid reign of his son, Otho the Great (936–973), nay, even under the first Frankish Emperors (1024–1056), the authority of the Roman hierarchy was considerably diminished, while on the other hand the influence of the German clergy at home had greatly increased; which circumstance was a powerful factor in the conflict between the iron Pope Gregory VII. and the impetuous and vacillating Emperor Henry IV. (1056–1106), and brought about in conjunction with the high-handed dealings of the self-dubbed "Roman Senators" of Germany, the degradation of the German Empire. The Papacy was now in the zenith of its power and glory, so that Gregory VII. could boastingly compare the Pope to the sun, and the Emperor to the moon; and although Henry IV. ultimately succeeded in taking revenge for his humiliation at Canossa, he never could wipe out its shame, and what is more, he was unable to suppress or eradicate the ideas represented by his defeated enemy, which had taken a firm hold on the minds of men. People believed in the supremacy of the Pope, even when he was driven from his seat of government; for his realm was of a spiritual kind and he had his invisible throne, as it were, in the hearts of Christian believers. An erring Pope was still the visible representative of the Church. The priests for the most part remained faithful to him under all circumstances. Such, however, was not the case with the Emperors and the Princes. In the first instance the former had no absolute power; secondly, they were elected by men, who considered themselves their equals, and lastly from the moment they lost their throne—no matter what the reasons were—they ceased to have a claim on the obedience of the people. The priests wished for a powerful Pope, because he was the natural guardian of their interests, whilst the German Princes objected to a powerful Emperor, because they trembled for their own independence and local authority.

If the German Emperors had not been constantly chasing the phantom of royal dignity in Italy, in order to be—plausibly at least—entitled to the vain-glorious designation of "Roman Kings," they might have directed their whole energy to the consolidation of their power at home, and have held their own against Popes and Prince-Electors. Unfortunately, however, they were constantly attracted by the delusive brilliancy of possessions in Italy, as if by an *ignis fatuus*; thus leading on the best forces of Germany to moral and physical ruin, and leaving their native country an easy prey to scheming priests and ambitious nobles. The result was that, towards the end of the eleventh century, the Emperor of Germany had neither any influence on the priests, who now depended entirely upon Rome, nor any power over the nobles, whose fiefs had become hereditary; nor did he possess any considerable domains, or actual revenue in his imperial capacity. He had nothing but the high-sounding titles of successor of the Cæsars and of ruler of the whole Christian world.

As a matter of course under these circumstances all progress of national life and culture was impeded. It did not spring spontaneously from within, nor did it receive any impulse from without. The Germans did not benefit intellectually in any way by their contact with the Italians. The conquered have often times become the teachers of their conquerors; but only when the latter settled in the vanquished country and made it their home. The German hordes, however, who crossed the Alps at the behests of their sovereigns, and urged on by the desire for adventure, warfare, and rapine, never permanently settled, as a body, in the flowery plains and flourishing towns of Italy. Numbers of those who survived the sanguinary battles fought in Italy, perished in the unused climate; the others returned home, frequently enriched by plunder and generally tainted by depraved morals. Thus the Germans did not even derive that small advantage from their connection with the Italians—who at that time did not themselves possess any literature or culture in the highest sense of the word—which a permanent settlement in Italy would have conferred on them.

The intellectual life of the Germans did not begin to flourish before the times of the Hohenstaufen (1138–1254). Unfortunately both Frederick I. (Barbarossa) and Frederick II. were almost constantly engaged in warfare with the Popes and the Italians, and both monarchs, especially the latter, utterly neglected the internal affairs of Germany, which country became a prey of the sanguinary contest between Guelphs and Ghibellines. The result was that Conrad IV., the last king from the Hohenstaufen dynasty in Germany, ruled without even a shadow of royal authority, and on his death, in 1254, the dissolution of the old German Empire may be said to have been complete.

During the lawless times of the *Interregnum* (1254–1273) the power of the German Princes consolidated itself more and more amidst the general anarchy. Order was restored, however, by Rudolf von Hapsburg (1273–1291), who concerned himself with the affairs of the country only. He had a right notion of what a King of Germany should be, and emancipated her—though temporarily only—from the fatal connection as an Empire with Rome. More than half a century later the Electoral Princes went a step further in this direction, by the formation of the Kurverein (1338) or "Election Union," of Rhens, when the principle was adopted that the election of German Kings depended upon the Electoral Princes alone, and that the Pope had no voice whatever in the matter. This patriotic proceeding received, however, a counter-check in the unworthy dealings of the mercenary Charles IV. (1347–1378), who repaired to Rome to receive there the crown from the Pope. He little thought that by resuming the connection with Rome he conjured up the greatest danger for his own son and successor, Wenceslaus, who was deposed through the conspiracy of Boniface IX. with the priests, and his influence over the Electoral Princes.

In the course of time a new power—the third Estate—arose in Germany; namely, the Middle Classes as represented by the thriving cities of the Empire. The burghers generally sided with the Emperors, to whom they looked up as their natural protectors against the exactions of priests and nobles. But being imbued with a true mercantile spirit, they did not give away their good will for nothing; they asked for sundry privileges as compensating equivalents. The Emperors had, therefore, now to contend against three powerful elements, the clergy, the nobles, and the burghers. The first were, through their chief representatives—as we have seen—at all times the most dangerous antagonists to Imperial authority, and generally achieved the victory in their contests with it. It was only during the time in which the Papacy had transferred its seat of government to Avignon, that the Romish hierarchy received a check, chiefly in consequence of the depravity of the Papal Court and its surroundings. With the return of the Popes to Rome by the Decree of the Council of Constance (1411–1418), the Papacy recovered its former ground; but this recovery of the lost authority was external only, for with the cruel execution of John Huss—which no sensible Roman Catholic ever thought of justifying—the Papacy received a most fatal blow. That scandalous crime could not have been committed at a more unpropitious time both for the Roman hierarchy and the dignity of the Councils, which latter pretended, at times at least, to have received their mandate immediately from Christ, as the sovereign representatives of the universal Roman Catholic Church. The reforms in the Church, advocated by the celebrated French theologians Cardinal Peter d'Ailly and Chancellor John Gerson, had already met with the approval of numerous thinking men, and the doctrines of Wycliffe had also found, through the teaching of John Huss and his disciples, a sympathetic echo in the hearts of a large portion of the Christian community. Had the Council of Constance shown itself, not magnanimous, but merely just, towards the Bohemian Reformer, the ascendancy of the Councils, in general, over the Popes, would probably have been for ever established; whilst as it was, the next great Council—at Basle (1431–1449)—had to give way to the Pope, and the Roman hierarchy was once more re-established in its former strength and power.

The results of the Councils of Constance and Basle were, however, particularly disastrous to Germany. The former brought about the terrible wars of the Hussites, while the latter was the indirect cause of placing the Imperial power in the hands of Frederick III. (1440–1493), who was a staunch adherent of the Pope and delivered over to him the few rights and privileges which were still left to the German Empire. The Imperial dignity existed now in name only; for Frederick, who, as Heeren says, "had slumbered away more than half a century on the throne," cared so little for Germany proper, that he remained absent from it for the space of full twenty-seven years. No wonder then that whilst the Imperial authority sank to the lowest level, the Papal supremacy rose higher than ever, and the Emperor became nothing more than the satellite of the Pope. Under these circumstances the German Princes began to raise the voice of opposition against their sluggish head; but as he was supported by the influential and subtle Pius II., all their efforts to make a stand against the encroachments of the Church were in vain.

A new order of things arose, however, when Maximilian, the son of Frederick III., was elected "Roman King" in 1486 by the Electoral Princes. The young King acquiesced in the constitutional demands of the Estates for concessions in return for various grants. Feuds were abolished for ever, an independent Chamber of Justice, *Kammergericht*, was established, and Germany received a new Imperial constitution. Nevertheless there were almost constant conflicts between the adventurous Maximilian and the Imperial Estates, so that the national unity, earnestly aimed at by both parties, could not be effected, in consequence of the absence of any connecting link between them. The only step which Maximilian took for the partial emancipation of Germany was his assumption of the title of "elected King of Rome" without being crowned by the Pope, and what is more, he also adopted the ancient title of *King of Germany*. This designation was, however, not intended to convey at the same time the notion of a severance from Rome in spiritual matters. This was now soon to be accomplished, but not by one bearing the imaginary crown of the Cæsars, nor by the decrees of a stately assembly. It was destined for one lowly born to break the fatal bondage in which Germany had been for centuries kept in durance vile by Rome.

II.

One of the few blessings which Germany derived in former times from her otherwise deplorable decentralization, was the establishment, throughout the country, of educational and other beneficial institutions, which even found their way into the most obscure nooks and corners, where under other political conditions no Government would have thought of founding any establishment of the kind. This is the reason why culture and learning—but more especially the latter—spread more generally in Germany than in other countries. What great centralized Government would ever have chosen the insignificant place of Wittenberg, which resembled more a village than a town, as the seat of an University? And this, too, by the side of the Universities of Leipzig and Erfurt which already enjoyed a high reputation and were well endowed? Yet this was done by the Prince Elector of Saxony, Frederick, surnamed the Wise. He had himself received a learned education, and it was his legitimate ambition to see his petty electoral principality adorned by a High School. The Elector himself was, as is well known, very poor. The only means at his disposal for such a learned foundation were the proceeds from the sale of Indulgences in his Electorate, which had been collected in 1501 for the purpose of a war against the Turks. Those moneys were deposited with him, and he refused to give them up to the Pope even at the intercession of the Emperor, unless they were employed for the purpose for which they had been collected. The war against the Turks was not undertaken at the time, and so Frederick employed the money for the endowment of the new University. It was also a significant fact, that Wittenberg was the first German University which did not receive its "Charter" from the Pope, but from the then Emperor of Germany—Maximilian I. The Prince Elector hit further upon the expedient of connecting several clerical benefices with some of the professorial chairs, and he hoped, moreover, that the members of the Augustine Order, settled at Wittenberg, would furnish some teachers for the learned institution, which was established by him in 1502. The connection of the new University with that Order was in many respects an intimate one. It was specially dedicated to St. Augustine; and Staupitz, the vicar of that Order at Erfurt, was the first Dean of the Theological Faculty. Through his influence it was that several Augustine monks received a call to the University, and among those who responded was the monk Martin Luther.

The early history of the poor miner's son may, in fact, serve as an illustration of the wholesome spread of education throughout Germany. Poor as his parents were, he had received a learned education, and became, in consequence of the religious turn of his mind, a monk. It was then in his double capacity of scholar and priest that he became connected with the University of Wittenberg (1508), and composed, and sent forth into the world, his famous 95 Theses,[6] against the wholesale disposal of Indulgences (31st Oct., 1517). Luther issued his challenge to the theological world from religious motives only, and it so happened that it fully coincided with the political views of the Elector; but, to the credit of both Prince and monk, it should be remembered that there was no mutual understanding between them. They had never seen each other before the publication of the 95 Theses; nor did they correspond on the subject, although they were of one accord about it. Frederick always viewed it with disfavour, and begrudged that such large amounts of money should be sent to Rome under the cloak of Indulgences, and we have

---

[6] Cp. pp. 1–12 in this volume.

seen how he had employed the proceeds resulting from their former sale. Now, however, he must have objected still more to the attempt to drain his poor country, because the object of the sale was not a holy war—if ever a war can be so called—but the alleged erection of St. Peter's Church. If such was really the case, it might be truly said that Leo X. undermined the Chair of St. Peter for the sake of the Church of St. Peter. But people were incredulous. It was whispered, that the Pope required the money for the benefit of his family. Another disagreeable element in the whole transaction was the then commonly known fact, that the Archbishop of Mentz had actually "farmed" the sale of the Indulgences in his own episcopal territory on condition that one half of the proceeds should fall to his share. He had promised to bear the expenses of obtaining the Pall himself, and having borrowed a considerable amount of money from the celebrated house of Fugger, he allowed their agents to travel about in company with the notorious Tetzel, as commercial controllers, and to take possession of half of the proceeds as they came in. Through this and other circumstances the affair assumed the ugly aspect of a very worldly and mercenary transaction, carried on in the meanest spirit. There was, besides, a tension between Frederick and the Prince Elector of Mentz; it was, therefore, natural that the step which Luther had taken should meet with his tacit approval. More than this Luther did not expect, for he well knew the lethargic character of Frederick; but under the circumstances that was quite sufficient, for the latter granted him shelter and protection, in spite of the urgent entreaties of zealots to deliver up the bold Augustinian monk at once to Rome.

The defence of the 95 Theses, which Luther transmitted to the Pope, was of no avail; for Leo X., urged by the fanatical Dominican Prierias—so notorious from the Reuchlin trial—cited the Wittenberg monk before an inquisitorial tribunal at Rome. Now for the first time it was seen how fortunate it was for Luther and the cause he defended, that he had found a prudent and humane protector in the Prince who exercised sovereign power in his own limited territory. To repair to Rome under the accusation of heresy would have been like plunging with open eyes into an abyss. Confiding and courageous as Luther was, he saw this himself very clearly, and it was at his request that the Saxon Court preacher, Spalatin, who was one of his most constant and zealous friends, persuaded the Emperor Maximilian as well as the Prince Elector—both of whom were at that time (1518) at the Diet of Augsburg—that the accused monk should be arraigned before a German tribunal. Frederick readily acquiesced, although, as he repeatedly declared, he did not fully share the views of Luther; and the Emperor also consented, partly because he required the moral support of the Prince Elector at the approaching election of a successor in the Imperial dignity, and partly because he hoped one day to make use of the enlightened monk, in his endeavour to bring about the much-needed reforms in the Church. In this sense it undoubtedly was, that he said to Frederick's councillor, Pfeffinger: "Luther is sure to begin a game with the priests. The Prince Elector should take good care of the monk, as he might one day be of use." It seems, therefore, that both friends and foes recognised (at an early stage) the great capacity which still lay hidden in the insignificant-looking monk. The Papal Nuncio, Cajetan, discovered at once, in his interview with him at Augsburg (1518), that he had to do with a superior power, when he heard the conclusive and thoughtful arguments of the Augustinian monk, and saw the divine fire of genius flashing from his eyes; and his friends already considered him of importance sufficient to induce them to bring about his sudden escape at night-time.

Urged by the wrathful Papal Legate not to disgrace the honour of his Electoral house by giving shelter to a heretic friar, Frederick, encouraged by his own University, drily replied that as no scholar, either in his own or in foreign lands, had as yet refuted the theories of Luther, he would continue to give him shelter until that was done. This was no subterfuge on the part of Frederick. It was the key-note of his conduct, from the beginning of the Reformation to the end of his own life, to have the teachings of Luther properly tested by a learned discussion. The Pope, being desirous of securing the Elector's co-operation at the impending Imperial election, humoured his learned whim, and tried to win him over by unctuous kindliness. Frederick was still a staunch Roman Catholic. He possessed a regular treasure of reliques—partly brought home from the Holy Land—which were displayed for the spiritual benefit of the devout on certain occasions, and it was known that he was yearning for the acquisition of the *Golden Rose*. Leo X. bestowed, therefore, on him that mark of apostolic favour, and dispatched to him as his Nuncio the Elector's own agent at Rome, Carl von Miltitz, a native of Saxony.

What the imperious haughtiness of the pompous Papal Legate was unable to achieve was, partly at least, effected by the shrewd *bonhomie* of Miltitz. He imploringly appealed to Luther's German good-nature, not to create any scandal in the Church, and after having agreed that the controversy should be submitted for investigation to the Archbishops of Würzburg and Treves, he obtained the promise of Luther to observe perfect silence on religious matters, *provided his enemies would do the same*, and to write an apologetic letter to the Pope. It is well known how badly the antagonists of Luther kept faith with him, and that he was obliged, in consequence, to break his conditionally promised silence, and to take part in the great public Disputation at Leipzig, in 1519. He now had to vindicate against Dr. Eck, his most bitter opponent, not only his own honour, but also that of his University, and this circumstance formed the subject of his justification before the Prince Elector, to whose personal esteem he attached the highest value. When, however, that Disputation ended, as is the case with most learned discussions, in something like a drawn battle, Luther was driven to a declaration virtually involving his secession from Rome.

III.

About the time when the celebrated Disputation was going on at Leipzig, in which two peasants' sons—for Dr. Eck was, like Martin Luther, the son of a peasant—took the most prominent part, another momentous gathering took place at Frankfort-on-the-Main. The Emperor Maximilian had died on 12th January, 1519, without being able to secure the succession in the royal dignity to his grandson Charles, Archduke of Austria and King of Spain and Naples. More than five months elapsed before the Electoral Princes assembled for the election of a new Emperor, and during that interval the "Vicariate of the Empire," as it was styled, was put into the hands of Lewis V. of the Palatinate, and of Frederick the Wise, in accordance with a provision of the "Golden Bull," which placed the Regency of the Empire, during a vacancy, in the hands of the rulers of those Electorates for the time being. The circumstance that the seat of the Imperial Government was at Wittenberg during the present short *Interregnum* bestowed not a little lustre both on Frederick and his University; but the work of the incipient Reformation was not particularly promoted by it, because it coincided with the truce which Luther faithfully kept until it was faithlessly broken by his antagonists.

There were three aspirants to the Imperial throne of Germany. First and foremost Maximilian's grandson Charles, Archduke of Austria; secondly, Francis I., King of France, and thirdly, Henry VIII. of England. The last-named monarch did not, however, seriously press his candidature. It was only when he saw the two other sovereigns contending for the prize that he deemed the moment favourable for securing it to himself. When he received, however, the practical hint that the barren honour would not be worth the trouble and the necessary expenditure, and when, moreover, it was taken into account, that since the introduction of Christianity into England this country did in no way belong to the "Holy Roman Empire," he prudently retired from all competition. Not so the ambitious Francis I., who spared neither promises nor bribes to secure his election, and obtained a party among the Electoral Princes.

If it should be asked, how it was actually possible that foreign kings ever thought of aspiring to a throne to which they had not even the shadow of a claim, the reason must be found in the above-mentioned circumstance, that the Imperial dignity of Germany was not a national institution, and that any Christian prince might think himself justified in aspiring to the crown of the "Holy Roman Empire," accidentally bestowed upon the "German nation." Were they not aware that in the thirteenth century two ecclesiastical Electoral Princes raised to the German throne, Richard of Cornwall and King Alfonso of Castile, respectively, in consideration of great bribes? And had not the French King sufficient wealth to buy the votes of both the secular and ecclesiastic Electoral Princes? He had, moreover, the precedent before him, that Philip VI. of Valois had, about a century before, endeavoured to transfer the dignity of the "Holy Roman Empire" from the Germans to the "Franks," to whom it originally belonged.

Both the French and Austrians lavishly distributed money in all directions. Frederick the Wise alone kept his hands pure, and he strictly prohibited even his officials and servants from accepting any presents. For a moment the Princes had turned their eyes to Frederick himself. But he had no confidence in his capability to sustain worthily and efficiently the functions incumbent upon the Imperial dignity. The Empire, as such, invested him with no material power and resources, and his own dynastic power was insignificant. How should he be able to hold his own against the ambitious and frequently turbulent Princes? Why, even under the "Imperial Vicariate," the peace of the land was broken. He, therefore, declined the proffered honour, and the Princes, fearing lest the powerful French King should curb their independence, suddenly remembered that he was a foreign sovereign, and that in order to keep up the national freedom of the Empire, they should give the preference to the Archduke Charles, who was, partially at least, of German descent. The latter, to whom also Frederick of Saxony finally gave his vote, was accordingly chosen Emperor, and he soon proved that it is not always the kinship which constitutes the sympathetic bond between a sovereign and his subjects.

The time which elapsed from the election of Charles to his arrival in Germany, more especially to his presence at the Diet of Augsburg in 1521, was most propitious for the spread of the work of Luther. It may be said that during that interval the Reformation assumed shape and form. Luther indefatigably continued to inculcate his religious principles on the minds of the people by sermons and numerous publications, and he found adherents so readily everywhere among all classes of the German nation, that Frederick, who still hoped the schism might be prevented by learned discussions, was of opinion, that if it should be attempted to suppress his teachings by force instead of by refutation, there would arise a great storm in Germany. Several distinguished members of the lower nobility, such as the brave Hutten and the martial Sickingen and many others, placed their swords at the disposal of Luther; the former was already active for him with the all-powerful weapon of the pen. Amidst this general commotion the humble Augustinian monk sent forth his powerful appeal, entitled: "To the Christian Nobility of the German Nation concerning the Reformation of the Christian Estate."[7] This production, which is rightly considered as the manifesto of the Reformation, clearly shows that Luther not only saw the clerical abuses, but also the political disadvantages under which Germany laboured and groaned. He was not what we should call a politician, but, unlike so many of his learned countrymen, he had a true patriotic instinct. The mere title of the appeal seems already to contain a protest against the designation of Germany as the Holy Roman Empire. That he addressed his appeal to the "Nobility" in general is only an additional proof of the remarkable tact which guided him throughout his career.

Some historians have blamed Luther for not having appealed to the "People." But the reproach is wrong. The German people in general had no power whatever in those days. It only obtained in the course of time a voice in the management of public affairs through the Reformation. It was Luther who proclaimed the freedom of man, or rather the "Christian man." The acknowledgment of political rights of the middle classes may, therefore, be said to date from the Reformation only. In appealing to the German Nobility, Luther addressed himself to the legitimate representatives of Germany; and he did so in the candid belief, that it was only necessary to open the eyes of those in power, in order to effect at once the abolition of any abuses. To address himself to the people, would have required his placing himself at the head of a revolution; but Luther was no revolutionist. It should also be remembered that a large number of noblemen had offered him support and shelter. Political power lay mainly in the hands of the nobles, who alone, in conjunction with the Emperor, could decide on the destiny of Germany. It is, however, a significant fact, that he wrote his appeal, not in Latin, but in German. In this way, indeed, he actually addressed himself to the German people.

In the meantime Leo X. had hurled his Bull of excommunication against Luther. When it arrived at Wittenberg both the University and the Government of the Prince Elector decided to take no notice of it, and now it again became manifest what a powerful support Luther had found in Frederick. On his return journey from the coronation of Charles V. at Aix-la-Chapelle, in 1520, the Papal Legates Aleander and Caraccioli demanded of the Elector, at Cologne, in the name of the Pope, to give effect to the Bull by burning the writings of Luther and punishing him as a heretic, or to deliver him to the Pope. The threat uttered on this occasion was certainly curious. In case the Papal Bull should not meet with ready obedience in Germany, the Legates menaced the country with the withdrawal of the title of the "Holy Roman Empire." Germany would forfeit that dignity in the same way as the Greeks had lost it after having seceded from the Pope. A more fortunate fate, in truth, could not have befallen the German Empire than its total political severance from Rome; but in those days the empty glory of the baneful union was still highly valued, and so the Elector asked time to consider.

Erasmus, whom Frederick consulted, clothed his opinion on the religious controversy in the humorous reply, "that Luther had sinned in two points: he had touched the crown of the Pope and the bellies of the monks." In his interview with Spalatin he was still more explicit, by expressing his conviction, that the attacks against Luther arose simply from hatred against the enlightenment of science and from tyrannical presumption. He further agreed with Luther in insisting on the question being examined and tried by the tribunal of public discussion. We know that this opinion fully coincided with the views of the Elector, and his answer to the threatening Papal Legates ran in

---

[7] Cp. pp. 15–92 in this volume.

accordance with his views. His additional and often-repeated assurance, that he had never made common cause with Luther, and that he would greatly disapprove of it, if the latter wrote anything adverse to the Pope, was of the greatest importance. This declaration was more decisive than if he had acknowledged himself openly in favour of the Reformer; he would then have been considered as a biassed partizan, whilst now he only played the part of an impartial patron, who wished to see his *protégé* judged by a fair trial. On his return to Saxony, Frederick sent to Luther a reassuring message, and the latter continued his work by teaching, writing and preaching, unmolested and without remission.

In other parts of Germany the Papal Bull was proclaimed with varying and unequal effect. Luther's works were in the first instance burnt at Louvain, by command of Charles V., in his capacity of hereditary sovereign of the Netherlands. The same fate befell them at Cologne and Mentz. It will, therefore, readily be acknowledged that it was the Pope and his overzealous adherents who drove Luther to the committal of perhaps the boldest act ever accomplished by a single individual, more especially by one in Luther's dependent position. By the public burning of the Papal Bull before the Elstergate of Wittenberg (1520), the act of secession from Rome was consummated. What no Emperor had dared before him, the humble Augustine monk accomplished courageously and deliberately. Well might he do so. He acted on conviction with that moral courage which knows no fear, and he had the German people at his back to support him.[8]

IV.

"Your majesty must go to Germany and show there some favour to a certain Martin Luther, who is at the Court of Saxony and causes anxiety to the Roman Court by his sermons." Such were the words which the shrewd Spanish ambassador, Don Juan Manuel, addressed to Charles V. from Rome in 1520. They were written at a time when it was still doubtful whether Leo X. would side in the impending struggle in Italy with the King of France or with the Emperor of Germany, and moreover at a time when the latter had reason to be dissatisfied with the course the Pope had taken. Leo X. had consented, in compliance with a petition from the Castilian Cortes, to introduce some reforms in the exercise of the Inquisition. This concession was, however, entirely opposed to the views of the young Emperor, who was completely guided by his Dominican confessor. Under these circumstances it was deemed expedient to make use of Luther as a kind of bugbear in order to frighten the Pope. To people not accustomed to the tortuous windings of politics it seems, of course, bewildering, that a heretic should be favoured in one country, in order to make it possible to enforce the rigours of the Inquisition in another country. In like manner Francis I. acted. In France he persecuted and burnt mercilessly the opponents of the Roman Catholic Church, whilst in Germany he befriended the adherents of the Reformation. This much, however, is certain, had Luther entertained the slightest suspicion at what price it was intended to extend indulgence to his work, he would have been the first to scorn that indulgence.

The advice of the diplomatic Spanish ambassador was, however, not followed. Pope and Emperor came to an amicable understanding. The former cancelled his concession to the Castilian Cortes, and promised the coveted assistance against Francis I., in Italy,

---

[8] In one of his letters to Dr. Eck—communicated in the *Documenta Lutherana* recently issued by the Vatican— the Papal Nuncio Aleander confesses, that the excitement in consequence of the burning of Luther's work was so great among the people, that he trembled for his own safety.

whilst the latter pledged himself to crush the Reformation and to issue an Edict for the execution of the Papal Bull against Luther. Now it came to light how ill-advised was the election of Charles V. as Emperor of Germany. At the time when the celebrated Diet of 1521 assembled at Worms, the Emperor had his whole attention directed across the Alps. The affairs of Germany had only in so far any importance for him as they had any influence or bearing on the affairs of Italy. He took no note of the great objects which then agitated the hearts and minds of the Germans, and had he been able to recognise them, they would have excited in him no corresponding sympathy for them. He did not even fully understand the cultured language—as far as it existed in those days—of Germany, being able to speak Low German only. The political institutions of the country—the lingering fragments of the ancient German liberty—were thoroughly distasteful to him. He was also a bigoted Roman Catholic at heart, and—as we have seen—entirely opposed to all religious reforms. It must, therefore, be acknowledged, that among the many historical misfortunes which have befallen Germany—and no country perhaps has been tried by so many—the accession of Charles V. to the throne of the German Empire was one of the greatest. What might a German sovereign, with a due appreciation of the political and religious aspirations of the people, not have achieved at that important epoch, which was the turning-point in the history of Germany!

After the Emperor had laid his Edict regarding the Papal Bull before the Estates, they made him earnest representations, alleging that the people were throughout Germany so thoroughly impregnated by the doctrines of Luther, that any violent measures undertaken against him would call forth the greatest commotion. They submitted, therefore, to Charles the opinion that the Reformer should be summoned to Worms, not for the sake of any argumentative or learned disputation, but merely for a summary interrogatory. In case he should recant his doctrines concerning the Christian faith, he might further be interrogated about the minor points in his writings, and whatever was advisable should be adopted. If, however, he persisted in his refusal to recant, the necessary steps would be taken against him. We see by this that the Estates drew a distinction in Luther's doctrines between those points which concerned the ecclesiastical administration only, and those which referred to the Christian faith proper and were chiefly contained in his work 'On the Babylonish Captivity of the Church.'[9]

Charles V. consented to this proposal, by which the Estates may be said to have betrayed the cause of the Reformation. Frederick was charged with the task of summoning Luther to Worms, but he prudently declined. As he was to be summoned in the name of the Emperor and the Estates, he ought to receive the citation direct from them. The stubborn character of the Elector being well known, the Emperor was obliged to yield also on this point, and in order to be consistent with official etiquette, Luther was addressed by Charles V. in the citation, issued on March 6, 1521, as "honourable, beloved, and pious!" A safe conduct for the journey to and from Worms accompanied the citation. A man less endowed with moral courage than Luther would nevertheless have shrunk from completing the journey. On his way to Worms he learned that a Mandate for the confiscation of his writings had been issued by the Emperor, and the Imperial herald actually asked him, whether he still intended to continue his journey. The Reformer undauntedly proceeded on his way, although the Imperial Mandate clearly showed him that his writings had already been unconditionally condemned, and that he was merely summoned to declare whether he would recant or not.

---

[9] See pp. 130–243 in the present volume.

Luther's appearance before the Diet of Worms may be considered as the first official recognition of the German people as a power; for it was only by representing the danger which would arise from the unconditional condemnation of the Reformer before being heard, that the Emperor was induced to consent to the step which was resented by the Papal Legate and his party. The wrath of Aleander greatly increased, when the Imperial Estates presented to Charles V. their *gravamina* respecting the abuses of the Church, the abolition of which they had a right to expect in accordance with the capitulation made at the time of the Emperor's election. That petition, which is generally regarded as a *pendant* to Luther's programme of the Reformation, as contained in his address to the "Christian Nobility of the German Nation," and which had even obtained the approval of George, Duke of Saxony (that great opponent of Luther), was, formally at least, "graciously" received by the Emperor.

When Luther arrived at Worms both his adherents and antagonists were startled. The former trembled for his safety, and the latter feared the influence of his presence—his eloquence and the victorious power of inner conviction. The Emperor's expectations of so remarkable a personage—who was capable of inspiring such a high degree of enthusiasm and aversion—must, therefore, have been very great, and we do not wonder at his disappointment on seeing before him an insignificant-looking monk. He did not believe in the power of the mind, and it was quite natural in the young monarch that he should have looked forward to a commanding, giantlike figure, with a thundering voice, somewhat like Dr. Eck, who derived no little benefit from these accessories, so advantageous both on the political and religious platform. Even after Luther had produced—on the second day of his appearance before the Diet—a deep impression on almost all his hearers, Charles V. could never be brought to believe that the meek Augustinian monk was the author of all the energetic and impetuous compositions which passed under his name.

Luther's public refusal to recant unless convinced of his error through the Scriptures, was the official proclamation of the Reformation, and well might he exclaim, on the evening of the 18th of April, on coming home from perhaps the most memorable sitting of any Diet—*"Ich bin durch!"* But the decision of the Emperor was also taken, and on the morning of the 19th of April he declared to the Diet—in a French document written in his own hand—"that as a descendant of the most Christian German Emperors, and the Catholic Kings of Spain, he had resolved to maintain everything which had been adopted by his ancestors, more especially at the Council of Constance. . . . That he will not hear Luther again, but let him go back to Wittenberg in accordance with his safe conduct, and *then he will proceed with him as a heretic*."

The fanatic advisers of the Emperor certainly wished that he should not only strictly adhere to the doctrines confirmed by the Diet of Constance, but that he also should follow its example, set by the execution of Huss, with respect to Luther; for the simple reason "that there is no need of keeping faith with heretics." Charles V. had, however, not been informed in vain of the disposition of the people regarding the Reformer. He also took into account the views of the Imperial Estates.

The times had evidently changed since the Council of Constance. It was no longer safe to burn a heretic after he had received Imperial protection; and it may be assumed futhermore that the young monarch also possessed too much sense of honour to listen to the ruthless suggestions of his fanatical advisers. After some more attempts to induce Luther to retract—all of which, of course, proved futile—he allowed him to depart; but as he had uttered the threat to treat the excommunicated monk as a heretic, after the expiration of his safe conduct, Frederick, who was not undeservedly called the Wise, considered it expedient to bring Luther, by means of a stratagem, to a place of safety.

The sudden disappearance of Luther naturally caused great anxiety among his adherents; but his opponents seemed to have instinctively guessed the truth. They knew very well how little they themselves were to be trusted, and suspected that his friends had secretly saved him from their clutches. Cardinal Eleander even went nearer the mark, and expressed his opinion, that the "Saxon fox" had hidden the monk. Charles V. himself took no cognisance of the occurrence; nay, he even cautiously deferred the promulgation of the Edict against Luther, and it was only after Frederick the Wise, accompanied by the Palatine Elector, had left Worms on account of illness, that the Emperor summoned to his private residence the three clerical Electors, together with the Elector of Brandenburg, and several other members of the Imperial Estates, and communicated to them the long-expected Edict. The Imperial ban was thus promulgated on May 25, without the formal sanction of the Diet. And in order to stamp it with the appearance of legality, it was postdated to the 8th of May, when the Estates were still together in good numbers. But it was at the same time an ominous date; for on that day an alliance was concluded between the Emperor and the Pope to the effect "to have the same friends and without exception the same enemies; the same willingness and unwillingness for defence and attack."

Another expedient was resorted to in order to gain some plausibility for the illegally issued Edict. It was sophistically averred that, as the Diet had already decided that Luther was to be proceeded against, in case he should not recant, there was no further necessity for obtaining the additional sanction of that body for the publication of the Edict. By this decree the Papal ban was confirmed, and Luther himself was now outlawed as a heretic, and his books were prohibited. The Emperor having accomplished this step, which was one of the most momentous in the eventful course of the Reformation, now hastened to the Netherlands, and strengthened by the league with the Pope and Henry VIII., soon began his great war against the King of France.

V.

It is an amiable trait in human nature, though frequently bordering on weakness, to endeavour to find out the good side of any evil. Thus it has been considered a propitious coincidence that the German Empire had some "claims" on certain territories in Italy. For it was, in a great measure, in consequence of this fact, that the war broke out between the Emperor of Germany and the King of France, which necessitated the absence of the former from his German domains for several years and gave the Reformation time for its consolidation and expansion. We will not deny the advantages which resulted from that political combination, but it is to a certain extent counterbalanced by the ill which it produced. Without the contingency of that war, Charles V. would have had no occasion for leaguing himself with the Pope, the Edict of Worms would, in all probability, never have been issued, and the pressing demand for a General Council would have been acceded to. Luther would not have been obliged to hide himself at the Wartburg, and the subsequent troubles at Wittenberg would certainly never have broken out; and finally the firm hand of a sovereign residing in the country would have stemmed the torrent of the Peasants' War at the outset. Another drawback resulting from the absence of Charles V. was his utter estrangement from Germany, whose aspirations he neither cared for nor understood.

During the first few months after the departure of Charles from Germany the work of the Reformation went on undisturbed. The Edict of Worms found, in general, no responsive reception there. Its effect quite vanished before the impression made by Luther's manly, nay heroic, conduct in presence of the Diet. The rumour which had got abroad that he had been captured by an enemy of the Elector Frederick and perchance killed, rather promoted than damaged his cause. It aroused warm sympathy for the Reformer and increased the hatred against his enemies, who were alleged to have resorted to brutal force, because they could not disprove his arguments. In fact, the adoption of the Reformation was now so general, that Luther's antagonists hardly dared to denounce them openly. It is well known, that the Elector of Mentz would not give permission to the Minorite monks to preach against Luther. The Edict of Worms was thus practically set at defiance, and in spite of its prohibition not to publish any thing in favour of the Reformation, numerous writings in its favour issued from the German printing presses.

Whilst the seed which Luther had sown on German soil began to produce a magnificent harvest, and he himself was busy at the Wartburg, under the disguise of *Junker Georg*, with various religious writings, but more especially with the great work of his life, the translation of the Bible from the original text, some of his adherents began to precipitate matters at Wittenberg under the leadership of the impassioned Carlstadt. A time of general dissolution suddenly came on, in which there was a violent rupture with the past. Mass was abrogated, monks left their convents, and priests married. Holy images were destroyed, and nearly all the usages of the Roman Catholic Church were abruptly abolished. Other innovations were introduced, and the movement tended towards the introduction of a Christian socialism, or rather communism. If Luther had not been absent, the movement would never have broken out, and Melanchthon, who was present, was quite perplexed and not energetic enough to be able to stem the surging tide of the Revolution. The Prince Elector, too, looked on quite bewildered, and, imbued with a sense of unbounded tolerance, he fancied that, after all, the revolutionary "saints" might be right.

When Luther heard of the local excesses at Wittenberg, he suddenly left his "Patmos," in order to find out for himself the real state of things. In travelling to and from Wittenberg, where he stayed a few days only, he had to pass the territory of his great opponent, the Duke of Saxony. This was at the beginning of December, 1521, consequently only a few months after the publication of the Edict of Worms, and his conduct shows both his moral courage, of which he has given so many striking proofs, and his anxiety for the cause of the Reformation.

Soon, however, he was to give still more striking proofs of both. For after the "prophets of Zwickau," those deluded and deluding disciples of Thomas Münzer had chosen the birthplace of the Reformation for their field of action, more especially when he heard of the innovations introduced in his own community since his furtive visit there, he defied all danger, and disregarded the remonstrances of the Elector Frederick not to leave his place of refuge. His heart was so devoid of fear and he had so much confidence in the righteousness of his cause, that he actually declared to the Prince Elector that he might give to the latter greater protection than he could receive from him. He apologised nevertheless for his disobedience to Frederick, and a few days after his arrival at Wittenberg at the beginning of March, 1522, he began the series of sermons by which he soon allayed the storm and extended both his influence and reputation.

Several of the religious innovations introduced during the absence of Luther were quite in accordance with his views, but he chiefly objected to the violent manner in which the established usages were thrown over. Thus he approved the abolition of the *Mass*, but considered that it ought not to have been done in a way which was vexatious to another portion of the Christian community. The secular authorities should have been consulted and everything done in a legal manner. Luther was, besides, tolerant in the highest degree. He did not wish to force others to adopt his theories; he merely wanted to convince them. His mode of acting was concisely summed up in the following words, which contain the keynote of his activity as a Reformer: "I will preach about it, speak about it, write about it; but I will compel and drive no one by force; for belief is to be accepted freely and spontaneously. Take me as an example. I have opposed the Indulgences and the Papists, but not with force. I have only worked, preached, and written the Word of the Lord; else I have done nothing . . . *I* have done nothing; the Word has done and accomplished everything. If I had wished to proceed turbulently, I could have caused great bloodshed in Germany, and I might have played such a game at Worms, that even the Emperor would not have been safe,"[10] etc.

These words, which Luther uttered in his celebrated sermons preached after his return to Wittenberg, not only fully reveal to us one of his principal characteristics as a Reformer, but contain at the same time a full revelation of the cause of the peaceful course of the Reformation during his lifetime. He held the reins in his firm hands, and it would only have required an encouraging signal on his part, and the furies of civil war would have been at once let loose. But those words also confirm the charge which has been brought forward against the Imperial Estates, that they had betrayed the cause of the Reformation at the Diet of Worms. They had the German people at their back, and the Emperor, with all his Spanish and Italian courtiers and Papal Legates, would have been powerless. Had only some of them given signs of energetic opposition, the Emperor would, in all probability, have yielded. That the Princes did not fully answer Luther's expectations caused him considerable grief, and now he had experienced another disappointment in the conduct of the middle classes—the people proper—a portion of whom eagerly supported the violent innovations of the extreme reformers. But the greatest disappointment with regard to the healthiest class of the people—the peasants— was yet in store for him.

The effect which resulted from Luther's return to Wittenberg was doubly beneficial. It allayed the turbulent excitement at home, and prevented the breaking out of a storm abroad, which had well-nigh been conjured up by Duke George of Saxony at the "Imperial Regency," or *Reichsregiment*; which body conducted the government of the Empire in the absence of the Emperor, and had assembled at Nuremberg during the troubles at Wittenberg. The Duke actually prevailed upon the members of the Imperial Regency to issue an Edict enjoining the Bishops of Naumburg, Meissen and Merseburg, energetically to suppress all religious innovations; but when quiet had been restored at Wittenberg the tide turned in Luther's favour, partly owing to the direct and indirect influence of the Elector of Saxony; and thus the Edict of Worms was virtually set at naught. The Imperial Regency did not rest satisfied, however, with the tacit approval of the doctrines of Luther, and when Adrian VI., who had succeeded Leo X. in 1522, demanded through his Nuncio that a check should be put to the Lutheran innovations, the

---

[10] That the above assertion was no mere boast is confirmed—if anything what so truthful a man as Luther said requires confirmation—by the above-mentioned *Documenta Lutherana*, in which we find a letter from the Nuncio Aleander, describing the great popularity of Luther throughout Germany, and in particular at Augsburg. "Know then," he writes to Dr. Eck, "there are so many Lutherans here, that not only the men, but also the very trees and stones cry: Luther!"

Imperial Regency replied by a Resolution in which it declared its refusal to carry out the Edict of Worms. On the other hand it demanded "the summoning of a General Council, if possible within a year's time, in a German town and under the co-operation of the Emperor." It was, of course, understood that the secular Estates should also take part in that council, and perfect immunity for a free expression of opinion was at the same time admitted. Moreover, one hundred gravamina with respect to the prevailing abuses of the Church were handed to the Legate.

One of the most remarkable features in the passing of the above Resolution was the circumstance that it even obtained the consent of the adherents of the Pope, and that the views of the latter regarding the necessity of Church reforms, in some degree at least, contributed to it. Adrian VI. was in almost every respect the opposite of Leo X. He had the welfare of the Church truly at heart, and fully saw the abuses which had crept in through the depravity of its representatives. He therefore energetically and earnestly urged the necessity of reforming the Church, or rather the clergy. He himself showed the way by setting, in his own person, the example of a true Apostolic Pontiff, by leading the life of a humble and austere monk, whereas Leo X. had surrounded himself with regal pomp and the luxuries of an Asiatic potentate. On the other hand Adrian was also an orthodox Dominican, and detested the religious innovations more intensely than his predecessor did, who, as a true Medici, being an enthusiastic admirer of art and a zealous cultivator of polite literature, was quite indifferent to ecclesiastical and religious matters. Leo X. was opposed to Luther because, as Erasmus expressed it, "he had touched the Papal crown," whilst Adrian took up the gauntlet against the Reformer because, in his opinion, the latter weakened the corner-stone of the Church and undermined its very foundations. For this reason he had sent his Nuncio Chieregati to the Imperial Regency at Nuremberg with the demand to have the Edict of Worms carried into effect. This demand was only consistent with the Pope's line of action; but the times had changed, even during the short space which had elapsed since Charles V. had issued his Edict against Luther by a shuffling proceeding, and the Imperial Regency openly refused to enact it.

That the Estates should have been able thus to act in defiance of both Pope and Emperor, was in itself the result of the influence which the Reformation exercised on the political status of the German people. The civic element now assumed a political importance which it never enjoyed before. The commoner began to feel his dignity, as a man, as a member of the State. The teachings of Luther had set free human intelligence and free thought, which had been so long held imprisoned and bound by political and religious tyranny, and the people began—to think and reason for themselves. From the moment this was done, they were free, and as soon as they obtained political rights, they well understood how to assert them. The re-establishment of an Imperial Regency on a "constitutional basis," formed one of the principal stipulations at the election of Charles V., and the Deputies having been chosen by the Electoral Princes and the various "Circles," or districts into which Germany was then divided, the commonwealth was for the first time officially represented at a German constitutional assembly. We have seen how worthily the members of the Imperial Regency had discharged their trust; and it may be said, that from that moment dates the political emancipation of Germany.

VI.

The answer of the Imperial Regency to Adrian VI. was the first political triumph of the Reformation, but its effect was considerably weakened by several events which occurred shortly after. First came the rising of the knights—who constituted the lower nobility—under the banner of the brave and restless Franz von Sickingen. Grave discontent reigned among the knights with the doings of the all-powerful "Suabian League," formed in 1488 by the Estates of Suabia for the maintenance of general peace, and also with the encroachments of the Princes; and Sickingen, aided by Ulrich von Hutten, united the lesser nobles into one body with the avowed object of breaking the power of the higher nobility, and of acknowledging one head only—the Emperor. It has been plausibly assumed, that Sickingen pursued a more ambitious aim, and he has therefore been compared with Wallenstein. Sickingen professed, however, another object in his enterprise: the furtherance of the cause of the Reformation; and at the head of a large and powerful army, he directed his first attack (Sept. 1522), against the Archbishop of Treves. The knights were defeated, their leader lost his life, and Hutten wandered away—outlawed and proscribed—to find an exile's grave in a small island of Switzerland. The enemies of Luther considered, or pretended to consider, the Reformation as the main cause of Sickingen's undertaking, and this circumstance estranged from the Reformer a number of his adherents and confirmed his antagonists in their enmity against him, although he had no immediate connection with the revolt of the nobles.

The first result of the rising and of the defeat of the knights was, that several Princes now assumed a somewhat hostile attitude towards the Imperial Regency, that had shown itself so tolerant respecting religious reforms; but a still severer blow threatened that body from another quarter. The wealthy German cities sent a deputation to Charles V. in Spain, with a petition against some ordinances which the Imperial Chamber had decided upon and which were considered detrimental to their commercial interests. The Emperor, dissatisfied with that liberal Institution, readily promised a new administration. This promise was fulfilled at the next Diet, in 1524, at Nuremberg, when it was decided to reorganise the Imperial Regency by electing for it entirely new members. Those who consented to this proceeding were influenced, partly by political and partly by commercial reasons, but as regards religious matters there was still a majority in favour of the Reformation. On this account it came to pass that a Resolution was carried at the Diet, to convoke another assembly of the Estates in the same year at Spires, the points to be discussed there being in the meantime drawn up for the Princes by scholars and counsellors. Till then the Resolution of the preceding Diet, "that the Gospel should be allowed to be freely preached," was to remain in force. Thus the mission of the Papal Nuncio Campeggi, who had been sent to Germany by Clement VII. (the successor of Adrian VI. since 1523) to bring about the enactment of the Edict of Worms, proved unsuccessful. It is true the Diet passed a Resolution, that the Edict of Worms should be executed, but this decision was rendered ineffective by the additional elastic clause: "As far as possible." At the same time the demand for a General Council was added.

The above Mandate now shared the fate of most compromises; inasmuch as it satisfied neither party. Luther himself and his followers saw in it an indirect confirmation of the Edict of Worms, and he expressed his indignation at it in an outspoken publication, in which he bitterly reproached the Emperor and the Princes for their treatment of him.

He had now lost all confidence in both. But the Emperor's indignation at the Nuremberg Mandate was not less strongly marked, and he issued an Edict, in which he energetically denied the Estates the right of interference in religious matters, demanding at the same time the strict execution of the Edict of Worms. The constant recurrence of the Emperor and the adherents of the Pope to that Edict must not surprise us. It is the point upon which the whole movement turned; for if the condemnation of Luther was confirmed, all his reforms and his adherents would be comprised in that condemnation.

Various circumstances now combined to strengthen the effect of the Emperor's new Edict. The Papal Nuncio Campeggi succeeded in inducing several influential forces, hostile to the Reformation, to form a League for the protection of the old faith. The Archduke Ferdinand and the Dukes of Bavaria—Princes who had for some time been conspiring with the Roman Curia—together with a number of Prelates, assembled for that purpose in the summer of 1524 at Ratisbon, and agreed upon stringent measures against the Reformation. They decided to give effect to the Edict of Worms, to proscribe again the works of Luther, and even to forbid to their subjects the attending of the University of Wittenberg.

The next step of the Ratisbon Convention was now to obtain the co-operation of Charles V., which was effected easily enough, inasmuch as the projected measures fully coincided with his own views; and being about to attack Francis I. in France itself, from the direction of Italy, he stood in great need of the Pope's tacit acquiescence. He issued, therefore, a stringent Edict, in which the convocation of a General Council was strictly prohibited, and all interference in religious matters was energetically forbidden. Those who dared to set at nought the provision of the Edict, would render themselves liable to a charge of high treason, and on conviction would be punished with the highest degree of the Imperial Ban, (Acht- und Aberacht). In that Imperial Order Luther himself—one of the noblest men who ever lived—was likened to some loathsome monster.

The Convention of Ratisbon, which was chiefly brought about by foreign influence, may be said to have caused the first violent rupture among the German people, and to be the origin of all the calamities which befell Germany in the sixteenth and seventeenth centuries. Without that Convention the projected General Council would, in all probability, have been held, the proposed reforms would have been peacefully and legally discussed, and there would not have occurred that violent disruption among the Germans, of which the evil effects, not only from a religious, but also from a political point of view, have not yet entirely disappeared. The only advantage which resulted from the Ratisbon Convention was the agreement to introduce a number of internal reforms in the Church. Thus the improved state of Roman Catholicism is entirely due to the doctrines of Luther and his Reformation.

VII.

The year 1525 was perhaps the most trying in Luther's career. He had hitherto been disappointed in the Princes and the burghers, and now he experienced the mortification of seeing that class of people, from which he sprang himself, entering on a path which must needs prove injurious to themselves, and to the cause for which he lived and worked. Various risings of the Peasants had taken place before the time of the Reformation, in consequence of the inhuman treatment to which they were subjected by the nobles. The exactions of the priests were likewise intolerable. Some local risings took place in 1524; but in the following year that terrible contest, known as "*The* Peasants' War," broke out in the south of Germany with all the fury of long-pent up despair. The origin of the insurrection must therefore be sought solely in the cause, which produced the risings of slaves or serfs in ancient and modern times. It was the revolt of men who felt their inner worth, and who were determined to shake off an unbearable yoke. The enemies of Luther attributed, however, the outbreak of the war to the influence of his teachings, in the same way as they attributed to these any other public calamity which then befell Germany; just as in modern times blinded political passions will trace the cause of the failure of a harvest, for instance, to the fact of this or that party being in power.

The first programme of the Peasants, as contained in the well-known Twelve Articles, was moderate enough. Even Luther did not entirely reject their demands, some of which he wished to see referred to the decision of legal authorities. He admonished the Peasants, however, not to have recourse to brutal violence, and at the same time he exhorted the nobles to lend a merciful ear to the cries of the sufferers. The last clause of the Twelve Articles must have struck in his heart a sympathetic chord. The Peasants declared that their demands shall not stand, in case they should be refuted by Scripture, which statement seems to be an echo of Luther's own declaration at the Diet of Worms. But it was just that external similarity which turned out so fatal for the cause of the Reformation. The Peasants borrowed the phraseology, as it were, of Luther; they clothed their grievances in the language of the Gospel, and thus gave to the enemies of the Reformation the plausible pretext of confounding it with their own insurrection. It was of little avail for Luther himself to protest against the allegation of the insurgents that their rising was founded on a religious basis, since his enemies persistently took the form for the substance.

If all the rebellious Peasants had strictly adhered to their first programme, their cause might yet have taken a favourable turn; but, as is generally the case with revolutionary movements, there soon arose an extreme party which aimed at the total subversion of the existing order of things. Here again it was unfortunate that some points started in the manifesto of that party had been previously advocated by Luther, for his unjust antagonists laid all their demands, which have been compared to the French revolutionary doctrines of 1783, to his charge. The climax of the insurrectionary outbreak was, however, reached by the doings of Thomas Münzer and his followers, who preached and practised evangelical communism, and who accelerated by their fanatic and fantastic conduct the tragic catastrophe in this sanguinary drama. Luther was now in a most critical position. He made every effort to stem the tide of the revolution—he energetically exhorted both Princes and Peasants, and travelled about as a missionary of peace; but all in vain. His influence seemed, for the first time, to have lost its effect, and friends and foes censured him alike. The former reproached him with having deserted his own cause, whilst the latter blamed him as the originator of this fatal war. Thomas Münzer and his followers even accused Luther of base servility towards the Princes; and one of the grossest calumnies perhaps ever brought forward against a man of Luther's stamp, was the charge that he had written his vehement publication, "against the murderous robber-bands of the Peasants," after their total defeat. But this was untrue. He wrote it, in fact, whilst the Peasants were in the ascendancy, and whilst they disgraced their victory by barbarous acts of cruelty. When the nobles got the upper hand, and wreaked their vengeance in a most inhuman manner on the vanquished, the wrath of Luther was turned against the cruel victors. He pleaded for mercy even for the guilty, and with some of the Princes his intercession was successful. Large numbers of defeated Peasants were allowed, by Landgrave Philip of Hesse and the Prince Elector John of Saxony, the brother and successor of the Elector Frederick, to return home unmolested, whilst the Bishop of Würzburg and other anti-Lutheran lords distinguished themselves by a most refined cruelty in their treatment of the Peasant prisoners.

VIII.

In addition to the various disasters which befell Luther—and in him the whole of Germany—in the calamitous year of 1525, he also had the misfortune to lose his friend and protector, the Elector of Saxony, who died in the spring of that year. Frederick had looked with true paternal compassion on the insurgent Peasants, and had life and health been spared him, he might have quelled the civil war by the dint of his authority, or at least have mitigated its evils. Besides him, there was no one in Germany who enjoyed the same universal respect, and both the Imperial Regency and the Estates were, as a body, powerless. If Germany had been ruled over at that time by a sovereign residing in the country, and caring for the welfare of his people, the Peasants' War would never have assumed such gigantic dimensions, nor would its consequences have been so fatal. But whilst Germany was convulsed by one of the most sanguinary of intestine wars, the Emperor resided in Spain, and his army fought and defeated the King of France before Pavia; which circumstance may serve as an additional proof of the evil caused by the election of Charles V. as head of the German Empire.

The only interest which the Emperor manifested with reference to Germany consisted in his relentless efforts to exterminate the Lutheran doctrines. Thus he again and again issued from Spain energetic admonitions to the Princes and Bishops to make a firm resistance against the Reformation; promising and threatening at the same time to come shortly to Germany himself, in order to crush the heretics. These acts, together with the consultation at Mentz at which a number of priests agreed on the suppression of Lutheran heresy, induced the Landgrave Philip of Hesse, and John the Elector of Saxony, in the spring of 1526, to form the so-called "League of Torgau" for the protection and defence of the Reformation. Luther himself, being, in principle, against all armed resistance to any constituted authority, had consistently opposed the formation of that or any other League, with a view to revolt.

Luther was of opinion that a bad Prince must be patiently borne with, like any other scourge or calamity sent by Heaven. In this sense it was, that he taught "that the badness and perversity of a government does not justify active resistance or rebellion." Indeed he considered the sufferings inflicted by a tyrannical ruler on his subjects as part and parcel of a man's destiny upon earth. It was his Christian duty to suffer. According to his opinion man was not destined to be happy in this world, where he has been placed as a martyr. Such were his honest convictions and his views of life; his denial of the right of resistance arose therefore from a purely religious feeling, and not from any servile instinct. Surely a man who speaks in the following strain of Princes cannot be accused of servility: "From the beginning of the world," says Luther, "a good Prince has been a rare bird and a pious Prince a still rarer one. They are as a rule the greatest fools and worst knaves upon earth. If there is a Prince who is a wise and pious man, or a Christian, it is a great miracle and the best sign of divine grace for a country. Therefore one must always expect the worst from them, and not hope for any good from them. They are the scourges and the executioners of God, and He employs them to punish the wicked and to maintain external peace."

Luther was well aware of the fact that Germany required a thorough reform as regards its civic or secular government, more especially as he had found out that both the Princes and the Emperor had betrayed the German people. With that dignified self-consciousness which is quite compatible with true modesty, he said: "At times it seems to me as if the Government and the Jurists also required a Luther." If there had been during his time a great man in Germany, capable of achieving in politics what he had himself achieved in religion, he would undoubtedly have co-operated with him. For Luther was a true German patriot, if ever there was one, as is evident from so many of his writings, and more especially from his appeal to the "Christian Nobility of the German Nation." What he abhorred was the use of brutal force, either by Princes or by the people, for the acquisition of political freedom, and this was—as we have seen—in strict accordance with his religious views. His notions of the individual freedom of man had also a religious basis. He regarded man as designed to be a free being, but it was only Christian belief which imparted to him that stamp of true freedom. This view Luther forcibly expressed in the well-known antithesis in his Treatise, 'Concerning Christian Liberty:' "A Christian man is the most free lord of all, and subject to none; a Christian man is the most dutiful servant of all, and subject to every one."[11]

The liberty of man, as interpreted by Luther, may be regarded by some persons as only of limited extent, and as having merely an ideal existence, but at any rate it marks a great progress in the history of civilization, and may be considered as the germ of the emancipation of the human race. It was the first step in the acknowledgment of the right of man as a human being. The principle of political freedom which now benefits the adherents of all creeds in civilized society must therefore be traced back to the Reformation. If the teachings of Luther had not first freed the *Christian* man, the liberty of man, in general—the equality of men—would scarcely have met with such a ready recognition in later centuries.

If Luther had not so strenuously opposed all active resistance against authority, the political course of the Reformation would certainly have taken a different turn; and it was fortunate enough for its consolidation, that some of the Princes, who otherwise followed his teachings, did not share his opinions on that subject. The formation of the above-mentioned League of Torgau was the first result of that difference of opinion; and when the Diet assembled, in the summer of 1526, at Spires, the Princes John and Philip, strengthened by their union, could dare to acknowledge and practise openly the doctrines of the Reformation in the face of the Diet. In vain did the Imperial Commissioners urge the Estates to carry out at last the Edict of Worms. The Diet was, however, so much the less inclined to obey the Emperor's behests on this point, because he was now himself at enmity with the Pope. Clement VII. being afraid of the ascendency of Charles V. after his victory at Pavia, released the French King from his solemn oath at the Peace of Madrid, and formed with him and several Italian Princes the League of Cognac, also blasphemously called the "Holy League," which was directed against Charles V. The Estates, therefore, eagerly seized the opportunity of declaring that the antagonism between Pope and Emperor made it impossible for them to give effect even indirectly to the Papal Excommunication against Luther. The Turk was also threatening from the East, and the Estates did not consider it prudent to cause dissensions among the German people. They resolved therefore to petition the Emperor, through an embassy, to come in

---

[11] See p. 102 in the present volume.

person to Germany and to convoke a General Council. They further decided that in matters of religion, perfect freedom and tolerance should prevail.

The Resolution of the Diet of Spires in 1526 was of considerable moment. The Reformation was now formally acknowledged and legalised, and had gained full time to recover lost ground and to obtain a firm footing throughout Germany. It also was a fortunate coincidence that Charles V. was now occupied in Italy with his war against the Pope and Francis I., whilst his brother Ferdinand, now King of Hungary and Bohemia, was encumbered by his troubles in those countries.

IX.

In consequence of the absence of both the Emperor and his *locum tenens* from Germany, the projected General Council was not convoked, and the next Diet did not assemble before the year 1529, at Spires. Till then the Reformation had full scope to expand; but after the armies of Charles V. had captured Rome, and a terrible pestilence had well-nigh destroyed the French troops in Italy, the Emperor was again free to terrorize over Germany. He concluded peace with Clement VII. at Barcelona, and with Francis I. at Cambray, and the first result of the diplomatic union between the three belligerents was a combination of their efforts to crush the "heresy" in Germany. Soon after the beginning of the Diet at Spires, a palpable proof was given that a great change had taken place in public affairs since 1526. On March 15, 1529, the Imperial Commissioners laid a Mandate before the Diet to the effect that the Resolution of the last Diet at Spires, which granted free exercise of religion, should be revoked, and that, on the other hand, the Edict of Worms should be enforced. The majority, though now consisting of adherents of the Pope, did not accept the proposal exactly in that form; but still they issued a Decree, the general acceptance of which would have implied a total condemnation of the Reformation on the part of its supporters.

In this emergency several German Princes and Imperial towns gave proof of a most praiseworthy moral courage. John, Prince Elector of Saxony, Philip, Landgrave of Hesse, George, Margrave of Brandenburg, Duke Ernest of Brunswick-Luneburg, Prince Wolfgang of Anhalt, and fourteen Imperial free towns, having in vain demurred against the decision of the Diet, laid before it a *Protest* against the pernicious decree, declaring at the same time, that in matters of religion and conscience the decision of majorities was not binding. How deep was the impression which that remarkable step had produced on the minds of the German people, may be inferred from the fact that it gave occasion to single out the adherents of Luther as a body and to apply to them the name of *Protestants.*

The rupture between the two religious parties was now complete. They no longer formed merely two different shades of the same party, but were distinguished from each other even as to the name. *Roman Catholics* stood opposite *Protestants.* In one respect the new appellation was a gain; for it embraced all the members of that Christian community, which did not acknowledge the supremacy of the Pope. On the other hand the name has the disadvantage that it is like the word "Reformation," of a *negative* character. It is true the *Protest* of the Princes actually was a *positive* assertion of the right of conscience, but popular interpretation applied to it the character of an aggressive document, and the adherents of Luther were consequently regarded henceforth in the light of a merely malcontent party. The term "Lutherans"—*Lutheraner*—does not embrace the whole body of those who seceded from the Roman Catholic Church. Luther himself deprecated, moreover, the distinction of being called a "founder of a religion," and although one of the greatest theological authorities of our times is still inclined to consider him as such, it seems to me—if I may venture to express an opinion on anything touching a theological subject—that Luther merely modified and reformed an established religious faith, but did not found one. The designation "Old Catholic" might perhaps have been the most appropriate, and would not perchance have caused such a violent disruption among the members of the great Christian community.

X.

At the Diet of 1529 the Protestants had gained a moral victory, but they had suffered a material defeat; for the government of the Empire was now entirely in the hands of their antagonists. It seemed, therefore, prudent to prepare for future emergencies, and some of the Protestant Princes began negotiations with several cities, both German and Swiss. A comprehensive scheme was devised which, if successfully carried out, would have entirely changed the political aspect of Germany, if not of Europe. Unfortunately this plan, the execution of which could alone have saved the cause of Protestantism, was frustrated by the well-known theological difference between the adherents of Luther and Zwingli. Thus, instead of first combining against the common enemy, and subsequently in firm union settling the theological differences, or even leaving them unsettled, the logical order of the proceeding was reversed. The Theologians first assembled to discuss their religious differences, and the result was that fatal schism which divided the camp of the Protestants, and permanently damaged their cause. Luther and his more immediate followers decided that it would not be justifiable to form an alliance with the Zwinglians, and further, that it would be an offence against law and religion to offer armed resistance to the Emperor. The co-operation of Upper Germany, Suabia and Switzerland was lost in consequence, and—in face of the armed and threatening enemy—all preparations for defence were neglected on account of religious scruples. "Surely," says Ranke, "this was not prudent, but it was grand."

Whilst the German Theologians discussed religious subjects and the "right of resistance," Charles V. strengthened his position in Italy, and Clement VII. placed on his head, at Bologna, the crown of Charles the Great. The Emperor was surrounded on this occasion chiefly by Italian Princes and Spanish Grandees, and only one or two German Princes were present. The coronation was, therefore, against the "ancient German custom," but Charles was crowned as a *Roman* and not as a *German* Emperor of Germany. He might have been like Henry the Fowler, another founder or regenerator of the German Empire, whereas he renovated the Imperial dignity only so far as his own personality was concerned. This step was very significant, and may serve as a clue to his subsequent course of action.

It is well known that the Pope and Emperor distrusted each other, but they were diplomatic enough to assume the mask of mutual friendship. There was, moreover, one powerful bond of union between them, namely, the determination to eradicate German "heresy." This resolve was one of the principal motives of the Emperor's journey to Germany, in the summer of 1530, for the purpose of holding a Diet at Augsburg. The writ issued on that occasion was peaceful and gracious enough. His avowed object was "to settle the prevailing discord, and to learn and graciously to consider everybody's conviction, opinion, and views, for the benefit of Christian truth."

It may reasonably be assumed that the Emperor was benevolently disposed, and would have preferred to see his point carried by gentle means. His benevolence was, however, of that conditional kind only, which first tries peaceful means, but subsequently has recourse to arbitrary and violent measures, should the gentle measures prove futile. He was not imbued with that absolute benevolence and clemency which shows mercy even to the guilty, or the supposed guilty. The Roman Catholic Princes were aware of this disposition of the Emperor, and of his secret agreement with the Pope, though the Protestant Princes implicitly believed in his peaceful and gracious assurances. The latter now hopefully looked forward to an amicable settlement of the prevailing discord, and at once proceeded to draw up a Programme, containing the substance of the reformed creed.

It did not take long however for the Protestants to see their error. Even before the Emperor's arrival at Augsburg he urged the Elector John of Saxony not to allow the preachers he had brought with him to preach in public. This demand was repeated in Augsburg, in the Emperor's presence, after his arrival in that city, to the Elector of Saxony, and several other Protestant Princes. The theological defence of the evangelical sermons by the Landgrave of Hesse merely served to arouse the wrath and indignation of Charles. When, however, the aged warrior, the Margrave George of Brandenburg emphatically exclaimed: "Sire, before renouncing the word of God, I would rather kneel down on this spot and let my head be cut off," the Emperor was deeply moved by this energetic protest, and uttered in his Low-German vernacular the reassuring words: "No heads off! no heads off, my dear Prince!"

The Protestant Princes also declined to join in the public procession on the festival of Corpus Christi, which was celebrated the following day, in spite of the Emperor's earnest invitation to attend it. Charles was startled by this stubborn resistance. He had cherished the hope that the halo of worldly glory which surrounded him, together with his brilliant entry into Augsburg, would dazzle and overawe the Protestant Princes; but they remained firm. Neither threats nor promises could move them. They were quite of a distinct caste from the Princes who had betrayed the cause of the Reformation at Worms; they were conscious of the risk they ran, and were ready to die for their religious convictions. It is true they were greatly encouraged by Luther, who, in order to be nearer to them while the Diet was held at Augsburg, had repaired to Coburg. He addressed to the Prince Elector of Saxony from his second "Patmos," as it were, letters of exhortation and comfort, full of energy and of that irresistible eloquence which is the result of inner conviction. Whenever the Princes and Melanchthon wavered, they were inspired by Luther's cheering and manly words, which proved particularly effective during the course of the Diet.

The religious contest being the first subject which was brought before the Diet, the Protestant Princes presented, on 25th June, 1530, their "Confession of Faith," which had been prepared by Melanchthon. There were two versions of it, one in German and another in Latin. The Emperor naturally desired to have the second version read, but the Protestant Princes advised him patriotically to admit on German soil the *German* version. This step may be considered as one of the results of the Reformation. Luther had awakened in the Germans the feelings of nationality and patriotism, and had also politically freed them from the fetters of Roman bondage.

The profession of faith of the Protestant Princes, known as the "Augsburg Confession," was drawn up in such a conciliatory spirit and contained so many concessions to Roman Catholicism, that some kind of agreement seemed to be possible, if not near at hand. The Protestants had now honestly fulfilled their duty. In accordance with the Imperial rescript they had laid their profession of faith before the Diet; and confidently expecting a similar profession on the part of the Roman Catholics, they looked forward to the promised mediation of the Emperor. But instead of drawing up a declaration in a defensive and conciliatory spirit, as had been done by the Protestants, the Catholic party at the Diet forming the majority, issued an aggressive "Refutation," which, receiving the Emperor's full approval, was issued in his name, with the appended threat, that in case the Protestants should henceforth not obediently return to the Roman Catholic faith, "the Emperor would proceed against them as befitted a *Roman* Emperor—the protector and defender of the Church." Manifest proofs that the admonitions of Charles V. were not mere empty threats were soon given. He made the Protestant Princes individually feel his displeasure, and he seemed fully determined to give effect to his threats by the force of arms. Fortunately the warning of the Prince Elector of Mentz in reference to the Turks of *Hannibal ad portas*, had the desirable effect of paving the way for mediation.

At the Conference which was held in August, 1530, for the purpose of effecting an agreement between the contending parties, a spirit of reconciliation prevailed. Both sides made concessions, and it was agreed to refer certain points of difference which were still pending to a General Council; so that there was a near prospect of a mutual understanding. Some agreement would, in all probability, have been brought about, but for the relentless spirit of fanaticism of the Roman Curia, as represented by the Legate Campeggi. It was he who frustrated the success of all further attempts at a reconciliation by inducing the Emperor and the majority of the Diet to make such conditions as the Protestants could not accept. The allied Princes remained firm, and as the attitude of the Imperial Court became more and more threatening, and the Theologians could not agree among themselves, the energetic Landgrave Philip of Hesse suddenly left Augsburg at the beginning of August. The Emperor was so startled by this unexpected event, that he ordered the gates of the city to be watched by his soldiers; but, too late, the bird had already flown. The Prince Elector of Saxony still remained behind, but his son, the hereditary Prince, had some time previously returned home and was now in perfect safety. It was, therefore, useless to attempt a *coup de main* against the leaders of the Protestant party.

The Emperor's disappointment was great, and the more so, as he was indignant against the Protestant Princes on account of their refusing to consent to the election of his brother Ferdinand as "King of Rome." Charles V. now proceeded to the last step which made the breach between the two great portions of the German nation irremediable. On the 22nd of September, 1530, he communicated to the Estates the draft of the Decree upon which he had resolved with reference to the religious contest, and which announced his determination "to carry out unconditionally the Edict of Worms." The Protestants were treated in that Decree as a mere sect, and their doctrines—of all shades—were indiscriminately condemned. All the usages of the old creed were to be maintained intact, and the rights of the Ecclesiastical Princes were to be fully restored, under pain of the Imperial ban. This Imperial Decree, which was virtually a total abolition of the work of the Reformation, was finally issued on the 19th of November with the additional clause—which savoured of mockery—that a time of respite should be granted to the Protestants until the 15th April, 1531, to enable them to declare their adhesion to the contested points. In the meantime the Emperor was to use his efforts with the Pope to convene a General Council to discuss the abolition of certain unquestionable abuses in the Church.

This amounted to an open declaration of war, and the Protestant Princes were prudent enough to take their measures accordingly.

XI.

The Diet of Augsburg in 1530 may be considered, in some respects, as the key-stone in the religious and political course of the Reformation. The "Augsburg Confession" practically completed the work of the Reformation from a religious point of view, whilst the Imperial Edict marked out in distinct features the line of action which the Papal and Imperial party was resolved to pursue towards the Protestants. It was an ultimatum in due form. All the subsequent events in the history of the Reformation—even as far down as the Peace of Westphalia in 1648—must, therefore, be regarded as merely the natural sequence of the Diet of Augsburg, and do not actually belong to the making or unmaking of the Reformation.

The stern necessity of self-defence caused at last the Protestant Princes to form the "Convention" or "League of Smalkald" in December 1530. Even Luther was induced to approve of it, and some of his writings, more especially his 'Warning to my beloved Germans,' showed that he no longer viewed self-defence in the light of rebellion. The schism among the Germans was now political as well as religious. A compact body stood armed, not against the sovereign power of the German Empire, but against the *Roman* Emperor of the German nation; against the monarch who identified himself with the Pope. Charles V. fully recognised the drift of the Protestant opposition, and it is not quite improbable that on account of it he insisted on the speedy election and coronation of his brother Ferdinand as "Roman King," which took place at Cologne at the end of 1530, and at Aix-la-Chapelle at the beginning of the following year. The Protestant Princes protested against this proceeding, as being contrary to the Imperial Constitution of Germany; but we have already seen that Charles cared very little either for the laws or the aspirations of the German people. The illegal election of Ferdinand necessarily widened the breach between the Emperor and the Protestant Princes, who plainly saw the danger impending from the supremacy of the house of Hapsburg.

The Dukes of Bavaria, who also aspired to the Imperial dignity, looked grudgingly on the ascendency of the Hapsburgs, and seemed inclined—staunch Roman Catholics though they were—to make common cause with the Protestants. Moreover the Turks were again threatening an invasion of the Austro-German provinces, and all these circumstances combined, induced the Emperor to conclude with the Protestant Princes, in the summer of 1532, the "Peace of Nuremberg." Considerable concessions were made to the Protestants, and the promise of a "General, free and Christian Council," was again held out; but of far greater moment was the fact, that by consenting to the "Peace of Nuremberg," the Emperor actually recognised the members of the "Smalkaldic League" as a regularly constituted power, with which it was desirable to come to an amicable understanding. The political element, which, as we have seen, had been at work throughout the course of the Reformation, became henceforth a more and more powerful factor in the struggle between the two hostile camps of the German nation.

After the Diet of Augsburg in 1530, Charles was again occupied with his military enterprises abroad, and remained absent from Germany for the space of nine years. His brother, King Ferdinand I., was likewise prevented from effectively interfering with religious affairs in consequence of the troubles in his hereditary dominions, and so the Reformation had again free scope to make its way through the greater portion of Germany. The indulgence granted to the Protestants was, however, apparent only. Both Charles and his brother treacherously bided their time to enter on the struggle of annihilation against them. That time seemed to them to have arrived when Charles, in conjunction with Henry VIII., had forced the King of France to sign the Peace of Crepy in 1544. It is true the Emperor consented to convene a Council in December, 1545, and so he did at Trent, but the Princes of Hesse and Saxony justly declined to attend it. The Emperor's hostile intentions against the Protestants now became patent, first by his renewed League with Paul III., the successor of Pope Clement VII., and afterwards by the mustering of his forces. If the Protestants had acted with energy and concord they might, with the greatest ease, have defeated the small Imperial forces in the summer of 1545; but instead of this they gave the Emperor full time to collect a considerable army.

In the meantime Martin Luther, the life and soul of the Reformation, had died on the 18th of February, 1546, and was spared the pain of witnessing the outbreak of the unfortunate Smalkaldic War, which laid Germany prostrate at the feet of the Emperor and his Spaniards. This calamity was, of course, due mostly to the fact that the old German Empire identified itself with the Papacy and considered itself bound to defend its cause. It is, however, a significant fact, that Charles V. was actually the last Roman Emperor of Germany crowned by a Pope. When he proceeded for his coronation, in 1530, to the Church of St. Petronio at Bologna, through a wooden structure which had been erected to connect his Palace with the church, the temporary passage gave way a few steps behind the Emperor. Popular superstition saw in this an evil omen—for Germany, it proved to be a happy one—and prophesied that Charles would be the last German Emperor thus crowned. The prophecy became true, but it was not in Italy that the link was broken which connected Germany with Rome. This was done in Germany itself, and as we have seen, by the humble peasants' son, Martin Luther.

Luther it was who actually freed Germany from the secular and spiritual bondage of Rome; for although the Protestants had been vanquished in the Smalkaldic war, they were not entirely crushed. The spirit of the Reformation survived, and exercised its beneficial influence not only throughout Germany, but over the whole of the civilised world, and it is in this sense that the Reformation is universally considered as the beginning of a New Era in the history of the world. The Reformation is the source, directly or indirectly, by action or by reaction, of everything great and noble which has taken place from about the beginning of the sixteenth century. Through the Reformation alone men of all creeds have become free and enlightened. And this is the reason why not only the Theologian, but also the political and literary Historian hails the work of the Reformation as one of the greatest blessings ever bestowed on mankind.

FIRST PRINCIPLES of THE REFORMATION.

THE NINETY-FIVE THESES.

INTRODUCTORY LETTER.

To the most Reverend Father in Christ and most illustrious Lord, Albert, Archbishop and Primate of the Churches of Magdeburg and Mentz, Marquis of Brandenburg, etc., his lord and pastor in Christ, most gracious and worthy of all fear and reverence—

Jesus.

The grace of God be with you, and whatsoever it is and can do.

Spare me, most reverend Father in Christ, most illustrious Prince, if I, the very dregs of humanity, have dared to think of addressing a letter to the eminence of your sublimity. The Lord Jesus is my witness that, in the consciousness of my own pettiness and baseness, I have long put off the doing of that which I have now hardened my forehead to perform, moved thereto most especially by the sense of that faithful duty which I feel that I owe to your most reverend Fatherhood in Christ. May your Highness then in the meanwhile deign to cast your eyes upon one grain of dust, and, in your pontifical clemency, to understand my prayer.

Papal indulgences are being carried about, under your most distinguished authority, for the building of St. Peter's. In respect of these I do not so much accuse the extravagant sayings of the preachers, which I have not heard, but I grieve at the very false ideas which the people conceive from them, and which are spread abroad in common talk on every side—namely, that unhappy souls believe that, if they buy letters of indulgences, they are sure of their salvation; also, that, as soon as they have thrown their contribution into the chest, souls forthwith fly out of purgatory; and furthermore, that so great is the grace thus conferred, that there is no sin so great—even, as they say, if, by an impossibility, any one had violated the Mother of God—but that it may be pardoned; and again, that by these indulgences a man is freed from all punishment and guilt.

O gracious God! it is thus that the souls committed to your care, most excellent Father, are being taught unto their death, and a most severe account, which you will have to render for all of them, is growing and increasing. Hence I have not been able to keep silence any longer on this subject, for by no function of a bishop's office can a man become sure of salvation, since he does not even become sure through the grace of God infused into him, but the Apostle bids us to be ever working out our salvation in fear and trembling. (Phil. ii. 12.) Even the righteous man—says Peter—shall scarcely be saved. (1 Pet. iv. 18.) In fine, so narrow is the way which leads unto life, that the Lord, speaking by the prophets Amos and Zachariah, calls those who are to be saved brands snatched from the burning, and our Lord everywhere declares the difficulty of salvation.

Why then, by these false stories and promises of pardon, do the preachers of them make the people to feel secure and without fear? since indulgences confer absolutely no good on souls as regards salvation or holiness, but only take away the outward penalty which was wont of old to be canonically imposed.

Lastly, works of piety and charity are infinitely better than indulgences, and yet they do not preach these with such display or so much zeal; nay, they keep silence about them for the sake of preaching pardons. And yet it is the first and sole duty of all bishops, that the people should learn the Gospel and Christian charity: for Christ nowhere commands that indulgences should be preached. What a dreadful thing it is then, what peril to a bishop, if, while the Gospel is passed over in silence, he permits nothing but the noisy outcry of indulgences to be spread among his people, and bestows more care on these than on the Gospel! Will not Christ say to them: "Straining at a gnat, and swallowing a camel"?

Besides all this, most reverend Father in the Lord, in that instruction to the commissaries which has been put forth under the name of your most reverend Fatherhood it is stated—doubtless without the knowledge and consent of your most reverend Fatherhood—that one of the principal graces conveyed by indulgences is that inestimable gift of God, by which man is reconciled to God, and all the pains of purgatory are done away with; and further, that contrition is not necessary for those who thus redeem souls or buy confessional licences.

But what can I do, excellent Primate and most illustrious Prince, save to entreat your reverend Fatherhood, through the Lord Jesus Christ, to deign to turn on us the eye of fatherly care, and to suppress that advertisement altogether and impose on the preachers of pardons another form of preaching, lest perchance some one should at length arise who will put forth writings in confutation of them and of their advertisements, to the deepest reproach of your most illustrious Highness. It is intensely abhorrent to me that this should be done, and yet I fear that it will happen, unless the evil be speedily remedied.

This faithful discharge of my humble duty I entreat that your most illustrious Grace will deign to receive in a princely and bishoplike spirit—that is, with all clemency—even as I offer it with a most faithful heart, and one most devoted to your most reverend Fatherhood, since I too am part of your flock. May the Lord Jesus keep your most reverend Fatherhood for ever and ever. Amen.

From Wittemberg, on the eve of All Saints, in the year 1517.

If it so please your most reverend Fatherhood, you may look at these Disputations, that you may perceive how dubious a matter is that opinion about indulgences, which they disseminate as if it were most certain.

To your most reverend Fatherhood.

Martin Luther.

DISPUTATION OF DR. MARTIN LUTHER
CONCERNING PENITENCE AND INDULGENCES.

In the desire and with the purpose of elucidating the truth, a disputation will be held on the underwritten propositions at Wittemberg, under the presidency of the Reverend Father Martin Luther, Monk of the Order of St. Augustine, Master of Arts and of Sacred Theology, and ordinary Reader of the same in that place. He therefore asks those who cannot be present and discuss the subject with us orally, to do so by letter in their absence. In the name of our Lord Jesus Christ. Amen.

1. Our Lord and Master Jesus Christ in saying: "Repent ye,"[12] etc., intended that the whole life of believers should be penitence.

---

[12] In the Latin, from the Vulgate, "*agite pœnitentiam*," sometimes translated "Do penance." The effect of the following theses depends to some extent on the double meaning of "*pœnitentia*"—penitence and penance.

2. This word cannot be understood of sacramental penance, that is, of the confession and satisfaction which are performed under the ministry of priests.

3. It does not, however, refer solely to inward penitence; nay such inward penitence is naught, unless it outwardly produces various mortifications of the flesh.

4. The penalty[13] thus continues as long as the hatred of self—that is, true inward penitence—continues; namely, till our entrance into the kingdom of heaven.

5. The Pope has neither the will nor the power to remit any penalties, except those which he has imposed by his own authority, or by that of the canons.

6. The Pope has no power to remit any guilt, except by declaring and warranting it to have been remitted by God; or at most by remitting cases reserved for himself; in which cases, if his power were despised, guilt would certainly remain.

7. God never remits any man's guilt, without at the same time subjecting him, humbled in all things, to the authority of his representative the priest.

8. The penitential canons are imposed only on the living, and no burden ought to be imposed on the dying, according to them.

9. Hence the Holy Spirit acting in the Pope does well for us, in that, in his decrees, he always makes exception of the article of death and of necessity.

10. Those priests act wrongly and unlearnedly, who, in the case of the dying, reserve the canonical penances for purgatory.

11. Those tares about changing of the canonical penalty into the penalty of purgatory seem surely to have been sown while the bishops were asleep.

12. Formerly the canonical penalties were imposed not after, but before absolution, as tests of true contrition.

13. The dying pay all penalties by death, and are already dead to the canon laws, and are by right relieved from them.

14. The imperfect soundness or charity of a dying person necessarily brings with it great fear, and the less it is, the greater the fear it brings.

15. This fear and horror is sufficient by itself, to say nothing of other things, to constitute the pains of purgatory, since it is very near to the horror of despair.

16. Hell, purgatory, and heaven appear to differ as despair, almost despair, and peace of mind differ.

17. With souls in purgatory it seems that it must needs be that, as horror diminishes, so charity increases.

18. Nor does it seem to be proved by any reasoning or any scriptures, that they are outside of the state of merit or of the increase of charity.

19. Nor does this appear to be proved, that they are sure and confident of their own blessedness, at least all of them, though we may be very sure of it.

20. Therefore the Pope, when he speaks of the plenary remission of all penalties, does not mean simply of all, but only of those imposed by himself.

21. Thus those preachers of indulgences are in error who say that, by the indulgences of the Pope, a man is loosed and saved from all punishment.

22. For in fact he remits to souls in purgatory no penalty which they would have had to pay in this life according to the canons.

23. If any entire remission of all penalties can be granted to any one, it is certain that it is granted to none but the most perfect, that is, to very few.

---

[13] I.e. "*Pœna*," the connection between "*pœna*" and "*pœnitentia*" being again suggestive.

24. Hence the greater part of the people must needs be deceived by this indiscriminate and high-sounding promise of release from penalties.

25. Such power as the Pope has over purgatory in general, such has every bishop in his own diocese, and every curate in his own parish, in particular.

26. The Pope acts most rightly in granting remission to souls, not by the power of the keys (which is of no avail in this case) but by the way of suffrage.

27. They preach man, who say that the soul flies out of purgatory as soon as the money thrown into the chest rattles.

28. It is certain that, when the money rattles in the chest, avarice and gain may be increased, but the suffrage of the Church depends on the will of God alone.

29. Who knows whether all the souls in purgatory desire to be redeemed from it, according to the story told of Saints Severinus and Paschal.

30. No man is sure of the reality of his own contrition, much less of the attainment of plenary remission.

31. Rare as is a true penitent, so rare is one who truly buys indulgences—that is to say, most rare.

32. Those who believe that, through letters of pardon, they are made sure of their own salvation, will be eternally damned along with their teachers.

33. We must especially beware of those who say that these pardons from the Pope are that inestimable gift of God by which man is reconciled to God.

34. For the grace conveyed by these pardons has respect only to the penalties of sacramental satisfaction, which are of human appointment.

35. They preach no Christian doctrine, who teach that contrition is not necessary for those who buy souls out of purgatory or buy confessional licences.

36. Every Christian who feels true compunction has of right plenary remission of pain and guilt, even without letters of pardon.

37. Every true Christian, whether living or dead, has a share in all the benefits of Christ and of the Church, given him by God, even without letters of pardon.

38. The remission, however, imparted by the Pope is by no means to be despised, since it is, as I have said, a declaration of the Divine remission.

39. It is a most difficult thing, even for the most learned theologians, to exalt at the same time in the eyes of the people the ample effect of pardons and the necessity of true contrition.

40. True contrition seeks and loves punishment; while the ampleness of pardons relaxes it, and causes men to hate it, or at least gives occasion for them to do so.

41. Apostolical pardons ought to be proclaimed with caution, lest the people should falsely suppose that they are placed before other good works of charity.

42. Christians should be taught that it is not the mind of the Pope that the buying of pardons is to be in any way compared to works of mercy.

43. Christians should be taught that he who gives to a poor man, or lends to a needy man, does better than if he bought pardons.

44. Because, by a work of charity, charity increases, and the man becomes better; while, by means of pardons, he does not become better, but only freer from punishment.

45. Christians should be taught that he who sees any one in need, and, passing him by, gives money for pardons, is not purchasing for himself the indulgences of the Pope, but the anger of God.

46. Christians should be taught that, unless they have superfluous wealth, they are bound to keep what is necessary for the use of their own households, and by no means to lavish it on pardons.

47. Christians should be taught that, while they are free to buy pardons, they are not commanded to do so.

48. Christians should be taught that the Pope, in granting pardons, has both more need and more desire that devout prayer should be made for him, than that money should be readily paid.

49. Christians should be taught that the Pope's pardons are useful, if they do not put their trust in them, but most hurtful, if through them they lose the fear of God.

50. Christians should be taught that, if the Pope were acquainted with the exactions of the preachers of pardons, he would prefer that the Basilica of St. Peter should be burnt to ashes, than that it should be built up with the skin, flesh, and bones of his sheep.

51. Christians should be taught that, as it would be the duty, so it would be the wish of the Pope, even to sell, if necessary, the Basilica of St. Peter, and to give of his own money to very many of those from whom the preachers of pardons extract money.

52. Vain is the hope of salvation through letters of pardon, even if a commissary—nay, the Pope himself—were to pledge his own soul for them.

53. They are enemies of Christ and of the Pope, who, in order that pardons may be preached, condemn the word of God to utter silence in other churches.

54. Wrong is done to the word of God when, in the same sermon, an equal or longer time is spent on pardons than on it.

55. The mind of the Pope necessarily is that, if pardons, which are a very small matter, are celebrated with single bells, single processions, and single ceremonies, the Gospel, which is a very great matter, should be preached with a hundred bells, a hundred processions, and a hundred ceremonies.

56. The treasures of the Church, whence the Pope grants indulgences, are neither sufficiently named nor known among the people of Christ.

57. It is clear that they are at least not temporal treasures, for these are not so readily lavished, but only accumulated, by many of the preachers.

58. Nor are they the merits of Christ and of the saints, for these, independently of the Pope, are always working grace to the inner man, and the cross, death, and hell to the outer man.

59. St. Lawrence said that the treasures of the Church are the poor of the Church, but he spoke according to the use of the word in his time.

60. We are not speaking rashly when we say that the keys of the Church, bestowed through the merits of Christ, are that treasure.

61. For it is clear that the power of the Pope is alone sufficient for the remission of penalties and of reserved cases.

62. The true treasure of the Church is the Holy Gospel of the glory and grace of God.

63. This treasure, however, is deservedly most hateful, because it makes the first to be last.

64. While the treasure of indulgences is deservedly most acceptable, because it makes the last to be first.

65. Hence the treasures of the Gospel are nets, wherewith of old they fished for the men of riches.

66. The treasures of indulgences are nets, wherewith they now fish for the riches of men.

67. Those indulgences, which the preachers loudly proclaim to be the greatest graces, are seen to be truly such as regards the promotion of gain.

68. Yet they are in reality in no degree to be compared to the grace of God and the piety of the cross.

69. Bishops and curates are bound to receive the commissaries of apostolical pardons with all reverence.

70. But they are still more bound to see to it with all their eyes, and take heed with all their ears, that these men do not preach their own dreams in place of the Pope's commission.

71. He who speaks against the truth of apostolical pardons, let him be anathema and accursed.

72. But he, on the other hand, who exerts himself against the wantonness and licence of speech of the preachers of pardons, let him be blessed.

73. As the Pope justly thunders against those who use any kind of contrivance to the injury of the traffic in pardons,

74. Much more is it his intention to thunder against those who, under the pretext of pardons, use contrivances to the injury of holy charity and of truth.

75. To think that Papal pardons have such power that they could absolve a man even if—by an impossibility—he had violated the Mother of God, is madness.

76. We affirm on the contrary that Papal pardons cannot take away even the least of venial sins, as regards its guilt.

77. The saying that, even if St. Peter were now Pope, he could grant no greater graces, is blasphemy against St. Peter and the Pope.

78. We affirm on the contrary that both he and any other Pope has greater graces to grant, namely, the Gospel, powers, gifts of healing, etc. (1 Cor. xii. 9.)

79. To say that the cross set up among the insignia of the Papal arms is of equal power with the cross of Christ, is blasphemy.

80. Those bishops, curates, and theologians who allow such discourses to have currency among the people, will have to render an account.

81. This licence in the preaching of pardons makes it no easy thing, even for learned men, to protect the reverence due to the Pope against the calumnies, or, at all events, the keen questionings of the laity.

82. As for instance:—Why does not the Pope empty purgatory for the sake of most holy charity and of the supreme necessity of souls—this being the most just of all reasons—if he redeems an infinite number of souls for the sake of that most fatal thing money, to be spent on building a basilica—this being a very slight reason?

83. Again; why do funeral masses and anniversary masses for the deceased continue and why does not the Pope return, or permit the withdrawal of the funds bequeathed for this purpose, since it is a wrong to pray for those who are already redeemed?

84. Again; what is this new kindness of God and the Pope, in that, for money's sake, they permit an impious man and an enemy of God to redeem a pious soul which loves God, and yet do not redeem that same pious and beloved soul, out of free charity, on account of its own need?

85. Again; why is it that the penitential canons, long since abrogated and dead in themselves in very fact and not only by usage, are yet still redeemed with money, through the granting of indulgences, as if they were full of life?

86. Again; why does not the Pope, whose riches are at this day more ample than those of the wealthiest of the wealthy, build the one Basilica of St. Peter with his own money, rather than with that of poor believers?

87. Again; what does the Pope remit or impart to those who, through perfect contrition, have a right to plenary remission and participation?

88. Again; what greater good would the Church receive if the Pope, instead of once, as he does now, were to bestow these remissions and participations a hundred times a day on any one of the faithful?

89. Since it is the salvation of souls, rather than money, that the Pope seeks by his pardons, why does he suspend the letters and pardons granted long ago, since they are equally efficacious.

90. To repress these scruples and arguments of the laity by force alone, and not to solve them by giving reasons, is to expose the Church and the Pope to the ridicule of their enemies, and to make Christian men unhappy.

91. If then pardons were preached according to the spirit and mind of the Pope, all these questions would be resolved with ease; nay, would not exist.

92. Away then with all those prophets who say to the people of Christ: "Peace, peace," and there is no peace.

93. Blessed be all those prophets, who say to the people of Christ: "The cross, the cross," and there is no cross.

94. Christians should be exhorted to strive to follow Christ their head through pains, deaths, and hells.

95. And thus trust to enter heaven through many tribulations, rather than in the security of peace.

Protestation.

I, Martin Luther, Doctor, of the Order of Monks at Wittemberg, desire to testify publicly that certain propositions against pontifical indulgences, as they call them, have been put forth by me. Now although, up to the present time, neither this most celebrated and renowned school of ours, nor any civil or ecclesiastical power has condemned me, yet there are, as I hear, some men of headlong and audacious spirit, who dare to pronounce me a heretic, as though the matter had been thoroughly looked into and studied. But on my part, as I have often done before, so now too I implore all men, by the faith of Christ, either to point out to me a better way, if such a way has been divinely revealed to any, or at least to submit their opinion to the judgment of God and of the Church. For I am neither so rash as to wish that my sole opinion should be preferred to that of all other men, nor so senseless as to be willing that the word of God should be made to give place to fables, devised by human reason.

THE THREE PRIMARY WORKS of DR. MARTIN LUTHER.

I. TO THE CHRISTIAN NOBILITY OF THE GERMAN NATION RESPECTING THE REFORMATION OF THE CHRISTIAN ESTATE.

JESUS.

DEDICATORY LETTER.

To the respected and worthy NICOLAUS VON AMSDORF, Licentiate in the Holy Scriptures and Canon of Wittenberg,[14] My particular and affectionate friend. Dr. MARTIN LUTHER.

The Grace and Peace of God be with you! Respected, worthy Sir and dear friend.

The time for silence is gone and the time to speak has come, as we read in Ecclesiastes (iii. 7.) I have in conformity with our resolve put together some few points concerning the *Reformation of the Christian Estate*, with the intent of placing the same before the *Christian Nobility of the German Nation*, in case it may please God to help His Church by means of the laity, inasmuch as the clergy, whom this task rather befitted, have become quite careless. I send all this to your worship, to judge and to amend where needed. I am well aware that I shall not escape the reproach of taking far too much upon me, in presuming, insignificant as I am, to address such high estates on such weighty and great subjects; as if there were no one in the world but Dr. Luther, to have a care for Christianity, and to give advice to such wise people.

Let who will blame me, I shall not offer any excuse. Perhaps I still owe God and the world another folly. This debt I have now resolved honestly to discharge, as well as may be, and to be court fool for once in my life: if I fail, I shall at any rate gain this advantage, that no one need buy me a fool's cap or shave my poll. But it remains to be seen which shall hang the bells on the other. I must fulfil the proverb: When anything is to be done in the world, a monk must be in it, were it only as a painted figure. I suppose, it has often happened that a fool has spoken wisely, and wise men have often done foolishly, as St. Paul says: "If any man among you seemeth to be wise in this world, let him become a fool, that he may be wise." (1 Cor. iii. 18.)

Now, inasmuch as I am not only a fool, but also a sworn doctor of the Holy Scriptures, I am glad that I have an opportunity of fulfilling my oath, just in this fool's way. I beg you to excuse me to the moderately wise: for I know not how to deserve the favour and grace of the supremely wise, which I have so often sought with much labour, but now for the future shall neither have nor regard.

God help us to seek not our glory, but His alone. Amen.

From Wittenberg, in the monastery of St. Augustine, on the eve of St. John the Baptist, in the year 1520.

---

[14] Nicolaus von Amsdorf (1483–1565) was a colleague of Luther at the University of Wittenberg, and one of his most zealous fellow-workers in the cause of the Reformation.

JESUS.

To his most Serene and Mighty Imperial Majesty, and to the Christian Nobility of the German Nation.

Dr. MARTINUS LUTHER.

The grace and might of God be with you, Most Serene Majesty! most gracious, well beloved gentlemen!

It is not out of mere arrogance and perversity that I, a single poor man, have taken upon me to address your lordships. The distress and misery that oppress all the Christian estates, more especially in Germany, have led not only myself, but every one else, to cry aloud and to ask for help, and have now forced me too, to cry out and to ask, if God would give His Spirit to any one, to reach a hand to His wretched people. Councils have often put forward some remedy, but through the cunning of certain men it has been adroitly frustrated, and the evils have become worse; whose malice and wickedness I will now, by the help of God, expose, so that, being known, they may henceforth cease to be so obstructive and injurious. God has given us a young and noble sovereign,[15] and by this has roused hope in many hearts: now it is right that we too should do what we can, and make good use of time and grace.

The first thing that we must do is to consider the matter with great earnestness, and, whatever we attempt, not to trust in our own strength and wisdom alone, even if the power of all the world were ours; for God will not endure that a good work should be begun, trusting to our own strength and wisdom. He destroys it; it is all useless: as we read in the xxxiii. Psalm. "There is no king saved by the multitude of an host: a mighty man is not delivered by much strength." And I fear it is for that reason, that those beloved Princes, the Emperors Frederick, the First and the Second, and many other German Emperors were, in former times, so piteously spurned and oppressed by the Popes, though they were feared by all the world. Perchance they trusted rather in their own strength than in God; therefore they could not but fall: and how would the sanguinary tyrant Julius II. have risen so high in our own days, but, that, I fear, France, the Germans and Venice trusted to themselves? The children of Benjamin slew forty-two thousand Israelites, for this reason, that these trusted to their own strength. (Judges xx. etc.)

That it may not happen thus to us and to our noble Emperor Charles, we must remember that in this matter we wrestle not against flesh and blood, but against the rulers of the darkness of this world (Eph. vi. 12), who may fill the world with war and bloodshed, but cannot themselves be overcome thereby. We must renounce all confidence in our natural strength, and take the matter in hand with humble trust in God; we must seek God's help with earnest prayer, and have nothing before our eyes but the misery and wretchedness of Christendom, irrespective of what punishment the wicked may deserve. If we do not act thus, we may begin the game with great pomp; but when we are well in it, the spirits of evil will make such confusion, that the whole world will be immersed in blood, and yet nothing be done. Therefore let us act in the fear of God, and prudently. The greater the might of the foe, the greater is the misfortune, if we do not act

[15] Charles V. was at that time not quite twenty years of age.

in the fear of God, and with humility. As Popes and Romanists have hitherto, with the Devil's help, thrown Kings into confusion, so will they still do, if we attempt things with our own strength and skill, without God's help.

I.

The Three Walls of the Romanists.

The Romanists have, with great adroitness, drawn three walls round themselves, with which they have hitherto protected themselves, so that no one could reform them, whereby all Christendom has fallen terribly.

Firstly, if pressed by the temporal power, they have affirmed and maintained that the temporal power has no jurisdiction over them, but on the contrary that the spiritual power is above the temporal.

Secondly, if it were proposed to admonish them with the Scriptures, they objected that no one may interpret the Scriptures but the Pope.

Thirdly, if they are threatened with a Council, they pretend that no one may call a Council but the Pope.

Thus they have secretly stolen our three rods, so that they may be unpunished, and entrenched themselves behind these three walls, to act with all wickedness and malice, as we now see. And whenever they have been compelled to call a Council, they have made it of no avail, by binding the Princes beforehand with an oath to leave them as they were. Besides this they have given the Pope full power over the arrangement of the Council, so that it is all one, whether we have many Councils, or no Councils, for in any case they deceive us with pretences and false tricks. So grievously do they tremble for their skin before a true, free Council; and thus they have overawed Kings and Princes, that these believe they would be offending God, if they were not to obey them in all such knavish, deceitful artifices.

Now may God help us, and give us one of those trumpets, that overthrew the walls of Jericho, so that we may blow down these walls of straw and paper, and that we may set free our Christian rods, for the chastisement of sin, and expose the craft and deceit of the devil, so that we may amend ourselves by punishment and again obtain God's favour.

The First Wall.

Let us, in the first place, attack the first wall.

It has been devised, that the Pope, bishops, priests and monks are called the Spiritual Estate; Princes, lords, artificers and peasants, are the Temporal Estate; which is a very fine, hypocritical device. But let no one be made afraid by it; and that for this reason: That all Christians are truly of the Spiritual Estate, and there is no difference among them, save of office alone. As St. Paul says (1 Cor. xii.), we are all one body, though each member does its own work, to serve the others. This is because we have one baptism, one gospel, one faith, and are all Christians alike; for baptism, gospel and faith, these alone make Spiritual and Christian people.

As for the unction by a pope or a bishop, tonsure, ordination, consecration, clothes differing from those of laymen—all this may make a hypocrite or an anointed puppet, but never a Christian, or a spiritual man. Thus we are all consecrated as priests by baptism, as St. Peter says: "Ye are a royal priesthood, a holy nation" (1 Peter ii. 9); and in the book of

Revelations: "and hast made us unto our God, kings and priests." (Rev. v. 10.) For, if we had not a higher consecration in us than Pope or bishop can give, no priest could ever be made by the consecration of Pope or bishop; nor could he say the mass, or preach, or absolve. Therefore the bishop's consecration is just as if in the name of the whole congregation he took one person out of the community, each member of which has equal power, and commanded him to exercise this power for the rest; in the same way as if ten brothers, co-heirs as king's sons, were to choose one from among them to rule over their inheritance; they would, all of them, still remain kings and have equal power, although one is ordered to govern.

And to put the matter even more plainly; If a little company of pious Christian laymen were taken prisoners and carried away to a desert, and had not among them a priest consecrated by a bishop, and were there to agree to elect one of them, married or unmarried, and were to order him to baptize, to celebrate the mass, to absolve and to preach; this man would as truly be a priest, as if all the bishops and all the Popes had consecrated him. That is why in cases of necessity every man can baptize and absolve, which would not be possible if we were not all priests. This great grace and virtue of baptism and of the Christian Estate, they have almost destroyed and made us forget by their ecclesiastical law. In this way the Christians used to choose their bishops and priests out of the community; these being afterwards confirmed by other bishops, without the pomp that we have now. So was it that St. Augustine, Ambrose, Cyprian, were bishops.

Since then the temporal power is baptized as we are, and has the same faith and gospel, we must allow it to be priest and bishop, and account its office an office that is proper and useful to the Christian community. For whatever issues from baptism, may boast that it has been consecrated priest, bishop, and Pope, although it does not beseem everyone to exercise these offices. For, since we are all priests alike, no man may put himself forward, or take upon himself, without our consent and election, to do that which we have all alike power to do. For, if a thing is common to all, no man may take it to himself without the wish and command of the community. And if it should happen that a man were appointed to one of these offices and deposed for abuses, he would be just what he was before. Therefore a priest should be nothing in Christendom but a functionary; as long as he holds his office, he has precedence of others; if he is deprived of it, he is a peasant and a citizen like the rest. Therefore a priest is verily no longer a priest after deposition. But now they have invented *characters indelebiles*,[16] and pretend that a priest after deprivation still differs from a simple layman. They even imagine that a priest can never be anything but a priest, that is, that he can never become a layman. All this is nothing but mere talk and ordinance of human invention.

It follows then, that between layman and priests, princes and bishops, or as they call it, between spiritual and temporal persons, the only real difference is one of office and function, and not of estate: for they are all of the same Spiritual Estate, true priests, bishops and Popes, though their functions are not the same: just as among priests and monks every man has not the same functions. And this St. Paul says (Rom. xii.; 1 Cor. xii.) and St. Peter (1 Peter ii.); "we being many are one body in Christ, and every one members one of another." Christ's body is not double or twofold, one temporal, the other spiritual. He is one head, and he has one body.

---

[16] In accordance with a doctrine of the Roman Catholic Church the act of ordination impresses upon the priest an indelible character; so that he immutably retains the sacred dignity of priesthood.

We see then that just as those that we call spiritual, or priests, bishops or popes, do not differ from other Christians in any other or higher degree, but in that they are to be concerned with the word of God, and the sacraments—that being their work and office—in the same way the temporal authorities hold the sword and the rod in their hands to punish the wicked and to protect the good. A cobbler, a smith, a peasant, every man has the office and function of his calling, and yet all alike are consecrated priests and bishops, and every man in his office must be useful and beneficial to the rest, that so many kinds of work may all be united into one community: just as the members of the body all serve one another.

Now see, what a Christian doctrine is this: that the temporal authority is not above the clergy, and may not punish it. This is, as if one were to say, the hand may not help, though the eye is in grievous suffering. Is it not unnatural, not to say unchristian, that one member may not help another, or guard it against harm? Nay, the nobler the member, the more the rest are bound to help it. Therefore I say: forasmuch as the temporal power has been ordained by God for the punishment of the bad, and the protection of the good, therefore we must let it do its duty throughout the whole Christian body, without respect of persons: whether it strike popes, bishops, priests, monks, or nuns. If it were sufficient reason for fettering the temporal power that it is inferior among the offices of Christianity to the offices of priest or confessor, or to the spiritual estate—if this were so, then we ought to restrain tailors, cobblers, masons, carpenters, cooks, servants, peasants, and all secular workmen, from providing the Pope, or bishops, priests and monks, with shoes, clothes, houses or victuals, or from paying them tithes. But if these laymen are allowed to do their work without restraint, what do the Romanist scribes mean by their laws? They mean that they withdraw themselves from the operation of temporal Christian power, simply in order that they may be free to do evil, and thus fulfil what St. Peter said: "There shall be false teachers among you, . . . and through covetousness shall they with feigned words make merchandize of you." (2 Peter ii. 1, etc.)

Therefore the temporal Christian power must exercise its office without let or hindrance, without considering whom it may strike, whether pope, or bishop, or priest: whoever is guilty let him suffer for it. Whatever the ecclesiastical law says in opposition to this, is merely the invention of Romanist arrogance. For this is what St. Paul says to all Christians: "Let every soul" (I presume including the Popes) "be subject unto the higher powers: for he beareth not the sword in vain: for he is the minister of God, a revenger to execute wrath upon him that doeth evil." (Rom. xiii. 1–4.) Also St. Peter: "Submit yourselves to every ordinance of man for the Lord's sake . . . for so is the will of God." (1 Peter ii. 13, 15.) He has also said, that men would come, who should despise government (2 Peter ii.); as has come to pass through ecclesiastical law.

Now I imagine, the first paper wall is overthrown, inasmuch as the temporal power has become a member of the Christian body, and although its work relates to the body, yet does it belong to the spiritual estate. Therefore it must do its duty without let or hindrance upon all members of the whole body, to punish or urge, as guilt may deserve, or need may require, without respect of Pope, bishops or priests; let them threaten or excommunicate as they will. That is why a guilty priest is deprived of his priesthood before being given over to the secular arm; whereas this would not be right, if the secular sword had not authority over him already by divine ordinance.

It is, indeed, past bearing that the spiritual law should esteem so highly the liberty, life and property of the clergy, as if laymen were not as good spiritual Christians, or not equally members of the Church. Why should your body, life, goods, and honour be free and not mine, seeing that we are equal as Christians, and have received alike baptism, faith, spirit and all things? If a priest is killed, the country is laid under an interdict:[17] why not also if a peasant is killed? Whence comes all this difference among equal Christians? Simply from human laws and inventions.

It can have been no good spirit, that devised these exceptions, and made sin to go unpunished. For, if as Christ and the Apostles bid us, it is our duty to oppose the evil one, and all his works and words, and to drive him away as well as may be; how then should we look on in silence, when the Pope and his followers are guilty of devilish works and words? Are we for the sake of men to allow the commandments and the truth of God to be defeated, which at our baptism we vowed to support with body and soul? Truly we should have to answer for all souls that are thus led away into error.

Therefore it must have been the archdevil himself who said, as we read in the ecclesiastical law: If the Pope were so perniciously wicked, as to be dragging souls in crowds to the devil, yet he could not be deposed. This is the accursed and devilish foundation on which they build at Rome, and think that the whole world is to be allowed to go to the devil, rather than they should be opposed in their knavery. If a man were to escape punishment simply because he is above the rest, then no Christian might punish another, since Christ has commanded each of us to esteem himself the lowest and the humblest. (Matt. xviii. 4; Luke ix. 48.)

Where there is sin, there remains no avoiding the punishment, as St. Gregory says: We are all equal, but guilt makes one subject to another. Now see, how they deal with Christendom, depriving it of its freedom without any warrant from the Scriptures, out of their own wickedness, whereas God and the Apostles made them subject to the secular sword; so that we must fear, that it is the work of Antichrist, or a sign of his near approach.

The Second Wall.

The second wall is even more tottering and weak: that they alone pretend to be considered masters of the Scriptures; although they learn nothing of them all their life, they assume authority, and juggle before us with impudent words, saying that the Pope cannot err in matters of faith, whether he be evil or good; albeit they cannot prove it by a single letter. That is why the canon law contains so many heretical and unchristian, nay, unnatural laws; but of these we need not speak now. For whereas they imagine the Holy Ghost never leaves them, however unlearned and wicked they may be, they grow bold enough to decree whatever they like. But were this true, where were the need and use of the Holy Scriptures? Let us burn them, and content ourselves with the unlearned gentlemen at Rome, in whom the Holy Ghost dwells, who however can dwell in pious souls only. If I had not read it, I could never have believed, that the Devil should have put forth such follies at Rome and find a following.

But not to fight them with our own words, we will quote the Scriptures. St. Paul says: "If anything be revealed to another that sitteth by, let the first hold his peace." (1 Cor. xiv. 30.) What would be the use of this commandment, if we were to believe him alone that teaches or has the highest seat? Christ Himself says: "And they shall be all taught of God." (St. John vi. 45.) Thus it may come to pass that the Pope and his

---

[17] By the *Interdict*, or general excommunication, whole countries, districts, or towns, were deprived of all the spiritual benefits of the Church, such as divine service, the administering of the sacraments, etc.

followers are wicked and not true Christians, and not being taught by God, have no true understanding, whereas a common man may have true understanding. Why should we then not follow him? Has not the Pope often erred? Who could help Christianity, in case the Pope errs, if we do not rather believe another, who has the Scriptures for him?

Therefore it is a wickedly devised fable, and they cannot quote a single letter to confirm it, that it is for the Pope alone to interpret the Scriptures or to confirm the interpretation of them: they have assumed the authority of their own selves. And though they say, that this authority was given to St. Peter when the keys were given to him, it is plain enough that the keys were not given to St. Peter alone, but to the whole community. Besides, the keys were not ordained for doctrine or authority, but for sin, to bind or loose; and what they claim besides this is mere invention. But what Christ said to St. Peter: "I have prayed for thee, that thy faith fail not" (St. Luke xxii. 32), cannot relate to the Pope, inasmuch as there have been many Popes without faith, as they are themselves forced to acknowledge. Nor did Christ pray for Peter alone, but for all the Apostles and all Christians, as He says, "Neither pray I for these alone, but for them also which shall believe on me through their word." (St. John xvii.) Is not this plain enough?

Only consider the matter. They must needs acknowledge that there are pious Christians among us, that have the true faith, spirit, understanding, word, and mind of Christ; why then should we reject their word and understanding, and follow a Pope who has neither understanding nor Spirit? Surely this were to deny our whole faith and the Christian Church. Moreover, if the article of our faith is right: *I believe in the Holy Christian Church*, the Pope cannot alone be right; else we must say: *I believe in the Pope of Rome*, and reduce the Christian Church to one man, which is a devilish and damnable heresy. Besides that, we are all priests, as I have said, and have all one faith, one gospel, one sacrament; how then should we not have the power of discerning and judging what is right or wrong in matters of faith? What becomes of St. Paul's words: "But he that is spiritual judgeth all things, yet he himself is judged of no man" (1 Cor. ii. 15); and also, "we having the same spirit of faith." (2 Cor. iv. 13.) Why then should we not perceive as well as an unbelieving Pope, what agrees, or disagrees with our faith?

By these and many other texts we should gain courage and freedom, and should not let the spirit of liberty (as St. Paul has it) be frightened away by the inventions of the Popes; we should boldly judge what they do and what they leave undone, by our own understanding of the Scriptures, and force them to follow the better understanding, and not their own. Did not Abraham in old days have to obey his Sarah, who was in stricter bondage to him than we are to any one on earth? Thus too Balaam's ass was wiser than the prophet. If God spoke by an ass against a prophet, why should He not speak by a pious man against the Pope? Besides, St. Paul withstood St. Peter as being in error. (Gal. ii.) Therefore it behoves every Christian to aid the faith by understanding and defending it, and by condemning all errors.

The Third Wall.

The third wall falls of itself, as soon as the first two have fallen; for if the Pope acts contrary to the Scriptures, we are bound to stand by the Scriptures, to punish and to constrain him, according to Christ's commandment; "Moreover if thy brother shall trespass against thee, go and tell him his fault between thee and him alone: if he shall hear thee, thou hast gained thy brother. But if he will not hear thee, then take with thee one or two more, that in the mouth of two or three witnesses every word may be established. And if he shall neglect to hear them, tell it unto the church: but if he neglect to hear the church, let him be unto thee as an heathen man and a publican." (St. Matt. xviii. 15–17.) Here each member is commanded to take care for the other; much more then should we do this, if it is a ruling member of the community that does evil, which by its evil doing, causes great harm and offence to the others. If then I am to accuse him before the church, I must collect the church together. Moreover they can show nothing in the Scriptures giving the Pope sole power to call and confirm councils; they have nothing but their own laws; but these hold good only so long as they are not injurious to Christianity and the laws of God. Therefore, if the Pope deserves punishment, these laws cease to bind us, since Christendom would suffer, if he were not punished by a council. Thus we read (Acts xv.), that the council of the Apostles was not called by St. Peter, but by all the Apostles and the elders. But if the right to call it had lain with St. Peter alone, it would not have been a Christian council, but a heretical *conciliabulum*. Moreover the most celebrated Nicene Council was neither called nor confirmed by the Bishop of Rome, but by the Emperor Constantine; and after him many other Emperors have done the same, and yet the councils called by them were accounted most Christian. But if the Pope alone had the power, they must all have been heretical. Moreover if I consider the councils that the Pope has called, I do not find that they produced any notable results.

Therefore when need requires and the Pope is a cause of offence to Christendom, in these cases whoever can best do so, as a faithful member of the whole body, must do what he can to procure a true free council. This no one can do so well as the temporal authorities, especially since they are fellow-Christians, fellow-priests, sharing one spirit, and one power in all things; and since they should exercise the office that they have received from God without hindrance, whenever it is necessary and useful that it should be exercised. Would it not be most unnatural, if a fire were to break out in a city, and everyone were to keep still and let it burn on and on, whatever might be burnt, simply because they had not the mayor's authority, or because the fire perhaps broke out at the mayor's house? Is not every citizen bound in this case to rouse and call in the rest? How much more should this be done in the spiritual city of Christ, if a fire of offence breaks out, either at the Pope's government or wherever it may! The like happens if an enemy attacks a town. The first to rouse up the rest earns glory and thanks. Why then should not he earn glory that announces the coming of our enemies from hell, and rouses and summons all Christians?

But as for their boasts of their authority, that no one must oppose it, this is idle talk. No one in Christendom has any authority to do harm, or to forbid others to prevent harm being done. There is no authority in the Church but for reformation. Therefore if the Pope wished to use his power to prevent the calling of a free council, so as to prevent the reformation of the Church, we must not respect him or his power; and if he should begin to excommunicate and fulminate, we must despise this as the ravings of a madman, and trusting in God, excommunicate and repel him, as best we may. For this his usurped power is nothing; he does not possess it, and he is at once overthrown by a text from the Scriptures. For St. Paul says to the Corinthians, "That God has given us authority for edification and not for destruction." (2 Cor. x. 8.) Who will set this text at naught? It is the power of the Devil and of Antichrist that prevents what would serve for the reformation of Christendom. Therefore we must not follow it, but oppose it with our body, our goods and all that we have. And even if a miracle were to happen in favour of the Pope, against the temporal power, or if some were to be stricken by a plague, as they sometimes boast has happened: all this is to be held as having been done by the Devil, for our want of faith in God, as was foretold by Christ: "There shall arise false Christs, and false prophets, and shall shew great signs and wonders; insomuch that, if it were possible, they shall deceive the very elect" (Matt. xxiv. 23); and St. Paul tells the Thessalonians that the coming of Antichrist shall be "after the working of Satan with all power and signs and lying wonders." (2 Thess. ii. 9.)

Therefore let us hold fast to this: that Christian power can do nothing against Christ, as St. Paul says: "for we can do nothing against Christ, but for Christ." (2 Cor. xiii. 8.) But, if it does anything against Christ, it is the power of Antichrist and the Devil, even if it rained and hailed wonders and plagues. Wonders and plagues prove nothing, especially in these latter evil days, of which false wonders are foretold in all the Scriptures. Therefore we must hold fast to the words of God with an assured faith; then the Devil will soon cease his wonders.

And now I hope we have laid the false, lying spectre with which the Romanists have long terrified and stupefied our consciences. And we have shown that, like all the rest of us, they are subject to the temporal sword; that they have no authority to interpret the Scriptures by force without skill; and that they have no power to prevent a council, or to pledge it in accordance with their pleasure, or to bind it beforehand, and deprive it of its freedom; and that if they do this, they are verily of the fellowship of Antichrist and the Devil, and have nothing of Christ but the name.

II.

Of the Matters to be Considered in the Councils.

Let us now consider the matters which should be treated in the councils, and with which popes, cardinals, bishops, and all learned men should occupy themselves day and night, if they loved Christ and His Church. But if they do not do so, the people at large and the temporal powers must do so, without considering the thunders of their excommunications. For an unjust excommunication is better than ten just absolutions, and an unjust absolution is worse than ten just excommunications. Therefore let us rouse ourselves, fellow-Germans, and fear God more than man, that we be not answerable for all the poor souls that are so miserably lost through the wicked, devilish government of the Romanists, through which also the dominion of the Devil grows day by day; if indeed this hellish government can grow any worse, which for my part I can neither conceive nor believe.

1. It is a distressing and terrible thing to see that the head of Christendom, who boasts of being the Vicar of Christ and the successor of St. Peter, lives in a worldly pomp that no king or emperor can equal: so that in him that calls himself most holy and most spiritual, there is more worldliness than in the world itself. He wears a triple crown, whereas the mightiest kings only wear one crown. If this resembles the poverty of Christ and St. Peter, it is a new sort of resemblance. They prate of its being heretical to object to this; nay, they will not even hear how unchristian and ungodly it is. But I think that if he should have to pray to God with tears, he would have to lay down his crowns; for God will not endure any arrogance. His office should be nothing else than to weep and pray constantly for Christendom, and to be an example of all humility.

However this may be, this pomp is a stumbling-block, and the Pope, for the very salvation of his soul, ought to put it off; for St. Paul says: "Abstain from all appearance of evil" (1 Thess. v. 21); and again: "Provide things honest in the sight of all men." (2 Cor.

viii. 21.) A simple mitre would be enough for the Pope: wisdom and sanctity should raise him above the rest; the crown of pride he should leave to Antichrist, as his predecessors did for some hundreds of years. They say: He is the ruler of the world. This is false; for Christ, whose vice-gerent and vicar he claims to be, said to Pilate: "My kingdom is not of this world." (John xviii. 36.) But no vice-gerent can have a wider dominion than his Lord. Nor is he a vice-gerent of Christ in His glory, but of Christ crucified, as St. Paul says: "For I determined not to know anything among you, save Jesus Christ, and him crucified" (2 Cor. ii. 2); and (Phil. ii. 7): "Let this mind be in you, which was also in Christ Jesus; who made himself of no reputation, and took upon himself the form of a servant." (Phil. ii. 5, 7.) Again (1 Cor. i.): "We preach Christ crucified." Now they make the Pope a vice-gerent of Christ exalted in heaven, and some have let the Devil rule them so thoroughly, that they have maintained that the Pope is above the angels in heaven, and has power over them; which is precisely the true work of the true Antichrist.

2. What is the use in Christendom of the people called "Cardinals"? I will tell you. In Italy and Germany there are many rich convents, endowments, fiefs and benefices, and as the best way of getting these into the hands of Rome, they created cardinals, and gave them the sees, convents, and prelacies, and thus destroyed the service of God. That is why Italy is almost a desert now: the convents are destroyed, the sees consumed, the revenues of the prelacies and of all the churches drawn to Rome; towns are decayed; the country and the people ruined, while there is no more any worship of God or preaching; why? Because the cardinals must have all the wealth. No Turk could have thus desolated Italy and overthrown the worship of God.

Now that Italy is sucked dry, they come to Germany and begin very quietly; but we shall see, that Germany is soon to be brought into the same state as Italy. We have a few cardinals already. What the Romanists mean thereby the drunken Germans[18] are not to see until they have lost everything—bishoprics, convents, benefices, fiefs, even to their last farthing. Antichrist must take the riches of the earth, as it is written. (Dan. xi. 8, 39, 43.) They begin by taking off the cream of the bishoprics, convents, and fiefs; and as they do not dare to destroy everything as they have done in Italy, they employ such holy cunning to join together ten or twenty prelacies, and take such a portion of each, annually, that the total amounts to a considerable sum. The priory of Würzburg gives one thousand guilders, those of Bamberg, Mayence, Treves and others also contribute. In this way they collect one thousand or ten thousand guilders, in order that a cardinal may live at Rome in a state like that of a wealthy monarch.

After we have gained this, we will create thirty or forty cardinals on one day, and give one St. Michael's Mount,[19] near Bamberg, and likewise the see of Würzburg, to which belong some rich benefices, until the churches and the cities are desolated; and then we shall say: We are the vicars of Christ, the shepherds of Christ's flocks; those mad, drunken Germans must submit to it. I advise, however, that there be made fewer cardinals, or that the Pope should have to support them out of his own purse. It would be amply sufficient, if there were twelve, and if each of them had an annual income of one thousand guilders. What has brought us Germans to such a pass, that we have to suffer this robbery and this destruction of our property by the Pope? If the kingdom of France has resisted it, why do we Germans suffer ourselves to be fooled and deceived? It would be more endurable, if they did nothing but rob us of our property; but they destroy the

---

[18] The epithet "drunken" was formerly often applied by the Italians to the Germans.
[19] Luther alludes here to the Benedictine convent standing on the Mönchberg, or St. Michael's Mount.

church and deprive Christ's flock of their good shepherds, and overthrow the service and word of God. Even if there were no cardinals at all, the Church would not perish; for they do nothing for the good of Christendom; all they do is to bargain and traffic in prelacies and bishoprics; which any robber could do as well.

3. If we took away ninety-nine parts of the Pope's court and only left one hundredth, it would still be large enough to answer questions on matters of belief. Now there is such a swarm of vermin at Rome, all called Papal, that Babylon itself never saw the like. There are more than three thousand Papal secretaries alone; but who shall count the other office-bearers, since there are so many offices that we can scarcely count them, and all waiting for German benefices, as wolves wait for a flock of sheep? I think Germany now pays more to the Pope, than it formerly paid the Emperors; nay, some think more than three hundred thousand guilders are sent from Germany to Rome every year, for nothing whatever; and in return we are scoffed at and put to shame. Do we still wonder why princes, noblemen, cities, foundations, convents and people are poor? We should rather wonder that we have anything left to eat.

Now that we have got well into our game, let us pause awhile and show that the Germans are not such fools, as not to perceive or understand this Romish trickery. I do not here complain, that God's commandments and Christian justice are despised at Rome; for the state of things in Christendom, especially at Rome, is too bad for us to complain of such high matters. Nor do I even complain that no account is taken of natural or secular justice and reason. The mischief lies still deeper. I complain that they do not observe their own fabricated canon law, though this is in itself rather mere tyranny, avarice and worldly pomp, than a law. This we shall now show.

Long ago the Emperors and Princes of Germany allowed the Pope to claim the annates[20] from all German benefices; that is, half of the first year's income from every benefice. The object at this concession was that the Pope should collect a fund with all this money, to fight against the Turks and infidels, and to protect Christendom, so that the nobility should not have to bear the burden of the struggle alone, and that the priests should also contribute. The Popes have made such use of this good simple piety of the Germans, that they have taken this money for more than one hundred years, and have now made of it a regular tax and duty; and not only have they accumulated nothing, but they have founded out of it many posts and offices at Rome, which are paid by it yearly, as out of a settled rent.

Whenever there is any pretence of fighting the Turks, they send out some commission for collecting money, and often send out indulgences under the same pretext of fighting the Turks. They think we Germans will always remain such great and inveterate fools, that we will go on giving money to satisfy their unspeakable greed, though we see plainly that neither *annates* nor absolution money, nor any other—not one farthing—goes against the Turks, but all goes into the bottomless sack. They lie and deceive, form and make covenants with us of which they do not mean to keep one jot. And all this is done in the holy name of Christ and St. Peter.

This being so, the German nation, the bishops and princes, should remember that they are Christians, and should defend the people, who are committed to their government and protection in temporal and spiritual affairs, from these ravenous wolves in sheep's clothing, that profess to be shepherds and rulers; and since the *annates* are so shamefully abused, and the covenants concerning them not carried out, they should not

---

[20] The duty of paying *annates* to the Pope was established by John XXII. in 1318.

suffer their lands and people to be so piteously and unrighteously flayed and ruined; but by an imperial or a national law they should either retain the *annates* in the country, or abolish them altogether. For since they do not keep to the covenants, they have no right to the *annates*; therefore bishops and princes are bound to punish this thievery and robbery, or prevent it, as justice demands. And herein should we assist and strengthen the Pope, who is perchance too weak to prevent this scandal by himself; or, if he wishes to protect or support it, restrain and oppose him as a wolf and tyrant; for he has no authority to do evil or to protect evil-doers. Even if it were proposed to collect any such treasure for use against the Turks, we should be wise in future, and remember that the German nation is more fitted to take charge of it than the Pope, seeing that the German nation by itself is able to provide men enough, if the money is forthcoming. This matter of the *annates* is like many other Romish pretexts.

Moreover the year has been divided among the Pope and the ruling bishops and foundations, in such wise, that the Pope has taken every other month—six in all—to give away the benefices that fall in his month; in this way almost all the benefices are drawn into the hands of Rome, and especially the best livings and dignities. And those that once fall into the hands of Rome never come out again, even if they never again fall vacant in the Pope's month. In this way the foundations come very short of their rights, and it is a downright robbery, by which it is intended that nothing of them should be left. Therefore it is now high time to abolish the Pope's months and to take back again all that has thereby fallen into the hands of Rome. For all the princes and nobles should insist, that the stolen property shall be returned, the thieves punished, and that those who abuse their powers shall be deprived of them. If the Pope can make a law on the day after his election, by which he takes our benefices and livings to which he has no right; the Emperor Charles should so much the more have a right to issue a law for all Germany on the day after his coronation,[21] that in future no livings and benefices are to fall to Rome by virtue of the Pope's month, but that those that have so fallen are to be freed and taken from the Romish robbers. This right he possesses by his office in virtue of his temporal sword.

But the see of avarice and robbery at Rome is unwilling to wait for the benefices to fall in one after another by means of the Pope's month; and in order to get them into its insatiable maw, as speedily as possible, they have devised the plan of taking livings and benefices in three other ways:

First, if the incumbent of a free living dies at Rome or on his way thither, his living remains for ever the property of the see of Rome, or I rather should say, the see of robbers, though they will not let us call them robbers, although no one has ever seen or read of such robbery.

Secondly, if a servant of the Pope, or of one of the cardinals, takes a living, or if having a living he becomes a servant of the Pope or of a cardinal, the living remains with Rome. But who can count the servants of the Pope and his cardinals, seeing that if he goes out riding, he is attended by three or four thousand mule-riders; more than any king or emperor. For Christ and St. Peter went on foot; in order that their vice-gerents might indulge the better in all manner of pomp. Besides, their avarice has devised and invented this, that in foreign countries also there are many called papal servants, as at Rome: so that in all parts this single crafty little word "papal servant" brings all benefices to the

---

[21] At the time when the above was written—June 1520—the Emperor Charles had been elected, but not yet crowned.

Chair of Rome and they are kept there for ever. Are not these mischievous, devilish devices? Let us only wait awhile. Mayence, Magdeburg, and Halberstadt will fall very nicely to Rome, and we shall have to pay dearly for our cardinal.[22] Hereafter, all the German bishops will be made cardinals, so that there shall remain nothing to ourselves.

Thirdly, whenever there is any dispute about a benefice; and this is, I think, well-nigh the broadest and commonest road by which benefices are brought to Rome. For where there is no dispute numberless knaves can be found at Rome, who are ready to scrape up disputes, and attack livings wherever they like. In this way many a good priest loses his living, or has to buy off the dispute for a time with a sum of money. These benefices, confiscated by right or wrong of dispute, are to be for ever the property of the see of Rome. It would be no wonder, if God were to rain sulphur and fire from heaven and cast Rome down into the pit, as he did formerly to Sodom and Gomorrah. What is the use of a Pope in Christendom, if the only use made of his power is to commit these supreme villainies under his protection and assistance? O noble princes and sirs, how long will you suffer your lands and your people to be the prey of these ravening wolves?

But these tricks did not suffice, and Bishoprics were too slow in falling into the power of Roman avarice. Accordingly our good friend Avarice made the discovery that all Bishoprics are abroad in name only; but that their land and soil is at Rome; from this it follows, that no bishop may be confirmed until he has bought the "Pall"[23] for a large sum, and has with a terrible oath bound himself a servant of the Pope. That is why no bishop dare oppose the Pope. This was the object of the oath, and this is how the wealthiest bishoprics have come to debt and ruin. Mayence, I am told, pays 20,000 guilders. These are true Roman tricks, it seems to me. It is true that they once decreed in the canon law, that the *Pall* should be given free, the number of the Pope's servants diminished, disputes made less frequent, that foundations and bishops should enjoy their liberty; but all this brought them no money. They have, therefore, reversed all this: bishops and foundations have lost all their power; they are mere cyphers, without office, authority or function; all things are regulated by the chief knaves at Rome; even the offices of sextons and bell-ringers in all churches. All disputes are transferred to Rome; each one does what he will, strong in the Pope's protection.

What has happened in this very year? The bishop of Strasburg, wishing to regulate his see in a proper way and reform it in the matter of divine service, published some divine and Christian ordinances for that purpose. But our worthy Pope and the holy Chair at Rome overturns altogether this holy and spiritual order on the accusation of the priests. This is what they call being the shepherd of Christ's sheep—supporting priests against their own bishops, and protecting their disobedience by divine decrees. Antichrist, I hope, will not insult God in this open way. There you have the Pope, as you have chosen to have him, and why? Why, because if the Church were to be reformed, many things would have to be destroyed, and possibly Rome among them. Therefore it is better to prevent priests from being at one with each other; they should rather, as they have done hitherto,

---

[22] Luther alludes here to the Archbishop Albert of Mayence, who was, besides, Archbishop of Magdeburg, and administrator of the bishopric of Halberstadt. In order to be able to defray the expense of the Archiepiscopal tax due to Rome, amounting to 30,000 guilders, he had farmed the sale of the Pope's indulgences—employing the notorious Tetzel as his agent, and sharing the profits with the Pope. In 1518 Albert was appointed Cardinal. See Ranke: *Deutsche Geschichte*, &c.; vol. i. p. 309, &c.

[23] The *Pallium* was since the fourth century the symbol of archiepiscopal power, and had to be redeemed from the Pope by means of a large sum of money and a solemn oath of obedience.

sow discord among kings and princes, flood the world with Christian blood, lest Christian unity should trouble the holy Roman See with reforms.

So far we have seen what they do with the livings that fall vacant. Now there are not enough vacancies for this delicate greed; therefore it has also taken prudent account of the benefices that are still held by their incumbents, so that they may become vacant, though they are in fact not vacant, and this they effect in many ways:

First, they lie in wait for fat livings or sees which are held by an old or sick man, or even by one afflicted by an imaginary incompetence; him the Roman See gives a coadjutor, that is an assistant without his asking or wishing it, for the benefit of the coadjutor, because he is a papal servant, or pays for the office, or has otherwise earned it by some menial service rendered to Rome. Thus there is an end of free election on the part of the chapter, or of the right of him that presents the living; and all goes to Rome.

Secondly, there is a little word: *commendam*, that is, when the Pope gives a rich and fat convent or church into the charge of a cardinal or any other of his servants, just as I might command you to take charge of one hundred guilders for me. In this way the convent is neither given, nor lent, nor destroyed, nor is its divine service abolished; but only entrusted to a man's charge: not, however, for him to protect and improve it, but to drive out the one he finds there; to take the property and revenue, and to instal some apostate[24] runaway monk, who is paid five or six guilders a year, and sits in the church all day and sells symbols and pictures to the pilgrims; so that neither chanting nor reading in the church goes on there any more. Now if we were to call this the destruction of convents and abolition of divine service, we should be accusing the Pope of destroying Christianity and abolishing divine service—for truly he is doing this effectually—but this would be thought harsh language at Rome, therefore it is called a *commendam*, or an order to take charge of the convent. In this way the Pope can make *commendams* of four or more convents a year, any one of which produces a revenue of more than six thousand guilders. This is the way divine service is advanced and convents kept up at Rome. This will be introduced into Germany as well.

Thirdly, there are certain benefices that are said to be *incompatible*, that is, they may not be held together according to the canon law; such as two cures, two sees and the like. Now the Holy See and avarice twists itself out of the canon law by making "glosses," or interpretations, called *Unio*, or *Incorporatio*, that is, several incompatible benefices are incorporated, so that one is a member of the other, and the whole is held to be one benefice; then they are no longer incompatible, and we have got rid of the holy canon law, so that it is no longer binding, except on those, who do not buy those glosses of the Pope, and his *Datarius*.[25] *Unio* is of the same kind: a number of benefices are tied together like a bundle of faggots, and on account of this coupling together, they are held to be one benefice. Thus there may be found many a courtling at Rome who alone holds twenty-two cures, seven priories, and forty-four prebends; all which is done in virtue of this masterly gloss, so as not to be contrary to law. Any one can imagine what cardinals and other prelates may hold. In this way the Germans are to have their purses emptied and be deprived of all comfort.

There is another *gloss* called *Administratio*, that is, that besides his see a man holds an abbey or other high benefice, and possesses all the property of it, without any other

---

[24] Monks who forsook their order without any legal dispensation were called "apostates."

[25] The Papal office for the issue and registration of certain documents was called Dataria, from the phrase appended to them, *Datum apud S. Petrum*. The chief of that office, usually a cardinal, bore the title of Datarius.

title but *administrator*. For at Rome it is enough that words should change and not deeds, just as if I said, a procuress was to be called a mayoress, yet may remain as good as she is now. Such Romish rule was foretold by St. Peter, when he said: "There shall be false teachers among you . . . and through covetousness shall they with feigned words make merchandize of you." (2 Pet. ii. 1, 3.)

This precious Roman avarice has also invented the practice of selling and lending prebends and benefices on condition that the seller or lender has the reversion, so that if the incumbent dies, the benefice falls to him that has sold it, lent it, or abandoned it; in this way they have made benefices heritable property, so that none can come to hold it unless the seller sells it to him, or leaves it to him at his death. Then there are many that give a benefice to another in name only; and on condition that he shall not receive a farthing. It is now too an old practice for a man to give another a benefice and to receive a certain annual sum, which proceeding was formerly called simony. And there are many other such little things which I cannot recount; and so they deal worse with the benefices than the heathens by the cross dealt with Christ's clothes.

But all this that I have spoken of is old and common at Rome. Their avarice has invented other device, which I hope will be the last and choke it. The Pope has made a noble discovery, called *Pectoralis Reservatio*, that is, "mental reservation"—*et proprius motus*, that is, "and his own will and power." The matter is managed in this way: Suppose a man obtains a benefice at Rome, which is confirmed to him in due form; then comes another, who brings money, or who has done some other service of which the less said the better, and requests the Pope to give him the same benefice, then the Pope will take it from the first and give it him. If you say, that is wrong; the Most Holy Father must then excuse himself, that he may not be openly blamed for having violated justice; and he says: "that in his heart and mind he reserved his authority over the said benefice;" whilst he never had heard or thought of the same in all his life. Thus he has devised a *gloss* which allows him in his proper person to lie and cheat and fool us all; and all this impudently and in open daylight, and nevertheless he claims to be the head of Christendom; letting the evil spirit rule him with manifest lies.

This "mere motion" and lying reservation of the Popes has brought about an unutterable state of things at Rome. There is a buying and a selling, a changing, exchanging, and bargaining, cheating and lying, robbing and stealing, debauchery, and villainy, and all kinds of contempt of God, that Antichrist himself could not rule worse. Venice, Antwerp, Cairo, are nothing to this fair and market at Rome, except that there things are done with some reason and justice, whilst here things are done as the Devil himself could wish. And out of this ocean a like virtue overflows all the world. Is it not natural that such people should dread a reformation and a free council, and should rather embroil all kings and princes, than that their unity should bring about a council? Who would like his villainy to be exposed?

Finally the Pope has built a special house for this fine traffic, that is, the house of the *Datarius* at Rome. Thither all must come that bargain in this way for prebends and benefices; from his they must buy the *glosses* and obtain the right to practise uch prime villainy. In former days it was fairly well at Rome, when justice had to be bought, or could only be put down by money; but now she has become so fastidious, that she does not allow any one to commit villainies, unless he has first bought the right to do it with great sums. If this is not a house of prostitution, worse than all houses of prostitution that can be conceived, I do not know what houses of prostitution really are.

If you bring money to this house, you can arrive at all that I have mentioned; and more than this, any sort of usury is made legitimate for money; property got by theft or robbery is here made legal. Here vows are annulled; here a monk obtains leave to quit his order; here priests can enter married life for money; here bastards can become legitimate; and dishonour and shame may arrive at high honours; all evil repute and disgrace is knighted and ennobled; here a marriage is suffered that is in a forbidden degree, or has some other defect. Oh, what a trafficking and plundering is there! one would think that the canon laws were only so many ropes of gold, from which he must free himself who would become a Christian man. Nay, here the Devil becomes a saint, and a God besides. What heaven and earth might not do, may be done by this house. Their ordinances are called *compositions*—compositions, forsooth! confusions rather.[26] Oh what a poor treasury is the toll on the Rhine,[27] compared with this holy house!

Let no one think that I say too much. It is all notorious, so that even at Rome they are forced to own that it is more terrible and worse than one can say. I have said and will say nothing of the foul dregs of private vices. I only speak of well-known public matters, and yet my words do not suffice. Bishops, priests, and especially the doctors of the universities, who are paid to do it, ought to have unanimously written and exclaimed against it. Yea, if you will turn the leaf, you will discover the truth.

I have still to give a farewell greeting. These treasures, that would have satisfied three mighty kings, were not enough for this unspeakable greed, and so they have made over and sold their traffic to Fugger[28] at Augsburg, so that the lending and buying and selling sees and benefices, and all this traffic in ecclesiastical property, has in the end come into the right hands, and spiritual and temporal matters have now become one business. Now I should like to know what the most cunning would devise for Romish greed to do that it has not done; except that Fugger might sell or pledge his two trades that have now become one. I think they must have come to the end of their devices. For what they have stolen and yet steal in all countries by Bulls of Indulgences, Letters of Confession, Letters of Dispensation[29] and other *confessionalia*, all this I think mere bungling work, and much like playing toss with a devil in hell. Not that they produce little, for a mighty king could support himself by them; but they are as nothing compared to the other streams of revenue mentioned above. I will not now consider what has become of that Indulgence money; I shall enquire into this another time, for *Campofiore* and *Belvedere*[30] and some other places probably know something about it.

Meanwhile since this devilish state of things is not only an open robbery, deceit and tyranny of the gates of hell, but also destroys Christianity, body and soul, we are bound to use all our diligence to prevent this misery and destruction of Christendom. If we wish to fight the Turks, let us begin here, where they are worst. If we justly hang thieves and behead robbers, why do we leave the greed of Rome so unpunished, who is the greatest thief and robber that has appeared or can appear on earth, and does all this in the holy name of Christ and St. Peter? Who can suffer this and be silent about it? Almost everything that he possesses has been stolen, or got by robbery, as we learn from all histories. Why, the Pope never bought those great possessions, so as to be able to raise

---

[26] Luther uses here the expressions *compositiones* and *confusiones* as a kind of pun.
[27] Tolls were levied at many places along the Rhine.
[28] The commercial House of Fugger was in those days the wealthiest in Europe.
[29] Luther uses the word *Butterbriefe*, i.e. letters of indulgence allowing the enjoyment of butter, cheese, milk, etc., during Lent. They formed part only of the *confessionalia*, which granted various other indulgences.
[30] Parts of the Vatican.

wellnigh ten hundred thousand ducats from his ecclesiastical offices, without counting his gold mines described above, and his land. He did not inherit it from Christ and St. Peter; no one gave it or lent it him, he has not acquired it by prescription. Tell me, where can he have got it? You can learn from this, what their object is, when they sent out legates to collect money to be used against the Turk.

III.

Twenty-seven Articles respecting the Reformation of the Christian Estate.

Now though I am too lowly to submit articles that could serve for the reformation of these fearful evils, I will yet sing out my fool's song, and will show, as well as my wit will allow, what might and should be done by the temporal authorities or by a General Council.

1. Princes, nobles and cities should promptly forbid their subjects to pay the *annates* and should even abolish them altogether. For the Pope has broken the compact, and turned the *annates* into robbery for the harm and shame of the German nation; he gives them to his friends; he sells them for large sums of money and founds benefices on them. Therefore he has forfeited his right to them, and deserves punishment. In this way the temporal power should protect the innocent and prevent wrongdoing, as we are taught by St. Paul (Rom. xiii.) and by St. Peter (1 Pet. ii.) and even by the canon law. (16. q. 7. de Filiis.) That is why we say to the Pope and his followers: *tu ora!* "thou shalt pray;" to the Emperor and his followers: *tu protege!* "thou shalt protect;" to the commons: *tu labora!* "thou shalt work;" not that each man should not pray, protect and work; for if a man fulfils his duty, that is prayer, protection and work; but every man must have his proper task.

2. Since by means of those Romish tricks commendams, coadjutors, reservations, expectations, Pope's months, incorporations, unions, Palls, rules of chancellery, and other such knaveries, the Pope takes unlawful possession of all German foundations, to give and sell them to strangers at Rome, that profit Germany in no way; so that the incumbents are robbed of their rights, and the bishops are made mere cyphers and anointed idols; and thus besides natural justice and reason the Pope's own canon law is violated; and things have come to such a pass, that prebends and benefits are sold at Rome to vulgar, ignorant asses and knaves, out of sheer greed, while pious learned men have no profit by their merit and skill, whereby the unfortunate German people must needs lack good, learned Prelates and suffer ruin—on account of these evils the Christian nobility should rise up against the Pope as a common enemy and destroyer of Christianity, for the sake of the salvation of the poor souls that such tyranny must ruin. They should ordain, order and decree that henceforth no benefice shall be drawn away to Rome, and that no benefice shall be claimed there in any fashion whatsoever; and after having once got these benefices out of the hands of Romish tyranny, they must be kept from them, and their lawful incumbents must be reinstated in them to administer them as best they may, within the German nation. And if a courtling came from Rome, he should receive the strict command to withdraw, or to leap into the Rhine, or whatever river be nearest, and to administer a cold bath to the Interdict, seal and letters and all. Thus those at Rome would learn, that we Germans are not to remain drunken fools for ever, but that we, too, are become Christians, and that as such, we will no longer suffer this shameful mockery of

Christ's holy name, that serves as a cloak for such knavery and destruction of souls, and that we shall respect God and the glory of God more than the power of men.

3. It should be decreed by an Imperial law, that no episcopal cloak, and no confirmation of any appointment shall for the future be obtained from Rome. The order of the most holy and renowned Nicene Council must again be restored, namely, that a bishop must be confirmed by the two nearest bishops, or by the archbishop. If the Pope cancels the decrees of these and all other councils, what is the good of councils at all? Who has given him the right thus to despise councils and to cancel them? If this is allowed, we had better abolish all bishops, archbishops and primates, and make simple rectors of all of them, so that they would have the Pope alone over them; as is indeed the case now; he deprives bishops, archbishops and primates of all the authority of their office, taking everything to himself, and leaving them only the name and the empty title; more than this: by his exemption he has withdrawn convents, abbots and prelates from the ordinary authority of the Bishops, so that there remains no order in Christendom. The necessary result of this must be, and has been, laxity in punishing, and such a liberty to do evil in all the world, that I very much fear one might call the Pope "the man of sin." Who but the Pope is to blame for this absence of all order, of all punishment, of all government, of all discipline in Christendom? By his own arbitrary power he ties the hands of all his prelates, and takes from them their rods, while all their subjects have their hands unloosed, and obtain license by gift or purchase.

But, that he have no cause for complaint, as being deprived of his authority, it should be decreed, that in cases where the primates and archbishops are unable to settle the matter, or where there is a dispute among them, the matters shall then be submitted to the Pope, but not every little matter; as was done formerly, and was ordered by the most renowned Nicene Council. His Holiness must not be troubled with small matters, that can be settled without his help; so that he may have leisure to devote himself to his prayers and study, and to his care of all Christendom, as he professes to do. As indeed the Apostles did, saying (Acts vi. 2, 4): "It is not reason that we should leave the word of God, and serve tables . . . But we will give ourselves continually to prayer, and to the ministry of the word." But now we see at Rome nothing but contempt of the Gospel and of prayer, and the service of tables, that is, the service of the goods of this world; and the government of the Pope agrees with the government of the Apostles as well as Lucifer with Christ, hell with heaven, night with day; and yet he calls himself Christ's Vicar, and the successor of the Apostles.

4. Let it be decreed that no temporal matter shall be submitted to Rome, but all shall be left to the jurisdiction of the temporal authorities. This is part of their own canon law, though they do not obey it. For this should be the Pope's office, that he, the most learned in the Scriptures, and the most holy, not in name only, but in fact, should rule in matters concerning the faith and the holy life of Christians; he should make primates and bishops attend to this, and should work and take thought with them to this end: as St. Paul teaches (1 Cor. vi.), severely upbraiding those that occupy themselves with the things of this world. For all countries suffer unbearable damage by this practice of settling such matters at Rome, since it involves great expense; and besides this, the judges at Rome, not knowing the manners, laws and customs of other countries, frequently pervert the matter according to their own laws and their own opinions, thus causing injustice to all parties. Besides this, we should prohibit in all foundations the grievous extortion of the ecclesiastical judges; they should only be allowed to consider matters concerning faith and good morals; but matters concerning money, property, life and honour, should be left

to the temporal judges. Therefore the temporal authorities should not permit excommunication or expulsion except in matters of faith and righteous living. It is only reasonable, that spiritual authorities should have power in spiritual matters; spiritual matters, however, are not money or matters relating to the body, but faith and good works.

Still we might allow matters respecting benefices or prebends to be treated before bishops, archbishops and primates. Therefore, when it is necessary to decide quarrels and strifes let the Primate of Germany hold a general consistory, with assessors and chancellors, who would have the control over *the signaturas gratiae* and *justitiae*,[31] and to whom matters arising in Germany might be submitted by appeal. The officers of such court should be paid out of the *annates*, or in some other way, and should not have to draw their salaries as at Rome from chance presents and offerings; whereby they grow accustomed to sell justice and injustice, as they must needs do at Rome, where the Pope gives them no salary, but allows them to fatten themselves on presents; for at Rome no one heeds what is right or what is wrong, but only what is money and what is not money. But this matter of salaries I must leave to men of higher understanding and of more experience in these things than I have. I am content with making these suggestions and giving some materials for consideration to those who may be able and willing to help the German nation to become a free people of Christians, after this wretched, heathen, unchristian misrule of the Pope.

5. Henceforth no reservations shall be valid, and no benefices shall be appropriated by Rome, whether the incumbent die, or there be a dispute, or the incumbent be a servant of the Pope, or of a cardinal; and all courtiers shall be strictly prohibited and prevented from causing a dispute about any benefice, so as to cite the pious priests, to trouble them and to drive them into a lawsuit. And if in consequence of this there comes an interdict from Rome, let it be despised, just as if a thief were to excommunicate any man because he would not allow him to steal in peace. Nay, they should be punished most severely, for making such a blasphemous use of Excommunication and of the name of God, to support their robberies, and for wishing by their false threats to drive us to suffer and approve this blasphemy of God's name, and this abuse of Christian authority; and thus to become sharers before God in their wrongdoing, whereas it is our duty before God to punish it, as St. Paul (Rom. i.) upbraids the Romans for not only doing wrong, but allowing wrong to be done. But above all that lying mental reservation (*pectoralis reservatio*) is unbearable, by which Christendom is so openly mocked and insulted, in that its head notoriously deals with lies, and impudently cheats and fools every man for the sake of accursed wealth.

6. The cases reserved[32] (*casus reservati*) should be abolished, by which not only are the people cheated out of much money, but besides many poor consciences are confused and led into error by the ruthless tyrants to the intolerable harm of their faith in God, especially those foolish and childish cases that are made important by the Bull 'In Coena Domini,'[33] and which do not deserve the name of daily sins; not to mention those great

---

[31] At the time when the above was written the function of the *signatura gratiæ* was to superintend the conferring of grants, concessions, favours, etc., whilst the *signatura justitiæ* embraced the general administration of ecclesiastical matters.

[32] "Reserved cases" refer to those great sins for which the Pope or the bishops only could give absolution.

[33] The celebrated Papal Bull known under the name of In *Cœna Domini*, containing anathemas and excommunications against all those who dissented in any way from the Roman Catholic creed, used, until the year 1770, to be read publicly at Rome on Maundy Thursday.

cases for which the Pope gives no absolution: such as preventing a pilgrim from going to Rome, furnishing the Turks with arms or forging the Pope's letters. They only fool us with these gross, mad and clumsy matters: Sodom and Gomorrah, and all sins that are committed and that can be committed against God's commandments are, not reserved cases; but what God never commanded and they themselves have invented—these must be made reserved cases; solely in order that none may be prevented from bringing money to Rome, that they may live in their lust without fear of the Turk, and may keep the world in their bondage by their useless Bulls and Briefs.

Now all priests ought to know, or rather it should be a public ordinance, that no secret sin constitutes a reserved case, if there be no public accusation; and that every priest has power to absolve from all sin, whatever its name, if it be secret, and that no abbot, bishop or Pope has power to reserve any such case; and lastly, that if they do this, it is null and void, and they should moreover be punished as interfering without authority in God's judgment and confusing and troubling without cause our poor witless consciences. But in respect to any great open sin, directly contrary to God's commandments, there is some reason for a reserved case; but there should not be too many, nor should they be reserved arbitrarily without due cause. For God has not ordained tyrants, but shepherds in His Church, as St. Peter says. (1 Pet. v. 2.)

7. The Roman See must abolish the Papal offices, and diminish that crowd of crawling vermin at Rome, so that the Pope's servants may be supported out of the Pope's own pocket, and that his court may cease to surpass all royal courts in its pomp and extravagance; seeing that all this pomp has not only been of no service to the Christian faith, but has also kept them from study and prayer, so that they themselves know hardly anything concerning matters of faith; as they proved clumsily enough at the last Roman Council,[34] where among many childishly trifling matters, they decided "that the soul is immortal," and that a priest is bound to pray once every month on pain of losing his benefice.[35] How are men to rule Christendom and to decide matters of faith, who, callous and blinded by their greed, wealth, and worldly pomp, have only just decided that the soul is immortal? It is no slight shame to all Christendom that they should deal thus scandalously with the faith at Rome. If they had less wealth and lived in less pomp, they might be better able to study and pray, that they might become able and worthy to treat matters of belief, as they were once, when they were content to be bishops and not kings of kings.

8. The terrible oaths must be abolished which bishops are forced, without any right, to swear to the Pope, by which they are bound like servants, and which are arbitrarily and foolishly decreed in the absurd and shallow chapter, *Significasti*.[36] Is it not enough that they oppress us in goods, body, and soul by all their mad laws, by which they have weakened faith and destroyed Christianity; but must they now take possession of the very persons of Bishops, with their offices and functions, and also claim the *investiture*[37] which used formerly to be the right of the German Emperors, and is still the right of the King in France and other kingdoms? This matter caused many wars and disputes with the

---

[34] The council alluded to above was held at Rome from 1512 to 1517.

[35] Luther's objection is not, of course, to the recognition of the immortality of the soul; what he objects to is (1) that it was thought necessary for a council to decree that the soul is immortal, and (2) that this question was put on a level with trivial matters of discipline.

[36] The above is the title of a chapter in the *Corpus juris canonici*.

[37] The right of investiture was the subject of the dispute between Gregory VII. and Henry IV., which led to the Emperor's submission at Canossa.

Emperors until the Popes impudently took the power by force; since which time they have retained it; just as if it were only right for the Germans, above all Christians on earth, to be the fools of the Pope and the Holy See, and to do and suffer what no one beside would suffer or do. Seeing then that this is mere arbitrary power, robbery, and a hindrance to the exercise of the bishop's ordinary power, and to the injury of poor souls; therefore it is the duty of the Emperor and his nobles to prevent and punish this tyranny.

9. The Pope should have no power over the Emperor, except to anoint and crown him at the altar, as a bishop crowns a king; nor should that devilish pomp be allowed, that the Emperor should kiss the Pope's feet, or sit at his feet, or, as it is said, hold his stirrup, or the reins of his mule, when he mounts to ride; much less should he pay homage to the Pope, or swear allegiance, as is impudently demanded by the Popes, as if they had a right to it. The chapter Solite,[38] in which the papal authority is exalted above the Imperial, is not worth a farthing, and so of all those that depend on it or fear it; for it does nothing but pervert God's holy words from their true meaning, according to their own imaginations, as I have proved in a Latin treatise.

All these excessive, over-presumptuous and most wicked claims of the Pope are the invention of the Devil, with the object of bringing in Antichrist in due course, and to raise the Pope above God; as indeed many have done and are now doing. It is not meet that the Pope should exalt himself above temporal authority, except in spiritual matters, such as preaching and absolution; in other matters he should be subject to it, according to the teaching of St. Paul (Rom. xiii.), and St. Peter (1 Pet. iii.), as I have said above. He is not the Vicar of Christ in heaven, but only of Christ upon earth. For Christ in heaven, in the form of a ruler, requires no vicar, but there sits, sees, does, knows, and commands all things. But He requires him "in the form of a servant" to represent Him as He walked upon earth, working, preaching, suffering and dying. But they reverse this; they take from Christ His power as a heavenly ruler, and give it to the Pope, and allow "the form of a servant" to be entirely forgotten. (Phil. ii. 7.) He should properly be called the counter-Christ, whom the Scriptures call *Antichrist*; for his whole existence, work, and proceedings are directed against Christ, to ruin and destroy the existence and will of Christ.

It is also absurd and puerile for the Pope to boast for such blind, foolish reasons, in his decretal Pastoralis, that he is the rightful heir to the Empire, if the throne be vacant. Who gave it to him? Did Christ do so, when He said: "The kings of the Gentiles exercise lordship over them, but ye shall not do so"? (Luke xxii. 25, 26.) Did St. Peter bequeath it to him? It disgusts me that we have to read and teach such impudent, clumsy, foolish lies in the canon law, and moreover to take them for Christian doctrine, while in reality they are mere devilish lies. Of this kind also is the unheard-of lie touching the "donation of Constantine."[39] It must have been a plague sent by God that induced so many wise people to accept such lies, though they are so gross and clumsy, that one would think a drunken boor could lie more skilfully. How could preaching, prayer, study and the care of the poor consist with the government of the Empire? These are the true offices of the Pope, which Christ imposed with such insistence that He forbade them to take either coat or scrip (Matt. x. 10), for he that has to govern a single house can hardly perform these duties. Yet the Pope wishes to rule an Empire and to remain a Pope. This is the invention of the

---

[38] The chapter *Solite* is also contained in the *Corpus juris canonici.*

[39] In order to legalise the secular power of the Pope, the fiction was invented during the latter part of the eighth century, that Constantine the Great had made over to the Popes the dominion over Rome and over the whole of Italy.

knaves that would fain become lords of the world in the Pope's name, and set up again the old Roman empire, as it was formerly, by means of the Pope and name of Christ, in its former condition.

10. The Pope must withdraw his hand from the dish, and on no pretence assume royal authority over Naples and Sicily. He has no more right to it than I, and yet claims to be the lord of it. It has been taken by force and robbery like almost all his other possessions. Therefore the Emperor should grant him no such fief, nor any longer allow him those he has, but direct him instead to his Bibles and Prayer-books, so that he may leave the government of countries and peoples to the temporal power, especially of those that no one has given him. Let him rather preach and pray! The same should be done with Bologna, Imola, Vicenza, Ravenna, and whatever the Pope has taken by force and holds without right in the Ancontine territory, in the Romagna and other parts of Italy, interfering in their affairs against all the commandments of Christ and St. Paul. For St. Paul says (2 Tim. ii. 4): "that he that would be one of the soldiers of Heaven must not entangle himself in the affairs of this life." Now the Pope should be the head and the leader of the soldiers of Heaven, and yet he engages more in worldly matters than any king or emperor. He should be relieved of his worldly cares and allowed to attend to his duties as a soldier of Heaven. Christ also, whose vicar he claims to be, would have nothing to do with the things of this world, and even asked one that desired of him a judgment concerning his brother: "Who made me a judge over you?" (St. Luke xii. 14.) But the Pope interferes in these matters unasked, and concerns himself with all matters, as though he were a god, until he himself has forgotten what this Christ is, whose vicar he professes to be.

11. The custom of kissing the Pope's feet must cease. It is an un-Christian, or rather an anti-Christian example, that a poor sinful man should suffer his foot to be kissed by one who is a hundred times better than he. If it is done in honour of his power, why does he not do it to others in honour of their holiness? Compare them together: Christ and the Pope. Christ washed His disciples' feet and dried them, and the disciples never washed His. The Pope, pretending to be higher than Christ, inverts this, and considers it a great favour to let us kiss his feet: whereas if any one wished to do so, he ought to do his utmost to prevent them, as St. Paul and Barnabas would not suffer themselves to be worshipped as Gods by the men at Lystra, saying: "We also are men of like passions with you." (Acts xiv. 14 seq.) But our flatterers have brought things to such a pitch, that they have set up an idol for us, until no one regards God with such fear, or honours Him with such reverence as they do the Pope. This they can suffer, but not that the Pope's glory should be diminished a single hair's-breadth. Now if they were Christians and preferred God's honour to their own, the Pope would never be willing to have God's honour despised and his own exalted, nor would he allow any to honour him, until he found that God's honour was again exalted above his own.

It is of a piece with this revolting pride, that the Pope is not satisfied with riding on horseback or in a carriage, but though he be hale and strong, is carried by men like an idol in unheard-of pomp. I ask you, how does this Lucifer-like pride agree with the example of Christ, who went on foot, as did also all His Apostles? Where has there been a king who lived in such worldly pomp as he does, who professes to be the head of all whose duty it is to despise and flee from all worldly pomp—I mean, of all Christians? Not that this need concern us for his own sake, but that we have good reason to fear God's wrath, if we flatter such pride and do not show our discontent. It is enough that the

Pope should be so mad and foolish; but it is too much that we should sanction and approve it.

For what Christian heart can be pleased at seeing the Pope, when he communicates, sit still like a gracious lord and have the sacrament handed to him on a golden reed, by a cardinal bending on his knees before him? Just as if the holy sacrament were not worthy that a Pope, a poor miserable sinner, should stand to do honour to his God, although all other Christians, who are much more holy than the Most Holy Father, receive it with all reverence? Could we be surprised if God visited us all with a plague, for that we suffer such dishonour to be done to God by our prelates, and approve it, becoming partners of the Pope's damnable pride by our silence or flattery? It is the same when he carries the sacrament in procession. He must be carried, but the sacrament stands before him like a cup of wine on a table. In short, at Rome Christ is nothing, the Pope is everything; yet they urge us and threaten us, to make us suffer and approve and honour this Antichristian scandal, contrary to God and all Christian doctrine. Now, may God so help a free Council, that it may teach the Pope that he too is a man, not above God as he makes himself out to be.

12. Pilgrimages to Rome must be abolished, or at least no one must be allowed to go from his own wish or his own piety, unless his priest, his town magistrate, or his lord has found that there is sufficient reason for his pilgrimage. This I say, not because pilgrimages are bad in themselves, but because at the present time they lead to mischief; for at Rome a pilgrim sees no good examples, but only offence. They themselves have made a proverb: "The nearer to Rome, the farther from Christ," and accordingly men bring home contempt of God and of God's commandments. It is said: "The first time one goes to Rome, he goes to seek a rogue; the second time he finds him; the third time he brings him home with him." But now they have become so skilful, that they can do their three journeys in one, and they have in fact brought home from Rome this saying:—It were better never to have seen or heard of Rome.

And even if this were not so, there is something of more importance to be considered; namely, that simple men are thus led into a false delusion and a wrong understanding of God's commandments. For they think that these pilgrimages are precious and good works; but this is not true. It is but a little good work; often a bad, misleading work, for God has not commanded it. But He has commanded that each man should care for his wife and children and whatever concerns the married state; and should, besides, serve and help his neighbour. Now it often happens that one goes on a pilgrimage to Rome, spends fifty or one hundred guilders, more or less, which no one has commanded him, while his wife and children, or those dearest to him, are left at home in want and misery; and yet he thinks, poor foolish man, to atone for this disobedience and contempt of God's commandments by his self-willed pilgrimage, while he is in truth misled by idle curiosity, or the wiles of the Devil. This the Popes have encouraged with their false and foolish inventions of *Golden Years*,[40] by which they have incited the people, have torn them away from God's commandments and turned them to their own delusive proceedings, and set up the very thing that they ought to have forbidden. But it brought them money and strengthened their false authority, and therefore it was allowed to continue, though against God's will and the salvation of souls.

---

[40] The Jubilees, during which plenary indulgences were granted to those who visited the churches of St. Peter and St Paul at Rome, were originally celebrated every hundred years and subsequently every twenty-five years. Those who were unable to go to Rome in person could obtain the plenary indulgences by paying the expenses of the journey to Rome into the Papal treasury.

That this false, misleading belief on the part of simple Christians may be destroyed, and a true opinion of good works may again be introduced, all pilgrimages should be done away with. For there is no good in them; no commandment; but countless causes of sin and of contempt of God's commandments. These pilgrimages are the reason for there being so many beggars, that commit numberless villainies, taught by them and accustomed to beg without need. Hence arises a vagabond life; besides other miseries which I cannot dwell on now. If any one wishes to go on a pilgrimage or to make a vow for a pilgrimage, he should first inform his priest or the temporal authorities of the reason, and if it should turn out that he wished to do it for the sake of good works, let this vow and work be just trampled upon by the priest or the temporal authority as an infernal delusion, and let them tell him to spend his money, and the labour a pilgrimage would cost, on God's commandments, and on a thousand-fold better work, namely, on his family and his poor neighbours. But if he does it out of curiosity, to see cities and countries, he may be allowed to do so. If he have vowed it in sickness, let such vows be prohibited, and let God's commandments be insisted upon in contrast to them; so that a man may be content with what he vowed in baptism, namely, to keep God's commandments. Yet, for this once he may be suffered, for a quiet conscience sake, to keep his silly vow. No one is content to walk on the broad high road of God's commandments; every one makes for himself new roads and new vows, as if he had kept all God's commandments.

13. Now we come to the great crowd that promises much and performs little. Be not angry, my good sirs, I mean well. I have to tell you this bitter and sweet truth: Let no more mendicant monasteries be built! God help us! there are too many as it is. Would to God they were all abolished, or at least made over to two or three orders. It has never done good, it will never do good, to go wandering about over the country. Therefore my advice is that ten, or as many as required, may be put together and made into one, which one, sufficiently provided for is not to beg. Oh! it is of much more importance to consider what is necessary for the salvation of the common people, than what St. Francis, or St. Dominic, or St. Augustine,[41] or any other man, laid down; especially, since things have not turned out as they expected. They should also be relieved from preaching and confession, unless specially required to do so by bishops, priests, the congregation or other authority. For their preaching and confession has led to nought but mere hatred and envy between priests and monks, to the great offence and hindrance of the people, so that it well deserves to be put a stop to, since its place may be very well supplied. It does not look at all improbable that the Holy Roman See had its own reasons for encouraging all this crowd of monks: the Pope perhaps feared that priests and bishops, growing weary of his tyranny, might become too strong for him, and begin a reformation unendurable to his Holiness.

Besides this, one should also do away with the sections and the divisions in the same order which, caused for little reason and kept up for less, oppose each other with unspeakable hatred and malice. The result being, that the Christian faith, which is very well able to stand without their divisions, is lost on both sides, and that a true Christian life is sought and judged only by outward rules, works and manners, from which arise only hypocrisy and the destruction of souls; as every one can see for himself. Moreover the Pope should be forbidden to institute or to confirm the institution of such new orders, nay, he should be commanded to abolish several and to lessen their number. For the faith

---

[41] The above-mentioned saints were the patrons of the well-known mendicant orders, Franciscans, Dominicans and Augustines.

of Christ, which alone is the important matter and can stand without any particular Order, incurs no little danger, lest men should be led away by these diverse works and manners, rather to live for such works and manners than to care for faith. And unless there are wise prelates in the monasteries who preach and urge faith rather than the rule of the order, it is inevitable that the order should be injurious and misleading to simple souls, who have regard to works alone.

Now in our own time all the prelates are dead that had faith and founded orders. Just as it was in old days with the children of Israel; when their fathers were dead, that had seen God's works and miracles, their children, out of ignorance of God's work and of faith, soon began to set up idolatry and their own human works. In the same way, alas! these orders, not understanding God's works and faith, grievously labour and torment themselves by their own rules and laws, and yet never arrive at a true understanding of a spiritual and good life; as was foretold by the Apostle, saying of them, "Having a form of godliness, but denying the power thereof. . . . Ever learning, and never able to come to the knowledge" of what a true spiritual life is. (2 Tim. iii. 2–7.) Better to have no convents, where there is no truly spiritual prelate, of understanding in Christian faith, to govern them; for such a prelate cannot but rule with injury and harm, and the greater the apparent holiness of his life in external works, the greater the harm.

It would be, I think, necessary, especially in these perilous times, that foundations and convents should again be organised as they were in the time of the Apostles and a long time after: namely, when they were all free, for every man to remain there as long as he wished. For what were they but Christian schools, in which the Scriptures and Christian life were taught, and where folk were trained to govern and to preach; as we read that St. Agnes went to school, and as we see, even now, in some nunneries, as at Quedlinburg and other places? Truly all foundations and convents ought to be free in this way, that they may serve God of a free will and not as slaves. But now they have been bound round with vows and turned into eternal prisons, so that these vows are regarded even more than the vows of baptism. But what fruit has come of this we daily see, hear, read and learn more and more.

I dare say that this my counsel will be thought very foolish, but I care not for this. I advise what I think best; reject it, who will. I know how these vows are kept, especially that of chastity, which is so general in all convents,[42] and yet was not ordered by Christ, and it is given to comparatively few to be able to keep it, as He says and St. Paul also: (Col. ii. 20.) I wish all to be helped, and that Christian souls should not be held in bondage, through customs and laws invented by men.

14. We see also how the priesthood is fallen, and how many a poor priest is encumbered with a woman and children, and burdened in his conscience, and no one does anything to help him, though he might very well be helped. Popes and bishops may let that be lost that is being lost, and that be destroyed which is being destroyed; I will save my conscience and open my mouth freely, let it vex Popes and bishops or whoever it may be; therefore I say: According to the ordinances of Christ and His Apostles every town should have a minister, as St. Paul plainly says (Tit. i.), and this minister should not be forced to live without a lawful wife, but should be allowed to have one, as St. Paul writes (1 Tim. iii.), saying that "A bishop then must be blameless, the husband of one wife . . . having his children in subjection with all gravity." For with St. Paul a bishop and a

---

[42] Luther alludes here, of course, to the vow of celibacy, which was curiously styled the vow of chastity; thus indirectly condemning marriage in general.

presbyter are the same thing, as St. Jerome also confirms. But as for the bishops that we now have, of these the Scriptures know nothing; they were instituted by the Christian congregations, so that one might rule over many ministers.

Therefore, we teach clearly according to the Apostle, that every town should elect a pious learned citizen from the congregation and charge him with the office of minister; the congregation should support him and he should be left at liberty to marry or not. He should have as assistants, several priests and deacons, married or not, as they please, who should help him to govern the people and the congregation with sermons and the ministration of the sacraments, as is still the case in the Greek Church. In these latter times, where there are somany persecutions and conflicts against heretics, there were many holy fathers, who voluntarily abstained from the marriage state, that they might study more, and might be ready at all times for death and conflict. Now the Roman See has interfered of its own perversity, and has made a general law by which priests are forbidden to marry. This must have been at the instigation of the Devil, as was foretold by St. Paul (1 Tim. iv. 1, 2, *seq.*), saying that "there shall come teachers giving heed to seducing spirits . . . forbidding to marry," etc. This has been the cause of so much misery that it cannot be told, and has given occasion to the Greek Church to separate from us, and has caused infinite disunion, sin, shame and scandal, like everything that the Devil does or suggests. Now what are we to do?

My advice is, to restore liberty, and to leave every man free to marry or not to marry. But if we did this we should have to introduce a very different rule and order for property; the whole canon law would be overthrown and but few benefices would fall to Rome. I am afraid greed was a cause of this wretched, unchaste chastity; for the result of it was that every man wished to become a priest, or to have his son brought up to the priesthood—not with the intention of living in chastity, for this could be done without the priestly state, but to obtain his worldly support without labour or trouble, contrary to God's command (Gen. iii.): "In the sweat of thy face shalt thou eat thy bread;" and they have given a colour to this commandment as though their work was praying and reading the mass. I am not here considering Popes, bishops, canons, clergy and monks, who were not ordained by God; they have laid burdens on themselves, and they may bear them. I speak of the office of parish priest, which God ordained, who must rule a congregation with sermons and the ministration of the sacraments, and must live with them and manage their own worldly affairs. These should have the liberty given them by a Christian Council to marry and to avoid danger and sin. For as God has not bound them, no one may bind them, though he were an angel from heaven—let alone the Pope; and whatever is contrary to this in the canon law is mere idle talk and invention.

My advice further is, whoever henceforth is ordained priest, he should in no wise take the vow of chastity, but should protest to the bishop that he has no authority to demand this vow, and that it is a devilish tyranny to demand it. But if one is forced, or wishes to say, as some do, "so far as human frailty permits," let every man interpret that phrase as a plain negative, that is, "I do not promise chastity;" for human frailty does not allow men to live an unmarried life, but only angelic fortitude and celestial virtue. In this way he will have a clear conscience without any vow. I offer no opinion, one way or the other, whether those who have at present no wife should marry, or remain unmarried. This must be settled by the general order of the Church and by each man's discretion. But I will not conceal my honest counsel, nor withhold comfort from that unhappy crowd who now live in trouble with wife and children, and remain in shame, with a heavy conscience, hearing their wife called a priest's harlot, and the children bastards. And this I say frankly, by my fool's privilege.

There is many a poor priest free from blame in all other respects, except that he has succumbed to human frailty and come to shame with a woman, both minded in their hearts to live together always in conjugal fidelity, if only they could do so with a good conscience, though, as it is, they live in public shame. I say, these two are surely married before God. I say, moreover, that when two are so minded, and so come to live together, they should save their conscience; let the man take the woman as his lawful wife, and live with her faithfully as her husband, without considering whether the Pope approve or not, or whether it is forbidden by canon law, or temporal. The salvation of your soul is of more importance than their tyrannous, arbitrary, wicked laws, which are not necessary for salvation, nor ordained by God. You should do as the children of Israel did, who stole from the Egyptians the wages they had earned; or as a servant steals his well-earned wages from a harsh master; in the same way do you also steal your wife and child from the Pope.

Let him who has faith enough to dare this, only follow me courageously: I will not mislead him. I may not have the Pope's authority, yet I have the authority of a Christian to help my neighbour and to warn him against his sins and dangers. And here there is good reason for doing so.

a. It is not every priest that can do without a woman, not only on account of human frailty, but still more for his household. If, therefore, he takes a woman, and the Pope allows this, but will not let them marry, what is this but expecting a man and a woman to live together and not to fall? Just as if one were to set fire to straw, and command it should neither smoke nor burn.

b. The Pope having no authority for such a command, any more than to forbid a man to eat and drink, or to digest or to grow fat, no one is bound to obey it, and the Pope is answerable for every sin against it, for all the souls that it has brought to destruction, and for all the consciences that have been troubled and tormented by it. He has long deserved to be driven out of the world, so many poor souls has he strangled with this Devil's rope; though I hope that God has shown many more mercy at their death than the Pope did in their life. No good has ever come and can ever come from the Papacy and its laws.

c. Even though the Pope's laws forbid it, still after the married state has been entered, the Pope's laws are superseded, and are valid no longer: for God has commanded that no man shall put asunder husband and wife, and this commandment is far above the Pope's laws, and God's command must not be cancelled or neglected for the Papal commands. It is true that mad lawyers have helped the Pope to invent impediments or hindrances to marriage, and thus troubled, divided, and perverted the married state: destroying the commandments of God. What need I say further? In the whole body of the Pope's canon law, there are not two lines that can instruct a pious Christian, and so many false and dangerous ones, that it were better to treat it as waste paper.

But if you object that this would give offence, and that one must first obtain the Pope's dispensation, I answer that if there is any offence in it, it is the fault of the See of Rome, which has made unjust and unholy laws. It is no offence to God and the Scriptures. Even where the Pope has power to grant dispensation for money by his covetous tyrannical laws, every Christian has power to grant dispensation in the same matter for the sake of Christ and the salvation of souls. For Christ has freed us from all human laws, especially when they are opposed to God and the salvation of souls, as St. Paul teaches. (Gal. v. 1, and 1 Cor. viii. 9, 10.)

15. I must not forget the poor convents. The evil spirit, who has troubled all estates of life by human laws, and made them unendurable, has taken possession of some Abbots, Abbesses, and Prelates, and led them so to rule their brothers and sisters, that they do but go soon to hell, and live a wretched life even upon earth, as is the case with all the Devil's martyrs. For they have reserved in confession all, or at least some, deadly sins, which are secret, and from these no brother may on pain of excommunication and on his obedience absolve another. Now we do not always find angels everywhere, but men of flesh and blood, who would rather incur all excommunication and menace than confess their secret sins to a prelate or the confessor appointed for them; consequently they receive the sacrament with these sins on their conscience, by which they become *irregular*[43] and suffer much misery. Oh blind shepherds! Oh foolish Prelates! Oh ravenous wolves! Now I say that in cases where a sin is public and notorious, it is only right that the Prelate alone should punish it, and such sins and no others he may reserve and except for himself; over private sins he has no authority, even though they may be the worst that can be committed or imagined. And if the Prelate excepts these, he becomes a tyrant and interferes with God's judgment.

Accordingly I advise these children, brothers and sisters: if your superiors will not allow you to confess your secret sins to whomsoever you will, then take them yourself, and confess them to your brother or sister, to whomsoever you will; be absolved and comforted, and then go or do what your wish or duty commands; only believe firmly that you have been absolved, and nothing more is necessary. And let not their threats of excommunication, or irregularity, or what not, trouble or disturb you; these only apply to public or notorious sins, if they are not confessed: you are not touched by them. How canst thou take upon thyself, thou blind Prelate, to restrain private sins by thy threats? Give up what thou canst not keep publicly; let God's judgment and mercy also have its place with thy inferiors. He has not given them into thy hands so completely as to have let them go out of His own; nay, thou hast received the smaller portion. Consider thy statutes as nothing more than thy statutes, and do not make them equal to God's judgment in Heaven.

16. It were also right to abolish annual festivals, processions, and masses for the dead, or at least to diminish their number; for we evidently see that they have become no better than a mockery, exciting the anger of God, and having no object but money getting, eating and drinking. How should it please God to hear the poor vigils and masses mumbled in this wretched way, neither read nor prayed? Even when they are properly read, it is not done freely for the love of God, but for the love of money and as payment of a debt. Now it is impossible that anything should please God, or win anything from Him that is not done freely, out of love for Him. Therefore, as true Christians, we ought to abolish or lessen a practice that we see is abused, and that angers God instead of appeasing Him. I should prefer, and it would be more agreeable to God's will, and far better for a foundation, church or convent, to put all the yearly masses and vigils together into one mass, so that they would every year celebrate, on one day, a true vigil and mass with hearty sincerity, devotion and faith, for all their benefactors. This would be better than their thousand upon thousand masses said every year—each for a particular benefactor—without devotion and faith. My dear fellow-Christians! God cares not for much prayer, but for good prayer. Nay, He condemns long and frequent prayers (Matt. vi.

---

[43] Luther uses the expression *irregulares*, which was applied to those monks who were guilty of heresy, apostasy, transgression of the vow of chastity, etc.

2, *seq.*), saying: "Verily I say unto you, they have their reward." But it is the greed that cannot trust God by which such practices are set up; it is afraid it will die of starvation.

17. One should also abolish certain punishments inflicted by the canon law, especially the interdict, which is doubtless the invention of the evil one. Is it not the mark of the Devil to wish to better one sin by more and worse sins? It is surely a greater sin to silence God's word and service, than if we were to kill twenty Popes at once, not to speak of a single priest or of keeping back the goods of the Church. This is one of those gentle virtues which are learnt in the Spiritual law; for the Canon or Spiritual law is so called because it comes from a spirit—not however from the Holy Spirit, but from the Evil Spirit.

Excommunication should not be used except where the Scriptures command it: that is, against those that have not the right faith, or that live in open sin, and not in matters of temporal goods. But now the case has been inverted; each man believes and lives as he pleases, especially those that plunder and disgrace others with excommunications; and all excommunications are now only in matters of worldly goods. For which we have no one to thank but the holy canonical injustice. But of all this I have spoken previously in a sermon.

The other punishments and penalties—suspension, irregularity, aggravation, re-aggravation, deposition,[44] thundering, lightning, cursing, damning and what not, all these should be buried ten fathoms deep in the earth, that their very name and memory may no longer live upon earth. The evil spirit, who was let loose by the spiritual law, has brought all this terrible plague and misery into the heavenly kingdom of the holy Church, and has thereby brought about nothing but the harm and destruction of souls, that we may well apply to it the words of Christ (Matt. xxiii. 13): "But woe unto you, scribes and Pharisees, hypocrites! for you shut up the kingdom of heaven against men: for ye neither go in yourselves, neither suffer ye them that are entering to go in."

18. One should abolish all saints' days, keeping only Sunday. But if it were desired to keep the festival of Our Lady and the greater saints, they should all be held on Sundays, or only in the morning with the mass; the rest of the day being a working day. My reason is this: with our present abuses of drinking, gambling, idling, and all manner of sin, we vex God more on holy days than on others. And the matter is just reversed; we have made holy days unholy, and working days holy, and do no service but great dishonour to God and His saints with all our holy days. There are some foolish prelates that think they have done a good deed, if they establish a festival to St. Otilia, or St. Barbara, and the like, each in his own blind fashion, whilst he would be doing a much better work to turn a saint's day into a working day, in honour of a saint.

Besides these spiritual evils, these saints' days inflict bodily injury on the common man in two ways: he loses a day's work and he spends more than usual, besides weakening his body and making himself unfit for labour, as we see every day, and yet no one tries to improve it. One should not consider whether the Pope instituted these festivals, or whether we require his dispensation or permission. If anything is contrary to God's will and harmful to men in body and soul, not only has every community, council or government authority to prevent and abolish such wrong without the knowledge or consent of Pope or bishop; but it is their duty, as they value their soul's salvation, to

---

[44] Luther enumerates here the various grades of punishment inflicted on priests. The *aggravation* consisted of a threat of excommunication, after a thrice-repeated admonition, whilst the consequence of *re-aggravation* was immediate excommunication.

prevent it, even though Pope and bishop (that should be the first to do so) are unwilling to see it stopped. And first of all we should abolish church wakes, since they are nothing but taverns, fairs and gaming places, to the greater dishonour of God and the damnation of souls. It is no good to make a talk about their having had a good origin and being good works. Did not God set aside His own law that He had given forth out of heaven, when He saw that it was abused? and does He not now reverse every day what He has appointed, and destroy what He has made, on account of the same perverse misuse, as it is written in the eighteenth Psalm (v. 26): "With the froward thou wilt show thyself froward."

19. The degrees of relationship in which marriage is forbidden must be altered, such as so-called spiritual relations[45] in the third and fourth degrees; and where the Pope at Rome can dispense in such matters for money, and make shameful bargains, every priest should have the power of granting the same dispensations freely for the salvation of souls. Would to God that all those things that have to be bought at Rome, for freedom from the golden noose of the canon law, might be given by any priest without payment, such as Indulgences, letters of Indulgences, letters of dispensation, mass letters, and all the other religious licences and knaveries at Rome by which the poor people are deceived and robbed! For if the Pope has the power to sell for money his golden snares, or canon nets (laws, I should say), much more has a priest the power to cancel them and to trample on them for God's sake. But if he has no such power, then the Pope can have no authority to sell them in his shameful fair.

Besides this, fasts must be made optional, and every kind of food made free, as is commanded in the Gospels. (Matt. xv. 11.) For whilst at Rome they laugh at fasts, they let us abroad eat oil which they would not think fit for greasing their boots, and then sell us the liberty of eating butter and other things, whereas the Apostle says, that the Gospel has given us freedom in all such matters. (1 Cor. x. 25 seq.) But they have caught us in their canon law and have robbed us of this right, so that we have to buy it back from them; they have so terrified the consciences of the people, that one cannot preach this liberty without rousing the anger of the people, who think the eating of butter to be a worse sin than lying, swearing and unchastity. We may make of it what we will; it is but the work of man, and no good can ever come of it.

20. The country chapels and churches must be destroyed, such as those to which the new pilgrimages have been set on foot, Wilsnacht, Sternberg, Treves, the Grimmenthal, and now Ratisbon, and many others. Oh what a reckoning there will be for those bishops that allow these inventions of the Devil and make a profit out of them! They should be the first to stop it; they think that it is a godly, holy thing, and do not see that the Devil does this to strengthen covetousness, to teach false beliefs, to weaken parish churches, to increase drunkenness and debauchery, to waste money and labour, and simply to lead the poor people by the nose. If they had only studied the Scriptures as much as their accursed canon law, they would know well how to deal with the matter.

The miracles performed there prove nothing, for the Evil One can also show wonders, as Christ has taught us. (Matt. xxiv. 24.) If they took up the matter earnestly, and forbade such doings, the miracles would soon cease; or if they were done by God, they would not be prevented by their commands. And if there were nothing else to prove that these are not works of God, it would be enough that people go about turbulently and irrationally like herds of cattle, which could not possibly come from God. God has not

---

[45] Those, namely, between Sponsors at Baptism and their Godchildren.

commanded it; there is no obedience, and no merit in it; and therefore it should be vigorously interfered with and the people warned against it. For what is not commanded by God and goes beyond God's commandments is surely the Devil's own work. In this way also the parish churches suffer, in that they are less venerated. In fine, these pilgrimages are signs of great want of faith in the people; for if they truly believed, they would find all things in their own churches, where they are commanded to go.

But what is the use of my speaking? Every man thinks only how he may get up such a pilgrimage in his own district, not caring whether the people believes and lives rightly. The rulers are like the people—blind leaders of the blind. Where pilgrimages are a failure, they begin to glorify their saints; not to honour the saints, who are sufficiently honoured without them, but to cause a concourse, and to bring in money. Then Pope and bishops help them; it rains indulgences, and every one can afford to buy them; but what God has commanded no one cares for; no one runs after it, no one can afford any money for it. Alas for our blindness, that we not only suffer the Devil to have his way with his phantoms, but support him! I wish one would leave the good saints alone and not lead the poor people astray. What spirit gave the Pope authority to "glorify" the saints? Who tells him whether they are holy, or not holy? Are there not enough sins on earth, as it is, but we must tempt God, interfere in His judgment, and make money-bags of his saints? Therefore my advice is to let the saints glorify themselves; or rather, God alone should glorify them, and every man should keep to his own parish, where he will profit more than in all these shrines, even if they were all put together into one shrine. Here a man finds Baptism, the Sacrament, preaching, and his neighbour, and these are more than all the saints in Heaven, for it is by God's word and sacrament that they have all been hallowed.

Our contempt for these great matters justifies God's anger in giving us over to the devil to lead us astray, to get up pilgrimages, to found churches and chapels, to glorify the saints and to commit other like follies, by which we are led astray from the true faith into new false beliefs; just as he did in old time with the people of Israel, whom he led away from the temple to countless other places; all the while in God's name, and with the appearance of holiness, against which all the prophets preached, suffering martyrdom for their words. But now no one preaches against it; and probably if he did, bishops, Popes, priests and monks would combine to martyr him. In this way Antonius of Florence and many others are made saints, so that their holiness may serve to produce glory and wealth, whereas otherwise they would have served simply as good examples for the glory of God.

Even if this glorification of the Saints had been good once, it is not good now; just as many other things were good once and are now occasion of offence and injurious, such as holidays, ecclesiastical treasures and ornaments. For it is evident that what is aimed at in the glorification of saints is not the glory of God, nor the bettering of Christendom, but money and fame alone; one church wishes to have an advantage over another, and would be sorry to see another church enjoying the same advantages. In this way they have in these latter days abused the goods of the Church so as to gain the goods of the world; so that everything, and even God Himself, must serve their avarice. Moreover these privileges cause nothing but dissensions and worldly pride; one church being different from the rest, they despise or magnify one another, whereas all goods that are of God should be common to all, and should serve to produce unity. This, too, is why they please the Pope, who would be sorry to see all Christians equal and at one with one another.

Here must be added that one should abolish, or treat as of no account, or give to all churches alike, the licences, bulls, and whatever the Pope sells at his flying-ground at Rome. For if he sells or gives to Wittenberg, to Halle, to Venice, and above all to his own city of Rome, special permissions, privileges, indulgences, graces, advantages, faculties, why does he not give them to all churches alike? Is it not his duty to do all that he can for all Christians without reward, solely for God's sake, nay, even to shed his blood for them? Why then, I should like to know, does he give or sell these things to one church and not to another? Or does this accursed gold make a difference in his Holiness's eyes between Christians who all alike have baptism, gospel, faith, Christ, God, and all things? Do they wish us to be blind, when our eyes can see, to be fools, when we have reason, that we should worship this greed, knavery and delusion? He is a shepherd forsooth—so long as you have money, no further; and yet they are not ashamed to practise all this knavery right and left with their bulls. They care only for that accursed gold and for nought besides.

Therefore my advice is this: If this folly is not done away with, let all pious Christians open their eyes and not be deceived by these Romish Bulls and seals, and all their specious pretences; let them stop at home in their own churches, and be satisfied with their Baptism, Gospel, Faith, Christ and God (who is everywhere the same), and let the Pope continue to be a blind leader of the blind. Neither Pope nor angel can give you as much as God gives you in your own parish; nay, he only leads you away from God's gifts, which you have for nothing, to his own gifts, which you must buy; giving you lead for gold, skin for meat, strings for a purse, wax for honey, words for goods, the letter for the spirit; as you can see for yourselves though you will not perceive it. If you try to ride to heaven on the Pope's wax and parchment, your carriage will soon break down and you will fall into hell, not in God's name.

Let this be a fixed rule for you, Whatever has to be bought of the Pope is neither good, nor of God. For whatever comes from God is not only given freely, but all the world is punished and condemned for not accepting it freely. So is it with the Gospel and the works of God. We have deserved to be led into these errors, because we have despised God's holy word and the grace of baptism, as St. Paul says: "And for this cause God shall send them strong delusion, that they should believe a lie: that they all might be damned who believed not the truth, but had pleasure in unrighteousness." (2 Thess. ii. 11, 12.)

21. It is one of the most urgent necessities to abolish all begging in Christendom. No one should go about begging among Christians. It would not be hard to do this, if we attempted it with good heart and courage: each town should support its own poor and should not allow strange beggars to come in—whatever they may call themselves: pilgrims or mendicant monks. Every town could feed its own poor; and if it were too small, the people in the neighbouring villages should be called upon to contribute. As it is, they have to support many knaves and vagabonds under the name of beggars. If they did what I propose, they would at least know who were really poor or not.

There should also be an overseer or guardian who should know all the poor, and should inform the town or council, or the priest, of their requirements; or some other similar provision might be made. There is no occupation, in my opinion, in which there is so much knavery and cheating as among beggars; and it could so easily be prevented. This general, unrestricted begging is, besides, injurious for the common people. I estimate that of the five or six orders of mendicant monks, each one visits every place more than six or seven times in the year; then there are the common beggars, messengers and pilgrims; in this way I calculate every city has a blackmail levied on it about sixty times a year, not counting rates and taxes paid to the civil government and the useless robberies of the Roman See; so that it is to my mind one of the greatest of God's miracles how we manage to live and support ourselves.

Some may think that in this way the poor would not be well cared for, and that such great stone houses and convents would not be built, and not so plentifully, and I think so too. But there would be no harm in that. If a man will be poor, he should not be rich; if he will be rich, let him put his hand to the plough, and get wealth himself out of the earth. It is enough to provide decently for the poor, that they may not die of cold and hunger. It is not right, that one should work that another may be idle, and live ill that another may live well, as is now the perverse abuse, for St. Paul says (2 Thess. iii. 10): "If any would not work, neither should he eat." God has not ordained that any one should live of the goods of others, except priests and ministers alone, as St. Paul says (1 Cor. ix. 14), for their spiritual work's sake; as also Christ says to the Apostles (Luke x. 7): "The labourer is worthy of his hire."

22. It is also to be feared that the *many masses* that have been founded in convents and foundations, instead of doing any good, arouse God's anger; wherefore it would be well to endow no more masses and to abolish many of those that have been endowed; for we see that they are only looked upon as sacrifices and good works, though in truth they are sacraments like baptism and confession, and as such profit him only that receives them. But now the custom obtains of saying masses for the living and the dead, and everything is based upon them. This is the reason why there are so many, and that they have come to be what we see.

But perhaps all this is a new and unheard of doctrine, especially in the eyes of those that fear to lose their livelihood, if these masses were abolished. I must therefore reserve what I have to say on this subject until men have arrived at a truer understanding of the mass, its nature and use. The mass has, alas! for so many years been turned into means of gaining a livelihood, that I should advise a man to become a shepherd, a labourer, rather than a priest, or monk, unless he knows what the mass is.

All this, however, does not apply to the old foundations and chapters; which were doubtless founded in order that, since according to the custom of Germany all the children of nobles cannot be landowners and rulers, they should be provided for in these foundations, and these serve God freely, study and become learned themselves, and help others to acquire learning. I am speaking only of the new foundations, endowed for prayers and masses, by the example of which the old foundations have become burdened with the like prayers and masses, making them of very little, if of any use. Through God's righteous punishment they have at last come down to the dregs as they deserve; that is, to the noise of singers and organs, and cold, spiritless masses, with no end but to gain and spend the money due to them. Popes, bishops and doctors should examine and report on such things; as it is they are the guiltiest, allowing anything that brings them money; the blind ever leading the blind. This comes of covetousness and the canon law.

It must, moreover, not be allowed in future that one man should have more than one endowment or prebend. He should be content with a moderate position in life, so that others may have something besides himself; and thus we must put a stop to the excuses of those that say that they must have more than one office to enable them to live in their proper station. It is possible to estimate one's proper station in such a way, that a whole kingdom would not suffice to maintain it. So it is that covetousness and want of faith in

God go hand in hand, and often men take for the requirements of their station what is mere covetousness and want of faith.

23. As for the fraternities, together with indulgences, letters of indulgence, dispensations, masses and all the rest of such things, let it all be drowned and abolished; there is no good in it at all. If the Pope has the authority to grant dispensation in the matter of eating butter and hearing masses, let him allow priests to do the same; he has no right to take the power from them. I speak also of the fraternities in which indulgences, masses, and good works are distributed. My friend, in baptism you joined a fraternity of which Christ, the angels, the saints and all Christians are members; be true to this, and satisfy it, and you will have fraternities enough. Let others make what show they wish; they are as counters compared to coins. But if there were a fraternity that subscribed money to feed the poor, or to help others in any way, this would be good, and it would have its indulgence and its deserts in Heaven. But now they are good for nothing but gluttony and drunkenness.

First of all we should expel from all German lands the Pope's legates with their faculties, which they sell to us for much money, though it is all knavery; as, for instance, their taking money for making goods unlawfully acquired to be good, for freeing from oaths, vows, and bonds, thus destroying and teaching others to destroy truth and faith mutually pledged; saying the Pope has authority to do so. It is the Evil Spirit that bids them talk thus, and so they sell us the Devil's teaching, and take money for teaching us sins and leading us to hell.

If there were nothing else to show that the Pope is Antichrist, this would be enough. Dost thou hear this, O Pope! not the most holy, but the most sinful? Would that God would hurl thy Chair headlong from heaven, and cast it down into the abyss of hell! Who gave you the power to exalt yourself above your God? To break and to loose what He has commanded? To teach Christians, more especially Germans, who are of noble nature, and are famed in all histories for uprightness and truth, to be false, unfaithful, perjured, treacherous and wicked? God has commanded to keep faith and observe oaths even with enemies; you dare to cancel this command, laying it down in your heretical, antichristian decretals, that you have power to do so; and through your mouth and your pen Satan lies as he never lied before, teaching you to twist and pervert the Scriptures according to your own arbitrary will. O, Lord Christ! look down upon this, let Thy day of judgment come and destroy the Devil's lair at Rome. Behold him of whom St. Paul spoke (2 Thess. ii., 3, 4), that he should exalt himself above Thee and sit in Thy Church, showing himself as God—the man of sin, and the child of damnation. What else does the Pope's power do, but teach and strengthen sin and wickedness, leading souls to damnation in Thy name?

The children of Israel in old times kept the oath that they had sworn, in ignorance and error, to the Gibeonites, their enemies. And King Zedekiah was destroyed utterly with his people, because he broke the oath that he had sworn to the King of Babylon. And among us, a hundred years ago, the noble King Ladislaus V. of Poland and Hungary was slain by the Turk with so many of his people, because he allowed himself to be misled by Papal legates and cardinals, and broke the good and useful treaty that he had made with the Turk. The pious Emperor Sigismond had no good fortune after the Council of Constance, in which he allowed the knaves to violate the safe conduct that he had promised to John Huss and Jerome; from this has followed all the miserable strife between Bohemia and ourselves. And in our own time, God help us! how much Christian blood has been shed on account of the oath and bond which Pope Julius made and unmade between the Emperor Maximilian and King Lewis of France! How can I tell all the misery the Popes have caused by such devilish insolence, claiming the power of breaking oaths between great lords, causing a shameful scandal for the sake of money! I hope the day of judgment is at hand; things cannot and will not become worse than the dealings of the Roman Chair. The Pope treads God's commandments under foot and exalts his own; if this is not Antichrist I do not know what is. But of this and to more purpose another time.

24. It is high time to take up earnestly and truthfully the cause of the Bohemians, to unite them with ourselves and ourselves with them, so that all mutual accusations, envy and hatred may cease. I will be the first, in my capacity of fool, to give my opinion, with all due deference to those of better understanding.

First of all, we must honestly confess the truth, without attempting self-justification, and own one thing to the Bohemians, namely, that John Huss and Jerome of Prague were burnt at Constance in violation of the Papal, Christian, and Imperial oath and safe conduct, and that thus God's commandment was broken and the Bohemians excited to great anger. And though, no doubt, they ought to have been perfect men, and have patiently endured this wrong and disobedience to God, yet we cannot expect them to approve it and think it right. Nay, even now they should run any danger of life and limb rather than own that it is right to break an Imperial, Papal, Christian safe conduct and act faithlessly in opposition to it. Therefore, though the Bohemians may be to blame for their impatience, yet the Pope and his followers are most to blame for all the misery, all the error and destruction of souls, that followed this Council of Constance.

It is not my intention here to judge John Huss's belief and to defend his errors; although my understanding has not been able to find any error in him, and I would willingly believe that men who violated a safe conduct and God's commandment (doubtless possessed rather by the evil spirit than by the Spirit of God) were unable to judge well or to condemn with truth. No one can imagine that the Holy Ghost can break God's commandments; no one can deny that it is breaking God's commandments to violate faith and a safe conduct, even though it were promised to the devil himself, much more then in the case of a heretic; it is also notorious that a safe conduct was promised to John Huss and the Bohemians, and that the promise was broken and Huss was burnt. I have no wish to make a saint or a martyr of John Huss (as some Bohemians do), though I own that he was treated unjustly, and that his books and his doctrines were wrongfully condemned; for God's judgments are inscrutable and terrible, and none but Himself may reveal or explain them.

All I say is this: Granting he was a heretic, however bad he may have been, yet he was burnt unjustly and in violation of God's commandments, and we must not require the Bohemians to approve this, if we wish ever to be at one with them. Plain truth must unite us, not obstinacy. It is no use to say, as they said at the time, that a safe conduct need not be kept, if promised to a heretic; that is as much as to say, one may break God's commandments, in order to keep God's commandments. They were infatuated and blinded by the Devil, that they could not see what they said or did. God has commanded us to observe a safe conduct; and this we must do though the world should perish, much more then where it is only a question of a heretic being let free. We should overcome heretics with books, not with fire, as the old Fathers did. If there were any skill in overcoming heretics with fire the executioner would be the most learned doctor in the world; and there would be no need to study, but he that could get another into his power could burn him.

Besides this, the Emperor and the Princes should send to Bohemia several pious, learned bishops and doctors, but, for their life, no cardinal or legate or inquisitor, for such people are far too unlearned in all Christian matters, and do not seek the salvation of souls; but like all the Papal hypocrites, they seek only their own glory, profit and honour; they were also the leaders in that calamitous affair at Constance. But those learned men should inquire into the faith of the Bohemians to ascertain whether it would be possible to unite all their sects into one. Moreover the Pope should (for their souls' sake) for a time abandon his supremacy and, in accordance with the statutes of the Nicene Council, allow the Bohemians to choose for themselves an Archbishop of Prague. This choice to be confirmed by the Bishops of Olmütz in Moravia, or of Grun in Hungary, or the Bishop of Gnesen in Poland, or the Bishop of Magdeburg in Germany. It is enough that it be confirmed by one or two of these bishops, as in the time of St. Cyprian. And the Pope has no authority to forbid it; if he forbids it, he acts as a wolf and a tyrant, and no one should obey him, but answer his excommunication by excommunicating him.

Yet if, for the honour of the Chair of St. Peter, any one prefers to do this with the Pope's knowledge, I do not object, provided that the Bohemians do not pay a farthing for it, and that the Pope do not bind them a single hair's breadth, or subject them to his tyranny by oath, as he does all other bishops, against God and justice. If he is not satisfied with the honour of his assent being asked, leave him alone by all means with his own rights, laws, and tyrannies; be content with the election, and let the blood of all the souls that are in danger be upon his head. For no man may countenance wrong, and we have already shown enough respect to tyranny. If we cannot do otherwise, we may consider the popular election and consent as equal to a tyrannical confirmation; but I hope this will not be necessary. Sooner or later some Romans, or pious bishops and learned men, must perceive and avert the Pope's tyranny.

I do not advise that they be forced to abandon the sacrament in both kinds, for it is neither unchristian nor heretical. They should be allowed to continue in their present way; but the new bishop must see that there be no dissensions about this matter, and they must learn that neither practice is actually wrong; just as there need be no disputes about the priests not wearing the same dress as the laity. In the same way, if they do not wish to submit to the canon laws of the Roman Church, we must not force them, but we must content ourselves with seeing that they live in faith and according to the Scriptures. For Christian life and Christian faith may very well exist without the Pope's unbearable laws; nay, they cannot well exist until there are fewer of those laws or none. Our baptism has freed us and made us subject to God's word alone, why then should we suffer a man to make us the slaves of his words? As St. Paul says: "Stand fast, therefore, in the liberty wherewith Christ hath made us free, and be not entangled again with the yoke of bondage." (Gal. v. 1.)

If I knew that the only error of the Hussites[46] was that they believe that in the sacrament of the altar there is true bread and wine, though under it the body and the blood of Christ; if, I say, this were their only error, I should not condemn them; but let the Bishop of Prague see to this. For it is not an article of faith that in the sacrament there is bread and wine in substance and nature, which is a delusion of St. Thomas and the Pope: but it is an article of faith, that in the natural bread and wine there is Christ's true flesh and blood. We should accordingly tolerate the views of both parties until they are at one;

---

[46] Luther uses here the word "Pickarten," which is a corruption of *Begharden,* i.e. "Beghards," a nickname frequently applied in those days to the Hussites.

for there is not much danger whether you believe there is, or there is not, bread in the sacrament. For we have to suffer many forms of belief and order that do not injure the Faith; but if they believe otherwise, it would be better not to unite with them, and yet to instruct them in the truth.

All other errors and dissensions to be found in Bohemia should be tolerated until the Archbishop has been reinstated, and has succeeded, in time, in uniting the whole people in one harmonious doctrine. We shall never unite them by force, by driving or hurrying them. We must be patient, and use gentleness. Did not Christ have to walk with His disciples, suffering their unbelief, until they believed in His resurrection? If they had but once more a regular bishop, and good discipline without Romish tyranny, I think matters would mend.

The temporal possessions of the Church should not be too strictly claimed; but since we are Christians and bound to help one another, we have the right to give them these things for the sake of unity, and to let them keep them, before God and the world; for Christ says: "Where two or three are gathered together in My name, there am I in the midst of them." Would to God, we helped on both sides to bring about this unity, giving our hands one to the other in brotherly humility, not insisting on our authority or our rights! Love is more, and more necessary than the Papacy at Rome; the Papacy can exist without love, and love can exist without the Papacy. I hope I have done my best for this end. If the Pope or his followers hinder this good work, they will have to give an account of their actions, for having, against the love of God, sought their own advantage more than their neighbours'. The Pope should abandon his Papacy, all his possessions and honours, if he could save a soul by so doing. But he would rather see the world go to ruin than give up a hair's breadth of the power he has usurped; and yet he would be our most holy father! Herewith am I at least excused.

25. The Universities also require a good, sound Reformation. I must say this, let it vex whom it may. The fact is that whatever the Papacy has ordered or instituted is only designed for the propagation of sin and error. What are the Universities, as at present ordered, but as the Book of Maccabees says: "Schools of 'Greek fashion' and 'heathenish manners.'" (2 Maccab. iv. 12, 13); full of dissolute living, where very little is taught of the Holy Scriptures and of the Christian faith, and the blind heathen teacher, Aristotle, rules even further than Christ. Now, my advice would be that the books of Aristotle, the 'Physics,' the 'Metaphysics,' 'Of the Soul,' 'Ethics,' which have hitherto been considered the best, be altogether abolished, with all others that profess to treat of nature, though nothing can be learned from them, either of natural or of spiritual things. Besides, no one has been able to understand his meaning, and much time has been wasted, and many noble souls vexed, with much useless labour, study, and expense. I venture to say that any potter has more knowledge of natural things than is to be found in these books. My heart is grieved to see how many of the best Christians this accursed, proud, knavish heathen has fooled and led astray with his false words. God sent him as a plague for our sins.

Does not the wretched man in his best book, 'Of the Soul,' teach that the soul dies with the body; though many have tried to save him with vain words, as if we had not the Holy Scriptures to teach us fully of all things, of which Aristotle had not the slightest perception. Yet this dead heathen has conquered, and has hindered and almost suppressed the books of the living God; so that, when I see all this misery, I cannot but think that the evil spirit has introduced this study.

Then there is the 'Ethics,' which is accounted one of the best, though no book is more directly contrary to God's will and the Christian virtues. Oh, that such books could be kept out of the reach of all Christians! Let no one object that I say too much, or speak without knowledge. My friend, I know of what I speak. I know Aristotle as well as you or men like you. I have read him with more understanding than St. Thomas or Scotus; which I may say without arrogance, and can prove if need be. It matters not that so many great minds have exercised themselves in these matters for many hundred years. Such objections do not affect me as they might have done once; since it is plain as day that many more errors have existed for many hundred years in the world and the Universities.

I would, however, gladly consent that Aristotle's books of Logic, Rhetoric and Poetic should be retained; or they might be usefully studied in a condensed form, to practise young people in speaking and preaching; but the notes and comments should be abolished, and just as Cicero's Rhetoric is read without note or comment, Aristotle's Logic should be read without such long commentaries. But now neither speaking nor preaching are taught out of them, and they are used only for disputation and confusion. Besides this there are languages, Latin, Greek and Hebrew, the Mathematics, History; but this I leave to men of higher understanding; if they seriously strive after reform, all these things will come of themselves. And truly it is an important matter! for it concerns the teaching and training of Christian youths and of our noble people, in whom Christianity still abides. Therefore I think that Pope and Emperor could have no better task than the reformation of the Universities, just as there is nothing more devilishly mischievous than an unreformed University.

Physicians I would leave to reform their own faculty; Lawyers and Theologians I take under my charge, and say firstly, that it would be right to abolish the canon law entirely, from beginning to end, more especially the decretals. We are taught quite sufficiently in the Bible how we ought to act; all this study only prevents the study of the Scriptures, and for the most part it is tainted with covetousness and pride. And even though there were some good in it, it should nevertheless be destroyed, for the Pope having the canon law in *scrinio pectoris*,[47] all further study is useless and deceitful. At the present time the canon law is not to be found in the books, but in the whims of the Pope and his sycophants. You may have settled a matter in the best possible way according to the canon law, but the Pope has his *scrinium pectoris,* to which all law must bow in all the world. Now this scrinium is oftentimes directed by some knave, and the devil himself, whilst it boasts that it is directed by the Holy Ghost. This is the way they treat Christ's poor people, imposing many laws and keeping none; forcing others to keep them, or to free themselves by money.

Therefore since the Pope and his followers have cancelled the whole canon law, despising it and setting their own will above all the world, we should follow them and reject the books. Why should we study them to no purpose? We should never be able to know the Pope's caprice, which has now become the canon law. Let it fall then in God's name, after having risen in the devil's name. Let there be henceforth no doctor *decretorum*, but let them all be *doctores scrinii papalis*, that is, the Pope's sycophants. They say that there is no better temporal government than among the Turks, though they have no canon nor civil law, but only their Koran; we must at least own that there is no worse government than ours with its canon and civil law, for no estate lives according to the Scriptures, or even according to natural reason.

---

[47] In the shrine of his heart.

The civil law, too, good God! what a wilderness it is become! It is, indeed, much better, more skilful and more honest than the canon law, of which nothing is good but the name. Still there is far too much of it. Surely good governors, judging according to the Scriptures, would be law enough, as St. Paul says: "Is it so, that there is not a wise man among you? No, not one that shall be able to judge between his brethren?" (1 Cor. vi. 5.) I think also that the common law and the usage of the country should be preferred to the law of the Empire, and that the law of the Empire should only be used in cases of necessity. And would to God that, as each land has its own peculiar character and nature, they could all be governed by their own simple laws, just as they were governed before the law of the Empire was devised, and as many are governed even now! Elaborate and far-fetched laws are only burdensome to the people, and a hindrance rather than a help to business. But I hope that others have thought of this, and considered it to more purpose than I could.

Our worthy Theologians have saved themselves much trouble and labour by leaving the Bible alone and only reading the Sentences.[48] I should have thought that young Theologians might begin by studying the Sentences and that Doctors should study the Bible. Now they invert this: the Bible is the first thing they study; this ceases with the Bachelor's degree; the Sentences are the last, and these they keep for ever with the Doctor's degree; and this too under such sacred obligation that one that is not a priest may read the Bible, but a priest must read the Sentences; so that, as far as I can see, a married man might be a Doctor in the Bible, but not in the Sentences. How should we prosper so long as we act so perversely, and degrade the Bible, the holy word of God? Besides this, the Pope orders with many stringent words that his laws be read and used in schools and courts; while the law of the Gospel is but little considered. The result is that in schools and courts the Gospel lies dusty on the shelf, so that the Pope's mischievous laws may alone be in force.

Since, then, we hold the name and title of teachers of the Holy Scriptures, we should verily be forced to act according to our title, and to teach the Holy Scriptures and nothing else. Although, indeed, it is a proud, presumptuous title, for a man to proclaim himself teacher of the Scriptures, still it could be suffered, if the works confirmed the title. But as it is, under the rule of the Sentences, we find among Theologians more human and heathenish fallacies than true holy knowledge of the Scriptures. What then are we to do? I know not, except to pray humbly to God to give us Doctors of Theology. Doctors of Arts, of Medicine, of Law, of the Sentences, may be made by Popes, Emperors and the Universities; but of this we may be certain, a Doctor of the Holy Scriptures can be made by none but the Holy Ghost, as Christ says: "They shall all be taught of God." (John vi. 45.) Now the Holy Ghost does not consider red caps or brown, or any other pomp; nor whether we are young or old, layman or priest, monk or secular, virgin or married; nay, he once spoke by an ass against the prophet that rode on it. Would to God we were worthy of having such Doctors given us, be they laymen or priests, married or virgin! but now they try to force the Holy Ghost to enter into Popes, Bishops or Doctors, though there is no sign to show that He is in them.

We must also lessen the number of theological books, and choose the best; for it is not the number of books that make the learned man; nor much reading, but good books

---

[48] Luther refers here to the 'Sentences' of *Petrus Lombardus*, the so-called *magister sententiarum*, which formed the basis of all dogmatic interpretation from about the middle of the 12th century down to the Reformation.

often read, however few, make a man learned in the Scriptures and pious. Even the Fathers should only be read for a short time as an introduction to the Scriptures. As it is, we read nothing else, and never get from them into the Scriptures, as if one should be gazing at the sign-posts and never follow the road. These good Fathers wished to lead us into the Scriptures by their writings, whereas we lead ourselves out by them, though the Scriptures are our vineyard in which we should all work and exercise ourselves.

Above all, in schools of all kinds the chief and most common lesson should be the Scriptures, and for young boys the Gospel; and would to God each town had also a girl's school in which girls might be taught the Gospel for an hour daily, either in German or Latin! In truth, schools, monasteries and convents, were founded for this purpose, and with good Christian intentions; as we read concerning St. Agnes, and other saints;[49] then were there holy virgins and martyrs; and in those times it was well with Christendom; but now it has been turned into nothing but praying and singing. Should not every Christian be expected by his ninth or tenth year to know all the holy Gospels, containing as they do his very name and life? A spinner or a seamstress teaches her daughter her trade, while she is young, but now even the most learned Prelates and Bishops do not know the Gospel.

Oh, how badly we treat all these poor young people that are entrusted to us for discipline and instruction! and a heavy reckoning shall we have to give for it that we keep them from the word of God; their fate is that described by Jeremiah: "Mine eyes do fail with tears, my bowels are troubled, my liver is poured upon the earth, for the destruction of the daughter of my people; because the children and the sucklings swoon in the streets of the city. They say to their mothers, Where is corn and wine? when they swooned as the wounded in the streets of the city, when their soul is poured out into their mothers' bosom." (Lamen. ii. 11, 12.) We do not perceive all this misery, how the young folk are being pitifully corrupted in the midst of Christendom, all for want of the Gospel, which we should always read and study with them.

However, if the high schools studied the Scriptures diligently we should not send every one to them, as we do now, when nothing is considered but numbers, and every man wishes to have a Doctor's title; we should only send the aptest pupils, well prepared in the lower schools. This should be seen to by princes or the magistrates of the towns, and they should take care none but apt pupils be sent. But where the Holy Scriptures are not the rule, I advise no one to send his child. Everything must perish where God's word is not studied unceasingly; and so we see what manner of men there are now in the high schools, and all this is the fault of no one but of the Pope, the Bishops and the Prelates, to whom the welfare of the young has been entrusted. For the High Schools should train men simply to be of good understanding in the Scriptures, fit to become bishops and priests, and to stand at our head against heretics and the Devil and all the world. But where do we find this? I greatly fear the High Schools are nothing but great gates of hell, unless they diligently study the Holy Scriptures and teach them to the young people.

26. I know well the Romish mob will object and loudly pretend that the Pope took the Holy Roman Empire from the Greek Emperor and gave it to Germany, for which honour and favour he is supposed to deserve submission and thanks and all other kinds of returns from the Germans. For this reason we are not to presume to make any attempt to reform them, and we are to consider nothing but these gifts of the Roman Empire. This is also the reason why they have so arbitrarily and proudly persecuted and oppressed many

---

[49] See above p. 58.

good Emperors, so that it were pity to tell, and with the same cleverness have they made themselves lords of all the temporal power and authority, in violation of the holy Gospel; and accordingly I must speak of this matter also.

There is no doubt that the true Roman Empire, of which the prophets (Num. xxiv. 24) and Daniel (ii. 44) spoke, was long ago destroyed, as Balaam clearly foretold, saying: "And ships shall come from the coast of Chittim, and shall afflict Asshur, and shall afflict Eber, and he also shall perish for ever." (Num. xxiv. 24.)[50] And this was done by the Goths, and more especially since the empire of the Turks was formed, about one thousand years ago, and so gradually Asia and Africa were lost, and subsequently France, Spain, and finally Venice arose, so that Rome retains no part of its former power.

Since, then, the Pope could not force the Greeks and the Emperor at Constantinople, who is the hereditary Roman Emperor, to obey his will, he invented this device to rob him of his empire and title, and to give it to the Germans, who were at that time strong and of good repute; in order that they might take the power of the Roman Empire and hold it of the Pope; and this is what actually has happened. It was taken from the Emperor at Constantinople, and the name and title were given to us Germans, and therewith we became subject to the Pope, and he has built up a new Roman Empire on the Germans. For the other Empire, the original, came to an end long ago, as was said above.

Thus the Roman See has got what it wished: Rome has been taken possession of, and the German Emperor driven out and bound by oaths not to dwell in Rome. He is to be Roman Emperor and nevertheless not to dwell in Rome; and moreover always to depend on the Pope and his followers, and to do their will. We are to have the title, and they are to have the lands and the cities. For they have always made our simplicity the tool of their pride and tyranny, and they consider us as stupid Germans to be deceived and fooled by them as they choose.

Well, for our Lord God it is a small thing to toss kingdoms and principalities hither and thither; He is so free with them, that He will sometimes take a kingdom from a good man and give it to a knave; sometimes through the treachery of false, wicked men; sometimes by inheritance, as we read concerning Persia, Greece, and nearly all kingdoms; and Daniel says: "Wisdom and might are His: and He changes the times and the seasons, and He removeth Kings and setteth up Kings." (Dan. ii. 20, 21.) Therefore, no one need think it a grand matter, if he has a kingdom given to him, especially if he be a Christian; and so we Germans need not be proud of having had a new Roman Empire given us. For in His eyes, it is a poor gift, that He sometimes gives to the least deserving; as Daniel says: "And all the inhabitants of the earth are reputed as nothing; and He does according to His will in the army of heaven, and among the inhabitants of the earth." (Dan. iv. 35.)

Now although the Pope has violently and unjustly robbed the true Emperor of the Roman Empire, or its name, and has given it to us Germans, yet it is certain that God has used the Pope's wickedness to give the German nation this Empire and to raise up a new Roman Empire, that exists now, after the fall of the old Empire. We gave the Pope no cause for this action, nor did we understand his false aims and schemes; but still, through the craft and knavery of the Popes, we have, alas! all too dearly, paid the price of this Empire with incalculable bloodshed, with the loss of our liberty, with the robbery of our wealth, especially of our churches and benefices, and with unspeakable treachery and

---

[50] Luther here follows the Vulgate, translating the above verse by: "Es werden die Römer kommen und die Juden verstören: und hernach werden sie auch untergehen."

insult. We have the Empire in name, but the Pope has our wealth, our honour, our bodies, lives and souls, and all that we have. This was the way to deceive the Germans, and with a double deceit. What the Popes wished was, to become Emperors; and as they could not do this, they put themselves above the Emperors.

Since, then, we have received this Empire through God's providence and the schemes of evil men, without our fault, I would not advise that we should give it up, but that we should govern it honestly, in the fear of God, so long as He is pleased to let us hold it. For, as I have said, it is no matter to Him how a kingdom is come by, but He will have it duly governed. If the Popes took it from others dishonestly, we, at least, did not come by it dishonestly. It was given to us through evil men, under the will of God, to whom we have more regard than the false intentions of the Popes, who wished to be Emperors and more than Emperors, and to fool and mock us with the name.

The King of Babylon obtained his kingdom by force and robbery. Yet God would have it governed by the holy princes, Daniel, Ananias, Asarias and Misael. Much more then does He require this Empire to be governed by the Christian princes of Germany, though the Pope may have stolen or robbed, or newly fashioned it. It is all God's ordering, which came to pass before we knew of it.

Therefore the Pope and his followers have no reason to boast, that they did a great kindness to the German nation in giving them this Roman Empire. Firstly, because they intended no good to us in the matter; but only abused our simplicity to strengthen their own power against the Roman Emperor at Constantinople, from whom, against God and justice, the Pope has taken what he had no right to.

Secondly, the Pope sought to give the Empire, not to us, but to himself, and to become lord over all our power, liberty, wealth, body and soul, and through us over all the world, if God had not prevented it; as he plainly says in his decretals, and has tried with many mischievous tricks in the case of many German Emperors. Thus we Germans have been prettily taught German: Whilst we expected to become lords, we have become the servants of the most crafty tyrants; we have the name, title and arms of the Empire, but the Pope has the treasure, authority, law and freedom; thus whilst the Pope eats the kernel, he leaves us the empty shells to play with.

Now may God help us (who, as I have said, assigned us this kingdom through crafty tyrants, and charged us to govern it) to act according to our name, title and arms, and to secure our freedom; and thus let the Romans see at last what we have received of God through them. If they boast that they have given us an Empire; well, be it so, by all means: then, let the Pope give up Rome, all he has of the Empire, and free our country from his unbearable taxes and robberies, and give back to us our liberty, authority, wealth, honour, body and soul, rendering to the Empire those things that are the Empire's; so as to act in accordance with his words and pretences.

But if he will not do this, what game is he playing with all his falsehoods and pretences? Was it not enough to lead this great people by the nose for so many hundred years? Because the Pope crowns or makes the Emperor, it does not follow that he is above him; for the prophet, St. Samuel, anointed and crowned King Saul and David, at God's command, and was yet subject to them. And the prophet Nathan anointed King Solomon, and yet was not placed over him; moreover St. Elisha let one of his servants anoint King Jehu of Israel; yet they obeyed him. And it has never yet happened in the whole world that any one was above the king, because he consecrated or crowned him, except in the case of the Pope.

Now he is himself crowned Pope by three cardinals; yet they are subject to him and he is above them. Why then, contrary to his own example, and to the doctrine and practice of the whole world and the Scriptures, should he exalt himself above the temporal authorities and the Empire, for no other reason than that he crowns and consecrates the Emperor? It suffices that he is above him in all divine matters, that is in preaching, teaching and the ministration of the sacrament, in which matters, however, every priest or bishop is above all other men; just as St. Ambrose in his Chair was above the Emperor Theodosius, and the prophet Nathan above David, and Samuel above Saul. Therefore let the German Emperor be a true free Emperor, and let not his authority or his sword be overborne by these blind pretences of the Pope's sycophants, as if they were to be exceptions, and be above the temporal sword in all things.

27. Let this be enough about the faults of the spiritual Estate, though many more might be found, if the matter were properly considered: we must now consider the defects of the temporal Estates. In the first place, we require a general law and consent of the German nation against profusion and extravagance in dress, which is the cause of so much poverty among the nobles and the people. Surely God has given to us, as to other nations, enough wool, fur, flax, and whatever else is required for the decent clothing of every class; and it cannot be necessary to spend such enormous sums for silk, velvet, cloth of gold and all other kinds of outlandish stuff. I think that even if the Pope did not rob us Germans with his unbearable taxes, we should be robbed more than enough by these secret thieves, the dealers in silk and velvet. As it is we see that every man wishes to be every other man's equal, and that this causes and increases pride and envy among us, as we deserve; all which would cease, with many other misfortunes, if our self-will would but let us be gratefully content with what God has given us.

It is similarly necessary to diminish the use of spices, which is one of the ships in which our gold is sent away from Germany. God's mercy has given us more food, and that both precious and good, than is to be found in other countries. I shall probably be accused of making foolish and impossible suggestions, as if I wished to destroy the great business of commerce. But I am only doing my part; if the community does not mend matters, every man must do it himself. I do not see many good manners that have ever come into a land through commerce, and therefore God let the people of Israel dwell far from the sea and not carry on much trade.

But without doubt the greatest misfortune of the Germans is buying on credit. But for this, many a man would have to leave unbought his silk, velvet, cloth of gold, spices and all other luxuries. The system has not been in force for more than one hundred years, and has already brought poverty, misery, and destruction on almost all princes, foundations, cities, nobles and heirs. If it continues for another hundred years Germany will be left without a farthing, and we shall be reduced to eating one another. The Devil invented this system, and the Pope has done an injury to the whole world by sanctioning it.

My request and my cry, therefore, is this: Let each man see to the destruction of himself and his family, which is no longer at the door, but has entered the house; and let Emperors, Princes, Lords and Corporations, see to the condemnation and prohibition of this kind of trade, without considering the opposition of the Pope and all his justice and injustice, nor whether livings or endowments depend upon it. Better a single foundation in a city based on a freehold estate or honest interest, than a hundred based on credit; yea, a single endowment on credit is worse and more grievous than twenty based on real estate. Truly this credit is a sign and warning, that the world has been given over to the

Devil for its sins; and that we are losing our spiritual and temporal welfare alike; yet we heed it not.

Doubtless we should also find some bridle for the *Fuggers* and similar companies. Is it possible that in a single man's lifetime such great wealth should be collected together, if all were done rightly and according to God's will? I am not skilled in accounts. But I do not understand how it is possible for one hundred guilders to gain twenty in a year, or how one guilder can gain another, and that not out of the soil, or by cattle, seeing that possessions depend not on the wit of men, but on the blessing of God. I commend this to those that are skilled in worldly affairs. I as a theologian blame nothing but the evil appearance, of which St. Paul says: "abstain from all appearance of evil." (1 Thess. v. 22.) All I know is that it were much more godly to encourage agriculture and lessen commerce; and that they do the best who, according to the Scriptures, till the ground to get their living, as we are all commanded in Adam: "Cursed is the ground for thy sake. . . . Thorns also and thistles shall it bring forth to thee. . . . In the sweat of thy face shalt thou eat bread." (Gen. iii. 17–19.) There is still much ground that is not ploughed or tilled.

Then there is the excess in eating and drinking, for which we Germans have an ill reputation in foreign countries, as our special vice, and which has become so common, and gained so much the upper hand, that sermons avail nothing. The loss of money caused by it is not the worst; but in its train come murder, adultery, theft, blasphemy and all vices. The temporal power should do something to prevent it; otherwise it will come to pass, as Christ foretold, that the last day shall come as a thief in the night, and shall find them eating and drinking, marrying and giving in marriage, planting and building, buying and selling (Matt. xxiv. 38; Luke xvii. 26)—just as things go on now; and that so strongly, that I apprehend lest the day of judgment be at hand, even now when we least expect it.

Lastly, is it not a terrible thing that we Christians should maintain public brothels, though we all vow chastity in our baptism? I well know all that can be said on this matter, that it is not peculiar to one nation, that it would be difficult to alter it, and that it is better thus than that virgins, or married women, or honourable women should be dishonoured. But should not the spiritual and temporal powers combine to find some means of meeting these difficulties without any such heathen practice? If the people of Israel existed without this scandal, why should not a Christian nation be able to do so? How do so many towns and villages manage to exist without these houses? Why should not great cities be able to do so?

In all, however, that I have said above, my object has been to show how much good temporal authority might do, and what should be the duty of all authorities, so that every man might learn what a terrible thing it is to rule and to have the chief place. What boots it though a ruler be in his own person as holy as St. Peter, if he be not diligent to help his subjects in these matters? His very authority will be his condemnation; for it is the duty of those in authority to seek the good of their subjects. But if those in authority considered how young people might be brought together in marriage, the prospect of marriage would help every man, and protect him from temptations.

But as it is, every man is urged to become a priest or a monk; and of all these I am afraid not one in a hundred has any other motive, but the wish of getting a livelihood, and the uncertainty of maintaining a family. Therefore they begin by a dissolute life and sow their wild oats (as they say), but I fear they rather gather in a store of wild oats.[51] I hold the proverb to be true: "Most men become monks and priests in desperation." That is why things are as we see them.

But in order that many sins may be prevented that are becoming too common, I would honestly advise that no boy or girl be allowed to take the vow of chastity, or to enter a religious life, before the age of thirty years. For this requires a special grace, as St. Paul says. Therefore, unless God specially urge any one to a religious life, he will do well to leave all vows and devotions alone. I say further: If a man has so little faith in God as to fear that he will be unable to maintain himself in the married state, and if this fear is the only thing that makes him become a priest, then I implore him, for his own soul's sake, not to become a priest, but rather to become a peasant, or what he will. For if simple trust in God be necessary to ensure temporal support, tenfold trust in God is necessary to live a religious life. If you do not trust to God for your worldly food, how can you trust to Him for your spiritual food? Alas, this unbelief and want of faith destroys all things, and leads us into all misery, as we see among all conditions of men.

Much might be said concerning all this misery. Young people have no one to look after them, they are left to go on just as they like, and those in authority are of no more use to them than if they did not exist; though this should be the chief care of the Pope, of Bishops, Lords and Councils. They wish to rule over everything, everywhere, and yet they are of no use. Oh, what a rare sight, for these reasons, will a lord or ruler be in Heaven, though he might build a hundred churches to God and raise all the dead! But this may suffice for the present.

For of what concerns the temporal authority and the nobles, I have, I think, said enough in my tract on 'Good Works.' For their lives and governments leave room enough for improvement; but there is no comparison between spiritual and temporal abuses, as I have there shown. I dare say I have sung a lofty strain, that I have proposed many things that will be thought impossible, and attacked many points too sharply. But what was I to do? I was bound to say this: if I had the power, this is what I would do. I had rather incur the world's anger than God's; they cannot take from me more than my life. I have hitherto made many offers of peace to my adversaries. But, as I see, God has forced me through them to open my mouth wider and wider, and, because they do not keep quiet, to give them enough cause for speaking, barking, shouting and writing. Well, then, I have another song still to sing concerning them and Rome; if they wish to hear it, I will sing it to them, and sing with all my might. Do you understand, my friend Rome, what I mean?

I have frequently offered to submit my writings for inquiry and examination, but in vain; though I know, if I am in the right, I must be condemned upon earth, and justified by Christ alone in Heaven. For all the Scriptures teach us, that the affairs of Christians and Christendom must be judged by God alone; they have never yet been justified by men in this world, but the opposition has always been too strong. My greatest care and fear is, lest my cause be not condemned by men; by which I should know for certain that it does not please God. Therefore let them go freely to work, Pope, bishop, priest, monk, or doctor; they are the true people to persecute the truth, as they have always done. May God grant us all a Christian understanding, and especially to the Christian nobility of the German nation true spiritual courage, to do what is best for our unhappy Church. Amen!

At Wittenberg, in the year 1520.

---

[51] Luther uses the expression *ausbuben* in the sense of *sich austoben*, viz., "to storm *out* one's passions," and then coins the word *sich einbuben*, viz., "to storm *in* one's passions."

II. CONCERNING CHRISTIAN LIBERTY

DEDICATORY

LETTER OF MARTIN LUTHER TO POPE LEO X.

Among those monstrous evils of this age, with which I have now for three years been waging war, I am sometimes compelled to look to you and to call you to mind, most blessed father Leo. In truth, since you alone are everywhere considered as being the cause of my engaging in war, I cannot at any time fail to remember you; and although I have been compelled by the causeless raging of your impious flatterers against me to appeal from your seat to a future council—fearless of the futile decrees of your predecessors Pius and Julius, who in their foolish tyranny prohibited such an action—yet I have never been so alienated in feeling from your Blessedness as not to have sought with all my might, in diligent prayer and crying to God, every best gift for you and for your See. But those who have hitherto endeavoured to terrify me with the majesty of your name and authority, I have begun quite to despise and triumph over. One thing I see remaining, which I cannot despise, and this has been the reason of my writing anew to your Blessedness; namely, that I find that blame is cast on me, and that that rashness, in which I am judged to have spared not even your person, is imputed to me as a great offence.

Now, to confess the truth openly, I am conscious that, whenever I have had to mention your person, I have said nothing of you but what was honourable and good. If I had done otherwise, I could by no means have approved my own conduct, but should have supported with all my power the judgment of those men concerning me; nor would anything have pleased me better, than to recant such rashness and impiety. I have called you Daniel in Babylon; and every reader thoroughly knows with what distinguished zeal I defended your conspicuous innocence against Silvester, who tried to stain it. Indeed the published opinion of so many great men, and the repute of your blameless life, are too widely famed and too much reverenced throughout the world to be assailable by any man of however great name, or by any arts. I am not so foolish as to attack one whom everybody praises; nay, it has been and always will be my desire not to attack even those whom public repute disgraces. I am not delighted at the faults of any man, since I am very conscious myself of the great beam in my own eye, nor can I be the first to cast a stone at the adulteress.

I have indeed inveighed sharply against impious doctrines, and I have not been slack to censure my adversaries on account, not of their bad morals, but of their impiety. And for this I am so far from being sorry, that I have brought my mind to despise the judgments of men, and to persevere in this vehement zeal, according to the example of Christ, who, in his zeal, calls his adversaries a generation of vipers, blind, hypocrites, and children of the devil. Paul too charges the sorcerer with being a child of the devil, full of all subtlety and all malice; and defames certain persons as evil workers, dogs, and deceivers. In the opinion of those delicate-eared persons, nothing could be more bitter or intemperate than Paul's language. What can be more bitter than the words of the prophets? The ears of our generation have been made so delicate by the senseless multitude of flatterers, that, as soon as we perceive that anything of ours is not approved of, we cry out that we are being bitterly assailed; and when we can repel the truth by no other pretence, we escape by attributing bitterness, impatience, intemperance, to our adversaries. What would be the use of salt, if it were not pungent? or of the edge of the sword, if it did not slay? Accursed is the man, who does the work of the Lord deceitfully.

Wherefore, most excellent Leo, I beseech you to accept my vindication, made in this letter, and to persuade yourself that I have never thought any evil concerning your person; further, that I am one who desires that eternal blessing may fall to your lot, and that I have no dispute with any man concerning morals, but only concerning the word of truth. In all other things I will yield to any one, but I neither can nor will forsake and deny the Word. He who thinks otherwise of me or has taken in my words in another sense, does not think rightly, and has not taken in the truth.

Your see, however, which is called the Court of Rome, and which neither you nor any man can deny to be more corrupt than any Babylon or Sodom, and quite, as I believe, of a lost, desperate, and hopeless impiety, this I have verily abominated, and have felt indignant that the people of Christ should be cheated under your name and the pretext of the Church of Rome; and so I have resisted, and will resist, as long as the spirit of faith shall live in me. Not that I am striving after impossibilities, or hoping that by my labours alone, against the furious opposition of so many flatterers, any good can be done in that most disordered Babylon, but that I feel myself a debtor to my brethren, and am bound to take thought for them, that fewer of them may be ruined, or that their ruin may be less complete, by the plagues of Rome. For many years now, nothing else has overflowed from Rome into the world—as you are not ignorant—than the laying waste of goods, of bodies, and of souls, and the worst examples of all the worst things. These things are clearer than the light to all men; and the Church of Rome, formerly the most holy of all churches, has become the most lawless den of thieves, the most shameless of all brothels, the very kingdom of sin, death, and hell; so that not even Antichrist, if he were to come, could devise any addition to its wickedness.

Meanwhile you, Leo, are sitting like a lamb in the midst of wolves, like Daniel in the midst of lions, and, with Ezekiel, you dwell among scorpions. What opposition can you alone make to these monstrous evils? Take to yourself three or four of the most learned and best of the Cardinals. What are these among so many? You would all perish by poison, before you could undertake to decide on a remedy. It is all over with the Court of Rome; the wrath of God has come upon her to the uttermost. She hates councils, she dreads to be reformed, she cannot restrain the madness of her impiety, she fills up the sentence passed on her mother, of whom it is said, "We would have healed Babylon, but she is not healed; let us forsake her." It had been your duty and that of your Cardinals, to apply a remedy to these evils, but this gout laughs at the physician's hand, and the chariot does not obey the reins. Under the influence of these feelings I have always grieved that you, most excellent Leo, who were worthy of a better age, have been made Pontiff in this. For the Roman Court is not worthy of you and those like you, but of Satan himself, who in truth is more the ruler in that Babylon than you are.

O would that, having laid aside that glory which your most abandoned enemies declare to be yours, you were living rather in the office of a private priest, or on your paternal inheritance! In that glory none are worthy to glory, except the race of Iscariot, the children of perdition. For what happens in your court, Leo, except that, the more wicked and execrable any man is, the more prosperously he can use your name and authority for the ruin of the property and souls of men, for the multiplication of crimes, for the oppression of faith and truth, and of the whole Church of God? O Leo! in reality most unfortunate, and sitting on a most perilous throne—I tell you the truth, because I wish you well; for if Bernard felt compassion for his Anastasius at a time when the

Roman See, though even then most corrupt, was as yet ruling with better hope than now, why should not we lament, to whom so much additional corruption and ruin has happened in three hundred years?

Is it not true that there is nothing under the vast heavens more corrupt, more pestilential, more hateful than the Court of Rome? She incomparably surpasses the impiety of the Turks, so that in very truth she, who was formerly the gate of heaven, is now a sort of open mouth of hell, and such a mouth as, under the urgent wrath of God, cannot be blocked up; one course alone being left to us wretched men, to call back and save some few, if we can, from that Roman gulf.

Behold, Leo my father, with what purpose and on what principle it is that I have stormed against that seat of pestilence. I am so far from having felt any rage against your person, that I even hoped to gain favour with you, and to aid in your welfare, by striking actively and vigorously at that your prison, nay, your hell. For whatever the efforts of all intellects can contrive against the confusion of that impious Court will be advantageous to you and to your welfare, and to many others with you. Those who do harm to her are doing your office; those who in every way abhor her are glorifying Christ; in short, those are Christians who are not Romans.

But, to say yet more, even this never entered my heart, to inveigh against the Court of Rome, or to dispute at all about her. For, seeing all remedies for her health to be desperate, I looked on her with contempt, and, giving her a bill of divorcement, said to her, "He that is unjust, let him be unjust still; and he that is filthy, let him be filthy still;" giving myself up to the peaceful and quiet study of sacred literature, that by this I might be of use to the brethren living about me.

While I was making some advance in these studies, Satan opened his eyes and goaded on his servant John Eccius, that notorious adversary of Christ, by the unchecked lust for fame, to drag me unexpectedly into the arena, trying to catch me in one little word concerning the primacy of the Church of Rome, which had fallen from me in passing. That boastful Thraso, foaming and gnashing his teeth, proclaimed that he would dare all things for the glory of God, and for the honour of the holy apostolic seat; and, being puffed up respecting your power, which he was about to misuse, he looked forward with all certainty to victory; seeking to promote, not so much the primacy of Peter, as his own pre-eminence among the theologians of this age; for he thought it would contribute in no slight degree to this, if he were to lead Luther in triumph. The result having proved unfortunate for the sophist, an incredible rage torments him; for he feels that whatever discredit to Rome has arisen through me, has been caused by the fault of himself alone.

Suffer me, I pray you, most excellent Leo, both to plead my own cause, and to accuse your true enemies. I believe it is known to you in what way Cardinal Cajetan, your imprudent and unfortunate, nay, unfaithful legate, acted towards me. When, on account of my reverence for your name, I had placed myself and all that was mine in his hands, he did not so act as to establish peace, which he could easily have established by one little word, since I at that time promised to be silent and to make an end of my case, if he would command my adversaries to do the same. But that man of pride, not content with this agreement, began to justify my adversaries, to give them free licence, and to order me to recant; a thing which was certainly not in his commission. Thus indeed, when the case was in the best position, it came through his vexatious tyranny into a much worse one. Therefore, whatever has followed upon this is the fault, not of Luther, but entirely of Cajetan, since he did not suffer me to be silent and remain quiet, which at that time I was intreating for with all my might. What more was it my duty to do?

Next came Charles Miltitz, also a nuncio from your Blessedness. He, though he went up and down with much and varied exertion, and omitted nothing which could tend to restore the position of the cause, thrown into confusion by the rashness and pride of Cajetan, had difficulty, even with the help of that very illustrious prince the Elector Frederick, in at last bringing about more than one familiar conference with me. In these I again yielded to your great name, and was prepared to keep silence, and to accept as my judge either the Archbishop of Treves, or the Bishop of Naumburg; and thus it was done and concluded. While this was being done with good hope of success, lo! that other and greater enemy of yours, Eccius, rushed in with his Leipsic disputation, which he had undertaken against Carlstadt, and, having taken up a new question concerning the primacy of the Pope, turned his arms unexpectedly against me, and completely overthrew the plan for peace. Meanwhile Charles Miltitz was waiting, disputations were held, judges were being chosen, but no decision was arrived at. And no wonder; for by the falsehoods, pretences, and arts of Eccius the whole business was brought into such thorough disorder, confusion, and festering soreness, that, whichever way the sentence might lean, a greater conflagration was sure to arise; for he was seeking, not after truth, but after his own credit. In this case too I omitted nothing which it was right that I should do.

I confess that, on this occasion, no small part of the corruptions of Rome came to light; but, if there was any offence in this, it was the fault of Eccius, who, in taking on him a burden beyond his strength, and in furiously aiming at credit for himself, unveiled to the whole world the disgrace of Rome.

Here is that enemy of yours, Leo, or rather of your Court; by his example alone we may learn that an enemy is not more baneful than a flatterer. For what did he bring about by his flattery, except evils, which no king could have brought about? At this day the name of the Court of Rome stinks in the nostrils of the world, the papal authority is growing weak, and its notorious ignorance is evil spoken of. We should hear none of these things, if Eccius had not disturbed the plans of Miltitz and myself for peace. He feels this clearly enough himself, in the indignation he shows, too late and in vain, against the publication of my books. He ought to have reflected on this at the time when he was all mad for renown, and was seeking in your cause nothing but his own objects, and that with the greatest peril to you. The foolish man hoped that, from fear of your name, I should yield and keep silence; for I do not think he presumed on his talents and learning. Now, when he sees that I am very confident and speak aloud, he repents too late of his rashness, and sees—if indeed he does see it—that there is One in Heaven who resists the proud, and humbles the presumptuous.

Since, then, we were bringing about by this disputation nothing but the greater confusion of the cause of Rome, Charles Miltitz for the third time addressed the Fathers of the Order, assembled in chapter, and sought their advice for the settlement of the case, as being now in a most troubled and perilous state. Since, by the favour of God, there was no hope of proceeding against me by force, some of the more noted of their number were sent to me, and begged me at least to show respect to your person, and to vindicate in a humble letter both your innocence and my own. They said that the affair was not as yet in a position of extreme hopelessness, if Leo X., in his inborn kindliness, would put his hand to it. On this I, who have always offered and wished for peace, in order that I might devote myself to calmer and more useful pursuits, and who for this very purpose have acted with so much spirit and vehemence, in order to put down by the strength and impetuosity of my words as well as of my feelings, men whom I saw to be very far from equal to myself—I, I say, not only gladly yielded, but even accepted it with joy and gratitude, as the greatest kindness and benefit, if you should think it right to satisfy my hopes.

Thus I come, most blessed Father, and in all abasement beseech you to put to your hand, if it is possible, and impose a curb upon those flatterers, who are enemies of peace, while they pretend peace. But there is no reason, most blessed Father, why any one should assume that I am to utter a recantation, unless he prefers to involve the case in still greater confusion. Moreover, I cannot bear with laws for the interpretation of the Word of God, since the Word of God, which teaches liberty in all other things, ought not to be bound. Saving these two things, there is nothing which I am not able, and most heartily willing, to do or to suffer. I hate contention; I will challenge no one; in return I wish not to be challenged; but, being challenged, I will not be dumb in the cause of Christ my Master. For your Blessedness will be able by one short and easy word to call these controversies before you and suppress them, and to impose silence and peace on both sides; a word which I have ever longed to hear.

Therefore, Leo my Father, beware of listening to those Sirens, who make you out to be not simply a man, but partly a God, so that you can command and require whatever you will. It will not happen so, nor will you prevail. You are the servant of servants, and, more than any other man, in a most pitiable and perilous position. Let not those men deceive you, who pretend that you are Lord of the world; who will not allow any one to be a Christian without your authority; who babble of your having power over heaven, hell, and purgatory. These men are your enemies and are seeking your soul to destroy it, as Isaiah says: "My people, they that call thee blessed are themselves deceiving thee." They are in error, who raise you above councils and the universal Church. They are in error, who attribute to you alone the right of interpreting Scripture. All these men are seeking to set up their own impieties in the Church under your name, and alas! Satan has gained much through them in the time of your predecessors.

In brief, trust not in any who exalt you, but in those who humiliate you. For this is the judgment of God: "He hath cast down the mighty from their seat, and hath exalted the humble." See how unlike Christ was to His successors, though all will have it that they are His vicars. I fear that in truth very many of them have been in too serious a sense His vicars, for a vicar represents a prince who is absent. Now if a Pontiff rules while Christ is absent and does not dwell in his heart, what else is he but a vicar of Christ? And then what is that Church but a multitude without Christ? What indeed is such a vicar but Antichrist and an idol? How much more rightly did the Apostles speak, who call themselves the servants of a present Christ, not the vicars of an absent one.

Perhaps I am shamelessly bold, in seeming to teach so great a head, by whom all men ought to be taught, and from whom, as those plagues of yours boast, the thrones of judges receive their sentence; but I imitate Saint Bernard in his book concerning "Considerations" addressed to Eugenius, a book which ought to be known by heart by every Pontiff. I do this, not from any desire to teach, but as a duty, from that simple and faithful solicitude, which teaches us to be anxious for all that is safe for our neighbours, and does not allow considerations of worthiness or unworthiness to be entertained, being intent only on the dangers or advantage of others. For since I know that your Blessedness is driven and tossed by the waves at Rome, while the depths of the sea press on you with infinite perils, and that you are labouring under such a condition of misery that you need even the least help from any the least brother, I do not seem to myself to be acting unsuitably, if I forget your majesty till I shall have fulfilled the office of charity. I will not flatter in so serious and perilous a matter; and if in this you do not see that I am your friend and most thoroughly your subject, there is One to see and judge.

In fine, that I may not approach you empty handed, Blessed Father, I bring with me this little treatise, published under your name, as a good omen of the establishment of peace, and of good hope. By this you may perceive in what pursuits I should prefer and be able to occupy myself to more profit, if I were allowed, or had been hitherto allowed, by your impious flatterers. It is a small matter, if you look to its exterior, but, unless I mistake, it is a summary of the Christian life put together in small compass, if you apprehend its meaning. I, in my poverty, have no other present to make you; nor do you need anything else than to be enriched by a spiritual gift. I commend myself to your Paternity and Blessedness, whom may the Lord Jesus preserve for ever. Amen.

Wittenberg; 6th September, 1520.

CONCERNING CHRISTIAN LIBERTY

Christian faith has appeared to many an easy thing; nay, not a few even reckon it among the social virtues, as it were; and this they do, because they have not made proof of it experimentally, and have never tasted of what efficacy it is. For it is not possible for any man to write well about it, or to understand well what is rightly written, who has not at some time tasted of its spirit, under the pressure of tribulation. While he who has tasted of it, even to a very small extent, can never write, speak, think, or hear about it sufficiently. For it is a living fountain, springing up unto eternal life, as Christ calls it in the 4th chapter of St. John.

Now, though I cannot boast of my abundance, and though I know how poorly I am furnished, yet I hope that, after having been vexed by various temptations, I have attained some little drop of faith, and that I can speak of this matter, if not with more elegance, certainly with more solidity than those literal and too subtle disputants who have hitherto discoursed upon it, without understanding their own words. That I may open, then, an easier way for the ignorant—for these alone I am trying to serve — I first lay down these two propositions, concerning spiritual liberty and servitude.

A Christian man is the most free lord of all, and subject to none; a Christian man is the most dutiful servant of all, and subject to every one.

Although these statements appear contradictory, yet, when they are found to agree together, they will be highly serviceable to my purpose. They are both the statements of Paul himself, who says: "Though I be free from all men, yet have I made myself servant unto all" (1 Cor. ix. 19), and: "Owe no man anything, but to love one another." (Rom. xiii. 8.) Now love is by its own nature dutiful and obedient to the beloved object. Thus even Christ, though Lord of all things, was yet made of a woman; made under the law; at once free and a servant; at once in the form of God and in the form of a servant.

Let us examine the subject on a deeper and less simple principle. Man is composed of a twofold nature, a spiritual and a bodily. As regards the spiritual nature, which they name the soul, he is called the spiritual, inward, new man; as regards the bodily nature, which they name the flesh, he is called the fleshly, outward, old man. The Apostle speaks of this: "Though our outward man perish, yet the inward man is renewed day by day." (2 Cor. iv. 16.) The result of this diversity is, that in the Scriptures opposing statements are made concerning the same man; the fact being that in the same man these two men are opposed to one another; the flesh lusting against the spirit, and the spirit against the flesh. (Gal. v. 17.)

We first approach the subject of the inward man, that we may see by what means a man becomes justified, free, and a true Christian; that is, a spiritual, new, and inward man. It is certain that absolutely none among outward things, under whatever name they may be reckoned, has any weight in producing a state of justification and Christian liberty, nor, on the other hand, an unjustified state and one of slavery. This can be shown by an easy course of argument.

What can it profit the soul, that the body should be in good condition, free, and full of life; that it should eat, drink, and act according to its pleasure; when even the most impious slaves of every kind of vice are prosperous in these matters? Again, what harm can ill-health, bondage, hunger, thirst, or any other outward evil, do to the soul, when even the most pious of men, and the freest in the purity of their conscience, are harassed by these things? Neither of these states of things has to do with the liberty or the slavery of the soul.

And so it will profit nothing that the body should be adorned with sacred vestments, or dwell in holy places, or be occupied in sacred offices, or pray, fast, and abstain from certain meats, or do whatever works can be done through the body and in the body. Something widely different will be necessary for the justification and liberty of the soul, since the things I have spoken of can be done by any impious person, and only hypocrites are produced by devotion to these things. On the other hand, it will not at all injure the soul that the body should be clothed in profane raiment, should dwell in profane places, should eat and drink in the ordinary fashion, should not pray aloud, and should leave undone all the things abovementioned, which may be done by hypocrites.

And, to cast everything aside, even speculations, meditations, and whatever things can be performed by the exertions of the soul itself, are of no profit. One thing, and one alone, is necessary for life, justification, and Christian liberty; and that is the most holy word of God, the Gospel of Christ, as He says: "I am the resurrection and the life; he that believeth in me shall not die eternally" (John xi. 25); and also (John viii. 36) "If the Son shall make you free, ye shall be free indeed;" and (Matt. iv. 4), "Man shall not live by bread alone, but by every word that proceedeth out of the mouth of God."

Let us therefore hold it for certain and firmly established, that the soul can do without everything, except the word of God, without which none at all of its wants are provided for. But, having the word, it is rich and wants for nothing; since that is the word of life, of truth, of light, of peace, of justification, of salvation, of joy, of liberty, of wisdom, of virtue, of grace, of glory, and of every good thing. It is on this account that the prophet in a whole psalm (Ps. cxix.), and in many other places, sighs for and calls upon the word of God with so many groanings and words.

Again, there is no more cruel stroke of the wrath of God than when He sends a famine of hearing His words (Amos viii. 11); just as there is no greater favour from Him than the sending forth of His word, as it is said: "He sent his word and healed them, and delivered them from their destructions." (Ps. cvii. 20.) Christ was sent for no other office than that of the word, and the order of apostles, that of bishops, and that of the whole body of the clergy, have been called and instituted for no object but the ministry of the word.

But you will ask:—"What is this word, and by what means is it to be used, since there are so many words of God?" I answer, the Apostle Paul (Rom. i.) explains what it is, namely, the Gospel of God, concerning His Son, incarnate, suffering, risen, and glorified through the Spirit, the sanctifier. To preach Christ is to feed the soul, to justify it, to set it free, and to save it, if it believes the preaching. For faith alone, and the efficacious use of the word of God, bring salvation. "If thou shalt confess with thy mouth the Lord Jesus, and shalt believe in thine heart that God hath raised him from the dead, thou shalt be saved." (Rom. x. 9.) And again: "Christ is the end of the law for righteousness to every one that believeth" (Rom. x. 4); and "The just shall live by faith." (Rom. i. 17.) For the word of God cannot be received and honoured by any works, but by faith alone. Hence it is clear that, as the soul needs the word alone for life and justification, so it is justified by faith alone and not by any works. For if it could be justified by any other means, it would have no need of the word, nor consequently of faith.

But this faith cannot consist at all with works; that is, if you imagine that you can be justified by those works, whatever they are, along with it. For this would be to halt between two opinions, to worship Baal, and to kiss the hand to him, which is a very great iniquity, as Job says. Therefore, when you begin to believe, you learn at the same time that all that is in you is utterly guilty, sinful, and damnable; according to that saying: "All have sinned, and come short of the glory of God." (Rom. iii. 23.) And also: "There is none righteous, no, not one; they are all gone out of the way; they are together become unprofitable; there is none that doeth good, no, not one." (Rom. iii. 10–12.) When you have learnt this, you will know that Christ is necessary for you, since He has suffered and risen again for you, that, believing on Him, you might by this faith become another man, all your sins being remitted, and you being justified by the merits of another, namely, of Christ alone.

Since then this faith can reign only in the inward man, as it is said: "With the heart man believeth unto righteousness" (Rom. x. 10); and since it alone justifies, it is evident that by no outward work or labour can the inward man be at all justified, made free, and saved; and that no works whatever have any relation to him. And so, on the other hand, it is solely by impiety and incredulity of heart that he becomes guilty, and a slave of sin, deserving condemnation; not by any outward sin or work. Therefore the first care of every Christian ought to be, to lay aside all reliance on works, and strengthen his faith alone more and more, and by it grow in the knowledge, not of works, but of Christ Jesus, who has suffered and risen again for him; as Peter teaches, when he makes no other work to be a Christian one. Thus Christ, when the Jews asked Him what they should do that they might work the works of God, rejected the multitude of works, with which He saw that they were puffed up, and commanded them one thing only, saying: "This is the work of God, that ye believe on him whom He hath sent, for him hath God the Father sealed." (John vi. 27, 29.)

Hence a right faith in Christ is an incomparable treasure, carrying with it universal salvation, and preserving from all evil, as it is said: "He that believeth and is baptized shall be saved; but he that believeth not shall be damned." (Mark xvi. 16.) Isaiah, looking to this treasure, predicted: "The consumption decreed shall overflow with righteousness. For the Lord God of hosts shall make a consumption, even determined, in the midst of the land." (Is. x. 22, 23.) As if he said:—"Faith, which is the brief and complete fulfilling of the law, will fill those who believe with such righteousness, that they will need nothing else for justification." Thus too Paul says: "For with the heart man believeth unto righteousness." (Rom. x. 10.)

But you ask how it can be the fact that faith alone justifies, and affords without works so great a treasure of good things, when so many works, ceremonies, and laws are prescribed to us in the Scriptures. I answer: before all things bear in mind what I have said, that faith alone without works justifies, sets free, and saves, as I shall show more clearly below.

Meanwhile it is to be noted, that the whole Scripture of God is divided into two parts, precepts and promises. The precepts certainly teach us what is good, but what they teach is not forthwith done. For they show us what we ought to do, but do not give us the power to do it. They were ordained, however, for the purpose of showing man to himself; that through them he may learn his own impotence for good, and may despair of his own strength. For this reason they are called the Old Testament, and are so.

For example: "thou shalt not covet," is a precept by which we are all convicted of sin; since no man can help coveting, whatever efforts to the contrary he may make. In order therefore that he may fulfil the precept, and not covet, he is constrained to despair of himself, and to seek elsewhere and through another the help which he cannot find in himself; as it is said: "O Israel, thou hast destroyed thyself; but in me is thine help." (Hosea xiii. 9.) Now what is done by this one precept, is done by all; for all are equally impossible of fulfilment by us.

Now when a man has through the precepts been taught his own impotence, and become anxious by what means he may satisfy the law—for the law must be satisfied, so that no jot or tittle of it may pass away; otherwise he must be hopelessly condemned— then, being truly humbled and brought to nothing in his own eyes, he finds in himself no resource for justification and salvation.

Then comes in that other part of Scripture, the promises of God, which declare the glory of God, and say: "If you wish to fulfil the law, and, as the law requires, not to covet, lo! believe in Christ, in whom are promised to you grace, justification, peace, and liberty." All these things you shall have, if you believe, and shall be without them, if you do not believe. For what is impossible for you by all the works of the law, which are many and yet useless, you shall fulfil in an easy and summary way through faith; because God the Father has made everything to depend on faith, so that whosoever has it, has all things, and he who has it not, has nothing. "For God hath concluded them all in unbelief, that He might have mercy upon all." (Rom. xi. 32.) Thus the promises of God give that which the precepts exact, and fulfil what the law commands; so that all is of God alone, both the precepts and their fulfilment. He alone commands. He alone also fulfils. Hence the promises of God belong to the New Testament; nay, are the New Testament.

Now since these promises of God are words of holiness, truth, righteousness, liberty, and peace, and are full of universal goodness; the soul, which cleaves to them with a firm faith, is so united to them, nay, thoroughly absorbed by them, that it not only partakes in, but is penetrated and saturated by, all their virtue. For if the touch of Christ was healing, how much more does that most tender spiritual touch, nay, absorption of the word, communicate to the soul all that belongs to the word. In this way, therefore, the soul, through faith alone, without works, is from the word of God justified, sanctified, endued with truth, peace, and liberty, and filled full with every good thing, and is truly made the child of God; as it is said: "To them gave he power to become the sons of God, even to them that believe on his name." (John i. 12.)

From all this it is easy to understand why faith has such great power, and why no good works, nor even all good works put together, can compare with it; since no work can cleave to the word of God, or be in the soul. Faith alone and the word reign in it; and such as is the word, such is the soul made by it; just as iron exposed to fire glows like fire, on account of its union with the fire. It is clear then that to a Christian man his faith suffices for everything, and that he has no need of works for justification. But if he has no need of works, neither has he need of the law; and, if he has no need of the law, he is certainly free from the law, and the saying is true: "The law is not made for a righteous man." (1 Tim. i. 9.) This is that Christian liberty, our faith, the effect of which is, not that we should be careless or lead a bad life, but that no one should need the law or works for justification and salvation.

Let us consider this as the first virtue of faith; and let us look also to the second. This also is an office of faith, that it honours with the utmost veneration and the highest reputation him in whom it believes, inasmuch as it holds him to be truthful and worthy of belief. For there is no honour like that reputation of truth and righteousness, with which we honour him, in whom we believe. What higher credit can we attribute to any one than truth and righteousness, and absolute goodness? On the other hand, it is the greatest insult to brand any one with the reputation of falsehood and unrighteousness, or to suspect him of these, as we do when we disbelieve him.

Thus the soul, in firmly believing the promises of God, holds Him to be true and righteous; and it can attribute to God no higher glory than the credit of being so. The highest worship of God is to ascribe to Him truth, righteousness, and whatever qualities we must ascribe to one in whom we believe. In doing this the soul shows itself prepared to do His whole will; in doing this it hallows His name, and gives itself up to be dealt with as it may please God. For it cleaves to His promises, and never doubts that He is true, just, and wise, and will do, dispose, and provide for all things in the best way. Is not such a soul, in this its faith, most obedient to God in all things? What commandment does there remain which has not been amply fulfilled by such an obedience? What fulfilment can be more full than universal obedience? Now this is not accomplished by works, but by faith alone.

On the other hand, what greater rebellion, impiety, or insult to God can there be, than not to believe His promises? What else is this, than either to make God a liar, or to doubt His truth—that is, to attribute truth to ourselves, but to God flasehood and levity? In doing this, is not a man denying God and setting himself up as an idol in his own heart? What then can works, done in such a state of impiety, profit us, were they even angelic or apostolic works? Rightly hath God shut up all—not in wrath nor in lust—but in unbelief; in order that those who pretend that they are fulfilling the law by works of purity and benevolence (which are social and human virtues), may not presume that they will therefore be saved; but, being included in the sin of unbelief, may either seek mercy, or be justly condemned.

But when God sees that truth is ascribed to Him, and that in the faith of our hearts He is honoured with all the honour of which He is worthy; then in return He honours us on account of that faith; attributing to us truth and righteousness. For faith produces truth and righteousness, in rendering to God what is His; and therefore in return God gives glory to our righteousness. It is a true and righteous thing, that God is true and righteous; and to confess this, and ascribe these attributes to Him, is to be ourselves true and righteous. Thus He says: "Them that honour me I will honour, and they that despise me shall be lightly esteemed." (1 Sam. ii. 30.) And so Paul says that Abraham's faith was imputed to him for righteousness, because by it he gave glory to God; and that to us also, for the same reason, it shall be reputed for righteousness, if we believe. (Rom. iv.)

The third incomparable grace of faith is this, that it unites the soul to Christ, as the wife to the husband; by which mystery, as the Apostle teaches, Christ and the soul are made one flesh. Now if they are one flesh, and if a true marriage— nay, by far the most perfect of all marriages—is accomplished between them (for human marriages are but feeble types of this one great marriage), then it follows that all they have becomes theirs in common, as well good things as evil things; so that whatsoever Christ possesses, that the believing soul may take to itself and boast of as its own, and whatever belongs to the soul, that Christ claims as his.

If we compare these possessions, we shall see how inestimable is the gain. Christ is full of grace, life, and salvation; the soul is full of sin, death, and condemnation. Let faith step in, and then sin, death, and hell will belong to Christ, and grace, life, and salvation to the soul. For, if he is a husband, he must needs take to himself that which is his wife's, and, at the same time, impart to his wife that which is his. For, in giving her his own body and himself, how can he but give her all that is his? And, in taking to himself the body of his wife, how can he but take to himself all that is hers?

In this is displayed the delightful sight, not only of communion, but of a prosperous warfare, of victory, salvation, and redemption. For since Christ is God and man, and is such a person as neither has sinned, nor dies, nor is condemned,—nay, cannot sin, die, or be condemned; and since his righteousness, life, and salvation are invincible, eternal, and almighty; when, I say, such a person, by the wedding-ring of faith, takes a share in the sins, death, and hell of his wife, nay, makes them his own, and deals with them no otherwise than as if they were his, and as if he himself had sinned; and when he suffers, dies, and descends to hell, that he may overcome all things, since sin, death, and hell cannot swallow him up, they must needs be swallowed up by him in stupendous conflict. For his righteousness rises above the sins of all men; his life is more powerful than all death; his salvation is more unconquerable than all hell.

Thus the believing soul, by the pledge of its faith in Christ, becomes free from all sin, fearless of death, safe from hell, and endowed with the eternal righteousness, life, and salvation of its husband Christ. Thus he presents to himself a glorious bride, without spot or wrinkle, cleansing her with the washing of water by the word; that is, by faith in the word of life, righteousness, and salvation. Thus he betrothes her unto himself "in faithfulness, in righteousness, and in judgment, and in lovingkindness, and in mercies." (Hosea ii. 19, 20.)

Who then can value highly enough these royal nuptials? Who can comprehend the riches of the glory of this grace? Christ, that rich and pious husband, takes as a wife a needy and impious harlot, redeeming her from all her evils, and supplying her with all His good things. It is impossible now that her sins should destroy her, since they have been laid upon Christ and swallowed up in Him, and since she has in her husband Christ a righteousness which she may claim as her own, and which she can set up with confidence against all her sins, against death and hell, saying: "If I have sinned, my Christ, in whom I believe, has not sinned; all mine is His, and all His is mine;" as it is written, "My beloved is mine, and I am his. (Cant. ii. 16.) This is what Paul says: "Thanks be to God, which giveth us the victory through our Lord Jesus Christ;" victory over sin and death, as he says: "The sting of death is sin, and the strength of sin is the law." (1 Cor. xv. 56, 57.)

From all this you will again understand, why so much importance is attributed to faith, so that it alone can fulfil the law, and justify without any works. For you see that the first commandment, which says, "Thou shalt worship one God only," is fulfilled by faith alone. If you were nothing but good works from the soles of your feet to the crown of your head, you would not be worshipping God, nor fulfilling the first commandment, since it is impossible to worship God, without ascribing to Him the glory of truth and of universal goodness, as it ought in truth to be ascribed. Now this is not done by works, but only by faith of heart. It is not by working, but by believing, that we glorify God, and confess Him to be true. On this ground faith is the sole righteousness of a Christian man, and the fulfilling of all the commandments. For to him who fulfils the first, the task of fulfilling all the rest is easy.

Works, since they are irrational things, cannot glorify God; although they may be done to the glory of God, if faith be present. But at present we are enquiring, not into the quality of the works done, but into him who does them, who glorifies God, and brings forth good works. This is faith of heart, the head and the substance of all our righteousness. Hence that is a blind and perilous doctrine which teaches that the commandments are fulfilled by works. The commandments must have been fulfilled, previous to any good works, and good works follow their fulfilment, as we shall see.

But, that we may have a wider view of that grace which our inner man has in Christ, we must know that in the Old Testament God sanctified to Himself every first-born male. The birthright was of great value, giving a superiority over the rest by the double honour of priesthood and kingship. For the first-born brother was priest and lord of all the rest.

Under this figure was foreshown Christ, the true and only first-born of God the Father and of the Virgin Mary, and a true king and priest, not in a fleshly and earthly sense. For His kingdom is not of this world; it is in heavenly and spiritual things that He reigns and acts as priest; and these are righteousness, truth, wisdom, peace, salvation, &c. Not but that all things, even those of earth and hell, are subject to Him—for otherwise how could He defend and save us from them?—but it is not in these, nor by these, that His kingdom stands.

So too His priesthood does not consist in the outward display of vestments and gestures, as did the human priesthood of Aaron and our ecclesiastical priesthood at this day, but in spiritual things, wherein, in His invisible office, He intercedes for us with God in heaven, and there offers Himself, and performs all the duties of a priest; as Paul describes Him to the Hebrews under the figure of Melchizedek. Nor does He only pray and intercede for us; He also teaches us inwardly in the spirit with the living teachings of His Spirit. Now these are the two special offices of a priest, as is figured to us in the case of fleshly priests, by visible prayers and sermons.

As Christ by His birthright has obtained these two dignities, so He imparts and communicates them to every believer in Him, under that law of matrimony of which we have spoken above, by which all that is the husband's is also the wife's. Hence all we who believe on Christ are kings and priests in Christ, as it is said: "Ye are a chosen generation, a royal priesthood, an holy nation, a peculiar people; that ye should shew forth the praises of him who hath called you out of darkness into his marvellous light." (1 Pet. ii. 9.)

These two things stand thus. First, as regards kingship, every Christian is by faith so exalted above all things, that, in spiritual power, he is completely lord of all things; so that nothing whatever can do him any hurt; yea, all things are subject to him, and are compelled to be subservient to his salvation. Thus Paul says: "All things work together for good to them who are the called" (Rom. viii. 28); and also; "Whether life, or death, or things present, or things to come: all are yours; and ye are Christ's. (1 Cor. iii. 22, 23.)

Not that in the sense of corporeal power any one among Christians has been appointed to possess and rule all things, according to the mad and senseless idea of certain ecclesiastics. That is the office of kings, princes, and men upon earth. In the experience of life we see that we are subjected to all things, and suffer many things, even death. Yea, the more of a Christian any man is, to so many the more evils, sufferings, and deaths is he subject; as we see in the first place in Christ the first-born, and in all His holy brethen.

This is a spiritual power, which rules in the midst of enemies, and is powerful in the midst of distresses. And this is nothing else than that strength is made perfect in my weakness, and that I can turn all things to the profit of my salvation; so that even the cross and death are compelled to serve me and to work together for my salvation. This is a lofty and eminent dignity, a true and almighty dominion, a spiritual empire, in which there is nothing so good, nothing so bad, as not to work together for my good, if only I believe. And yet there is nothing of which I have need—for faith alone suffices for my salvation—unless that, in it, faith may exercise the power and empire of its liberty. This is the inestimable power and liberty of Christians.

Nor are we only kings and the freest of all men, but also priests for ever, a dignity far higher than kingship, because by that priesthood we are worthy to appear before God, to pray for others, and to teach one another mutually the things which are of God. For these are the duties of priests, and they cannot possibly be permitted to any unbeliever. Christ has obtained for us this favour, if we believe in Him, that, just as we are His brethren, and co-heirs and fellow kings with Him, so we should be also fellow priests with Him, and venture with confidence, through the spirit of faith, to come into the presence of God, and cry "Abba, Father!" and to pray for one another, and to do all things which we see done and figured in the visible and corporeal office of priesthood. But to an unbelieving person nothing renders service or works for good. He himself is in servitude to all things, and all things turn out for evil to him, because he uses all things in an impious way for his own advantage, and not for the glory of God. And thus he is not a priest, but a profane person, whose prayers are turned into sin; nor does he ever appear in the presence of God, because God does not hear sinners.

Who then can comprehend the loftiness of that Christian dignity which, by its royal power, rules over all things, even over death, life, and sin, and, by its priestly glory, is all powerful with God; since God does what He Himself seeks and wishes; as it is written: "He will fulfil the desire of them that fear Him: He also will hear their cry, and will save them"? (Ps. cxlv. 19.) This glory certainly cannot be attained by any works, but by faith only.

From these considerations any one may clearly see how a Christian man is free from all things; so that he needs no works in order to be justified and saved, but receives these gifts in abundance from faith alone. Nay, were he so foolish as to pretend to be justified, set free, saved, and made a Christian, by means of any good work, he would immediately lose faith with all its benefits. Such folly is prettily represented in the fable, where a dog, running along in the water, and carrying in his mouth a real piece of meat, is deceived by the reflection of the meat in the water, and, in trying with open mouth to seize it, loses the meat and its image at the same time.

Here you will ask: "If all who are in the Church are priests, by what character are those, whom we now call priests, to be distinguished from the laity?" I reply: By the use of these words, "priest," "clergy," "spiritual person," "ecclesiastic," an injustice has been done, since they have been transferred from the remaining body of Christians to those few, who are now, by a hurtful custom, called ecclesiastics. For Holy Scripture makes no distinction between them, except that those, who are now boastfully called popes, bishops, and lords, it calls ministers, servants, and stewards, who are to serve the rest in the ministry of the Word, for teaching the faith of Christ and the liberty of believers. For though it is true that we are all equally priests, yet we cannot, nor, if we could, ought we all to minister and teach publicly. Thus Paul says: "Let a man so account of us as of the ministers of Christ, and stewards of the mysteries of God." (1 Cor. iv. 1.)

This bad system has now issued in such a pompous display of power, and such a terrible tyranny, that no earthly government can be compared to it, as if the laity were something else than Christians. Through this perversion of things it has happened that the knowledge of Christian grace, of faith, of liberty, and altogether of Christ, has utterly perished, and has been succeeded by an intolerable bondage to human works and laws; and, according to the Lamentations of Jeremiah, we have become the slaves of the vilest men on earth, who abuse our misery to all the disgraceful and ignominious purposes of their own will.

Returning to the subject which we had begun, I think it is made clear by these considerations that it is not sufficient, nor a Christian course, to preach the works, life, and words of Christ in a historic manner, as facts which it suffices to know as an example how to frame our life; as do those who are now held the best preachers: and much less so, to keep silence altogether on these things, and to teach in their stead the laws of men and the decrees of the Fathers. There are now not a few persons who preach and read about Christ with the object of moving the human affections to sympathise with Christ, to indignation against the Jews, and other childish and womanish absurdities of that kind.

Now preaching ought to have the object of promoting faith in Him, so that He may not only be Christ, but a Christ for you and for me, and that what is said of Him, and what He is called, may work in us. And this faith is produced and is maintained by preaching why Christ came, what He has brought us and given to us, and to what profit and advantage He is to be received. This is done, when the Christian liberty which we have from Christ Himself is rightly taught, and we are shown in what manner all we Christians are kings and priests, and how we are lords of all things, and may be confident that whatever we do in the presence of God is pleasing and acceptable to Him.

Whose heart would not rejoice in its inmost core at hearing these things? Whose heart, on receiving so great a consolation, would not become sweet with the love of Christ, a love to which it can never attain by any laws or works? Who can injure such a heart, or make it afraid? If the consciousness of sin, or the horror of death, rush in upon it, it is prepared to hope in the Lord, and is fearless of such evils, and undisturbed, until it shall look down upon its enemies. For it believes that the righteousness of Christ is its own, and that its sin is no longer its own, but that of Christ, for, on account of its faith in Christ, all its sin must needs be swallowed up from before the face of the righteousness of Christ, as I have said above. It learns too, with the Apostle, to scoff at death and sin, and to say: "O death, where is thy sting? O grave, where is thy victory? The sting of death is sin, and the strength of sin is the law. But thanks be to God, which giveth us the victory through our Lord Jesus Christ." (1 Cor. xv. 55–57.) For death is swallowed up in victory; not only the victory of Christ, but ours also; since by faith it becomes ours, and in it we too conquer.

Let it suffice to say this concerning the inner man and its liberty, and concerning that righteousness of faith, which needs neither laws nor good works; nay, they are even hurtful to it, if any one pretends to be justified by them.

And now let us turn to the other part, to the outward man. Here we shall give an answer to all those who, taking offence at the word of faith and at what I have asserted, say: "If faith does everything, and by itself suffices for justification, why then are good works commanded? Are we then to take our ease and do no works, content with faith?" Not so, impious men, I reply; not so. That would indeed really be the case, if we were thoroughly and completely inner and spiritual persons; but that will not happen until the last day, when the dead shall be raised. As long as we live in the flesh, we are but beginning and making advances in that which shall be completed in a future life. On this account the Apostle calls that which we have in this life, the first-fruits of the Spirit. (Rom. viii. 23.) In future we shall have the tenths, and the fulness of the Spirit. To this part belongs the fact I have stated before, that the Christian is the servant of all and subject to all. For in that part in which he is free, he does no works, but in that in which he is a servant, he does all works. Let us see on what principle this is so.

Although, as I have said, inwardly, and according to the spirit, a man is amply enough justified by faith, having all that he requires to have, except that this very faith and abundance ought to increase from day to day, even till the future life; still he remains in this mortal life upon earth, in which it is necessary that he should rule his own body, and have intercourse with men. Here then works begin; here he must not take his ease; here he must give heed to exercise his body by fastings, watchings, labour, and other moderate discipline, so that it may be subdued to the spirit, and obey and conform itself to the inner man and faith, and not rebel against them nor hinder them, as is its nature to do if it is not kept under. For the inner man, being conformed to God, and created after the image of God through faith, rejoices and delights itself in Christ, in whom such blessings have been conferred on it; and hence has only this task before it, to serve God with joy and for nought in free love.

In doing this he offends that contrary will in his own flesh, which is striving to serve the world, and to seek its own gratification. This the spirit of faith cannot and will not bear; but applies itself with cheerfulness and zeal to keep it down and restrain it; as Paul says: "I delight in the law of God after the inward man; but I see another law in my members, warring against the law of my mind, and bringing me into captivity to the law of sin." (Rom. vii. 22, 23.) And again: "I keep under my body, and bring it into subjection, lest that by any means, when I have preached to others, I myself should be a castaway." (1 Cor. ix. 27.) And: "They that are Christ's have crucified the flesh with the affections and lusts." (Gal. v. 24.)

These works, however, must not be done with any notion that by them a man can be justified before God—for faith, which alone is righteousness before God, will not bear with this false notion—but solely with this purpose, that the body may be brought into subjection, and be purified from its evil lusts, so that our eyes may be turned only to purging away those lusts. For when the soul has been cleansed by faith and made to love God, it would have all things to be cleansed in like manner; and especially its own body, so that all things might unite with it in the love and praise of God. Thus it comes that, from the requirements of his own body, a man cannot take his ease, but is compelled on its account to do many good works, that he may bring it into subjection. Yet these works are not the means of his justification before God he does them out of disinterested love to the service of God; looking to no other end than to do what is well-pleasing to Him whom he desires to obey most dutifully in all things.

On this principle every man may easily instruct himself in what measure, and with what distinctions, he ought to chasten his own body. He will fast, watch, and labour, just as much as he sees to suffice for keeping down the wantonness and concupiscence of the body. But those who pretend to be justified by works are looking, not to the mortification of their lusts, but only to the works themselves; thinking that, if they can accomplish as many works and as great ones as possible, all is well with them, and they are justified. Sometimes they even injure their brain, and extinguish nature, or at least make it useless.

This is enormous folly, and ignorance of Christian life and faith, when a man seeks, without faith, to be justified and saved by works.

To make what we have said more easily understood, let us set it forth under a figure. The works of a Christian man, who is justified and saved by his faith out of the pure and unbought mercy of God, ought to be regarded in the same light as would have been those of Adam and Eve in Paradise, and of all their posterity, if they had not sinned. Of them it is said: "The Lord God took the man, and put him into the garden of Eden to dress it and to keep it." (Gen. ii. 15.) Now Adam had been created by God just and righteous, so that he could not have needed to be justified and made righteous by keeping the garden and working in it; but, that he might not be unemployed, God gave him the business of keeping and cultivating Paradise. These would have indeed been works of perfect freedom, being done for no object but that of pleasing God, and not in order to obtain justification, which he already had to the full, and which would have been innate in us all.

So it is with the works of a believer. Being by his faith replaced afresh in Paradise and created anew, he does not need works for his justification, but that he may not be idle, but may keep his own body and work upon it. His works are to be done freely, with the sole object of pleasing God. Only we are not yet fully created anew in perfect faith and love; these require to be increased, not however through works, but through themselves.

A bishop, when he consecrates a church, confirms children, or performs any other duty of his office, is not consecrated as bishop by these works; nay, unless he had been previously consecrated as bishop, not one of those works would have any validity; they would be foolish, childish, and ridiculous. Thus a Christian, being consecrated by his faith, does good works; but he is not by these works made a more sacred person, or more a Christian. That is the effect of faith alone; nay, unless he were previously a believer and a Christian, none of his works would have any value at all; they would really be impious and damnable sins.

True then are these two sayings: Good works do not make a good man, but a good man does good works. Bad works do not make a bad man, but a bad man does bad works. Thus it is always necessary that the substance or person should be good before any good works can be done, and that good works should follow and proceed from a good person. As Christ says: "A good tree cannot bring forth evil fruit, neither can a corrupt tree bring forth good fruit." (Matt. vii. 18.) Now it is clear that the fruit does not bear the tree, nor does the tree grow on the fruit; but, on the contrary, the trees bear the fruit and the fruit grows on the trees.

As then trees must exist before their fruit, and as the fruit does not make the tree either good or bad, but, on the contrary, a tree of either kind produces fruit of the same kind; so must first the person of the man be good or bad, before he can do either a good or a bad work; and his works do not make him bad or good, but he himself makes his works either bad or good.

We may see the same thing in all handicrafts. A bad or good house does not make a bad or good builder, but a good or bad builder makes a good or bad house. And in general, no work makes the workman such as it is itself; but the workman makes the work such as he is himself. Such is the case too with the works of men. Such as the man himself is, whether in faith or in unbelief, such is his work; good if it be done in faith, bad if in unbelief. But the converse is not true—that, such as the work is, such the man becomes in faith or in unbelief. For as works do not make a believing man, so neither do they make a justified man; but faith, as it makes a man a believer and justified, so also it makes his works good.

Since, then, works justify no man, but a man must be justified before he can do any good work, it is most evident that it is faith alone which, by the mere mercy of God through Christ, and by means of His word, can worthily and sufficiently justify and save the person; and that a Christian man needs no work, no law, for his salvation; for by faith he is free from all law, and in perfect freedom does gratuitously all that he does, seeking nothing either of profit or of salvation—since by the grace of God he is already saved and rich in all things through his faith—but solely that which is well-pleasing to God.

So too no good work can profit an unbeliever to justification and salvation; and on the other hand no evil work makes him an evil and condemned person, but that unbelief, which makes the person and the tree bad, makes his works evil and condemned. Wherefore, when any man is made good or bad, this does not arise from his works, but from his faith or unbelief, as the wise man says: "The beginning of sin is to fall away from God;" that is, not to believe. Paul says: "He that cometh to God must believe" (Heb. xi. 6); and Christ says the same thing: "Either make the tree good, and his fruit good; or else make the tree corrupt, and his fruit corrupt." (Matt. xii. 33.) As much as to say: He who wishes to have good fruit, will begin with the tree, and plant a good one; even so he who wishes to do good works must begin, not by working, but by believing, since it is this which makes the person good. For nothing makes the person good but faith, nor bad but unbelief.

It is certainly true that, in the sight of men, a man becomes good or evil by his works; but here "becoming" means that it is thus shown and recognised who is good or evil; as Christ says: "By their fruits ye shall know them." (Matt. vii. 20.) But all this stops at appearances and externals; and in this matter very many deceive themselves, when they presume to write and teach that we are to be justified by good works, and meanwhile make no mention even of faith, walking in their own ways, ever deceived and deceiving, going from bad to worse, blind leaders of the blind, wearying themselves with many works, and yet never attaining to true righteousness; of whom Paul says: "Having a form of godliness, but denying the power thereof; ever learning, and never able to come to the knowledge of the truth." (2 Tim. iii. 5, 7.)

He then, who does not wish to go astray with these blind ones, must look further than to the works of the law or the doctrine of works; nay, must turn away his sight from works, and look to the person, and to the manner in which it may be justified. Now it is justified and saved, not by works or laws, but by the word of God, that is, by the promise of His grace; so that the glory may be to the Divine majesty, which has saved us who believe, not by works of righteousness which we have done, but according to His mercy, by the word of His grace.

From all this it is easy to perceive on what principle good works are to be cast aside or embraced, and by what rule all teachings put forth concerning works are to be understood. For if works are brought forward as grounds of justification, and are done under the false persuasion that we can pretend to be justified by them, they lay on us the yoke of necessity, and extinguish liberty along with faith, and by this very addition to their use, they become no longer good, but really worthy of condemnation. For such works are not free, but blaspheme the grace of God, to which alone it belongs to justify and save through faith. Works cannot accomplish this, and yet, with impious presumption, through our folly, they take it on themselves to do so; and thus break in with violence upon the office and glory of grace.

We do not then reject good works; nay, we embrace them and teach them in the highest degree. It is not on their own account that we condemn them, but on account of this impious addition to them, and the perverse notion of seeking justification by them. These things cause them to be only good in outward show, but in reality not good; since by them men are deceived and deceive others, like ravening wolves in sheep's clothing.

Now this Leviathan, this perverted notion about works, is invincible, when sincere faith is wanting. For those sanctified doers of works cannot but hold it, till faith, which destroys it, comes and reigns in the heart. Nature cannot expel it by her own power; nay, cannot even see it for what it is, but considers it as a most holy will. And when custom steps in besides, and strengthens this pravity of nature, as has happened by means of impious teachers, then the evil is incurable, and leads astray multitudes to irreparable ruin. Therefore, though it is good to preach and write about penitence, confession, and satisfaction, yet if we stop there, and do not go on to teach faith, such teaching is without doubt deceitful and devilish. For Christ, speaking by His servant John, not only said: "Repent ye;" but added: "for the kingdom of heaven is at hand." (Matt. iii. 2.)

For not one word of God only, but both, should be preached; new and old things should be brought out of the treasury, as well the voice of the law, as the word of grace. The voice of the law should be brought forward, that men may be terrified and brought to a knowledge of their sins, and thence be converted to penitence and to a better manner of life. But we must not stop here; that would be to wound only and not to bind up, to strike and not to heal, to kill and not to make alive, to bring down to hell and not to bring back, to humble and not to exalt. Therefore the word of grace, and of the promised remission of sin, must also be preached, in order to teach and set up faith; since, without that word, contrition, penitence, and all other duties, are performed and taught in vain.

There still remain, it is true, preachers of repentance and grace, but they do not explain the law and the promises of God to such an end, and in such a spirit, that men may learn whence repentance and grace are to come. For repentance comes from the law of God, but faith or grace from the promises of God, as it is said: "Faith cometh by hearing, and hearing by the word of God." (Rom. x. 17.) Whence it comes, that a man, when humbled and brought to the knowledge of himself by the threatenings and terrors of the law, is consoled and raised up by faith in the Divine promise. Thus "weeping may endure for a night, but joy cometh in the morning." (Ps. xxx. 5.) Thus much we say concerning works in general, and also concerning those which the Christian practises with regard to his own body.

Lastly, we will speak also of those works which he performs towards his neighbour. For man does not live for himself alone in this mortal body, in order to work on its account, but also for all men on earth; nay, he lives only for others and not for himself. For it is to this end that he brings his own body into subjection, that he may be able to serve others more sincerely and more freely; as Paul says: "None of us liveth to himself, and no man dieth to himself. For whether we live, we live unto the Lord; and whether we die, we die unto the Lord." (Rom. xiv. 7, 8.) Thus it is impossible that he should take his ease in this life, and not work for the good of his neighbours; since he must needs speak, act, and converse among men; just as Christ was made in the likeness of men, and found in fashion as a man, and had His conversation among men.

Yet a Christian has need of none of these things for justification and salvation, but in all his works he ought to entertain this view, and look only to this object, that he may serve and be useful to others in all that he does; having nothing before his eyes but the necessities and the advantage of his neighbour. Thus the Apostle commands us to work with our own hands, that we may have to give to those that need. He might have said, that we may support ourselves; but he tells us to give to those that need. It is the part of a Christian to take care of his own body for the very purpose that, by its soundness and wellbeing, he may be enabled to labour, and to acquire and preserve property, for the aid of those who are in want; that thus the stronger member may serve the weaker member, and we may be children of God, thoughtful and busy one for another, bearing one another's burdens, and so fulfilling the law of Christ.

Here is the truly Christian life; here is faith really working by love; when a man applies himself with joy and love to the works of that freest servitude, in which he serves others voluntarily and for nought; himself abundantly satisfied in the fulness and riches of his own faith.

Thus, when Paul had taught the Philippians how they had been made rich by that faith in Christ, in which they had obtained all things, he teaches them further in these words—"If there be therefore any consolation in Christ, if any comfort of love, if any fellowship of the Spirit, if any bowels and mercies, fulfil ye my joy, that ye be like-minded, having the same love, being of one accord, of one mind. Let nothing be done through strife or vainglory; but in lowliness of mind let each esteem other better than themselves. Look not every man on his own things, but every man also on the things of others." (Phil. ii. 1–4.)

In this we see clearly that the Apostle lays down this rule for a Christian life, that all our works should be directed to the advantage of others; since every Christian has such abundance through his faith, that all his other works and his whole life remain over and above, wherewith to serve and benefit his neighbour of spontaneous good will.

To this end he brings forward Christ as an example, saying: "Let this mind be in you, which was also in Christ Jesus: who, being in the form of God, thought it not robbery to be equal with God: but made himself of no reputation, and took upon him the form of a servant, and was made in the likeness of men; and being found in fashion as a man, he humbled himself, and became obedient unto death." (Phil. ii. 5–8.) This most wholesome saying of the Apostle has been darkened to us by men who, totally misunderstanding the expressions: "form of God," "form of a servant," "fashion," "likeness of men," have transferred them to the natures of Godhead and manhood. Paul's meaning is this: Christ, when He was full of the form of God, and abounded in all good things, so that He had no need of works or sufferings to be justified and saved—for all these things He had from the very beginning—yet was not puffed up with these things, and did not raise Himself above us, and arrogate to Himself power over us, though He might lawfully have done so, but on the contrary so acted in labouring, working, suffering, and dying, as to be like the rest of men, and no otherwise than a man in fashion and in conduct, as if he were in want of all things, and had nothing of the form of God; and yet all this He did for our sakes, that He might serve us, and that all the works He should do under that form of a servant, might become ours.

Thus a Christian, like Christ his head, being full and in abundance through his faith, ought to be content with this form of God, obtained by faith; except that, as I have said, he ought to increase this faith, till it be perfected. For this faith is his life, justification, and salvation, preserving his person itself and making it pleasing to God, and bestowing on him all that Christ has; as I have said above, and as Paul affirms: "The life which I now live in the flesh I live by the faith of the Son of God." (Gal. ii. 20.) Though he is thus free from all works, yet he ought to empty himself of this liberty, take on him the form of a servant, be made in the likeness of men, be found in fashion as a man, serve, help, and in every way act towards his neighbour as he sees that God through Christ has acted and is acting towards him. All this he should do freely, and with regard to nothing but the good pleasure of God, and he should reason thus:

Lo! my God, without merit on my part, of His pure and free mercy, has given to me, an unworthy, condemned, and contemptible creature, all the riches of justification and salvation in Christ, so that I no longer am in want of anything, except of faith to believe that this is so. For such a Father then, who has overwhelmed me with these inestimable riches of His, why should I not freely, cheerfully, and with my whole heart and from voluntary zeal, do all that I know will be pleasing to Him, and acceptable in His sight? I will therefore give myself, as a sort of Christ, to my neighbour, as Christ has given Himself to me; and will do nothing in this life, except what I see will be needful, advantageous, and wholesome for my neighbour, since by faith I abound in all good things in Christ.

Thus from faith flow forth love and joy in the Lord, and from love a cheerful, willing, free spirit, disposed to serve our neighbour voluntarily, without taking any account of gratitude or ingratitude, praise or blame, gain or loss. Its object is not to lay men under obligations, nor does it distinguish between friends and enemies, or look to gratitude or ingratitude, but most freely and willingly spends itself and its goods, whether it loses them through ingratitude, or gains good will. For thus did its Father, distributing all things to all men abundantly and freely; making His sun to rise upon the just and the unjust. Thus too the child does and endures nothing, except from the free joy with which it delights through Christ in God, the giver of such great gifts.

You see then that, if we recognise those great and precious gifts, as Peter says, which have been given to us, love is quickly diffused in our hearts through the Spirit, and by love we are made free, joyful, all-powerful, active workers, victors over all our tribulations, servants to our neighbour, and nevertheless lords of all things. But for those who do not recognise the good things given to them through Christ, Christ has been born in vain; such persons walk by works, and will never attain the taste and feeling of these great things. Therefore, just as our neighbour is in want, and has need of our abundance, so we too in the sight of God were in want, and had need of His mercy. And as our heavenly Father has freely helped us in Christ, so ought we freely to help our neighbour by our body and works, and each should become to other a sort of Christ, so that we may be mutually Christs, and that the same Christ may be in all of us; that is, that we may be truly Christians.

Who then can comprehend the riches and glory of the Christian life? It can do all things, has all things, and is in want of nothing; is lord over sin, death, and hell, and at the same time is the obedient and useful servant of all. But alas! it is at this day unknown throughout the world; it is neither preached nor sought after, so that we are quite ignorant about our own name, why we are and are called Christians. We are certainly called so from Christ, who is not absent, but dwells among us, provided, that is, that we believe in Him, and are reciprocally and mutually one the Christ of the other, doing to our neighbour as Christ does to us. But now, in the doctrine of men, we are taught only to seek after merits, rewards, and things which are already ours, and we have made of Christ a task-master far more severe than Moses.

The Blessed Virgin, beyond all others, affords us an example of the same faith, in that she was purified according to the law of Moses, and like all other women, though she was bound by no such law, and had no need of purification. Still she submitted to the law voluntarily and of free love, making herself like the rest of women, that she might not offend or throw contempt on them. She was not justified by doing this; but, being already justified, she did it freely and gratuitously. Thus ought our works too to be done, and not in order to be justified by them; for, being first justified by faith, we ought to do all our works freely and cheerfully for the sake of others.

St. Paul circumcised his disciple Timothy, not because he needed circumcision for his justification, but that he might not offend or contemn those Jews, weak in the faith, who had not yet been able to comprehend the liberty of faith. On the other hand, when they contemned liberty, and urged that circumcision was necessary for justification, he resisted them, and would not allow Titus to be circumcised. For as he would not offend or contemn any one's weakness in faith, but yielded for the time to their will, so again he would not have the liberty of faith offended or contemned by hardened self-justifiers, but walked in a middle path, sparing the weak for the time, and always resisting the hardened, that he might convert all to the liberty of faith. On the same principle we ought to act, receiving those that are weak in the faith, but boldly resisting these hardened teachers of works, of whom we shall hereafter speak at more length.

Christ also, when His disciples were asked for the tribute money, asked of Peter, whether the children of a king were not free from taxes. Peter agreed to this; yet Jesus commanded him to go to the sea, saying: "Lest we should offend them, go thou to the sea, and cast a hook, and take up the fish that first cometh up; and when thou hast opened his mouth, thou shalt find a piece of money; that take, and give unto them for me and thee." (Matt. xvii. 27.)

This example is very much to our purpose; for here Christ calls Himself and His disciples free men, and children of a king, in want of nothing; and yet He voluntarily submits and pays the tax. Just as far then as this work was necessary or useful to Christ for justification or salvation, so far do all His other works or those of His disciples avail for justification. They are really free and subsequent to justification, and only done to serve others and set them an example.

Such are the works which Paul inculcated; that Christians should be subject to principalities and powers, and ready to every good work (Tit. iii. 1); not that they may be justified by these things, for they are already justified by faith, but that in liberty of spirit they may thus be the servants of others, and subject to powers, obeying their will out of gratuitous love.

Such too ought to have been the works of all colleges, monasteries, and priests; every one doing the works of his own profession and state of life, not in order to be justified by them, but in order to bring his own body into subjection, as an example to others, who themselves also need to keep under their bodies; and also in order to accommodate himself to the will of others, out of free love. But we must always guard most carefully against any vain confidence or presumption of being justified, gaining merit, or being saved by these works; this being the part of faith alone, as I have so often said.

Any man possessing this knowledge may easily keep clear of danger among those innumerable commands and precepts of the Pope, of bishops, of monasteries, of churches, of princes, and of magistrates, which some foolish pastors urge on us as being necessary for justification and salvation, calling them precepts of the Church, when they are not so at all. For the Christian freeman will speak thus: I will fast, I will pray, I will do this or that, which is commanded me by men, not as having any need of these things for justification or salvation, but that I may thus comply with the will of the Pope, of the bishop, of such a community or such a magistrate, or of my neighbour as an example to him; for this cause I will do and suffer all things, just as Christ did and suffered much more for me, though He needed not at all to do so on His own account, and made Himself for my sake under the law, when He was not under the law. And although tyrants may do me violence or wrong in requiring obedience to these things, yet it will not hurt me to do them, so long as they are not done against God.

From all this every man will be able to attain a sure judgment and faithful discrimination between all works and laws, and to know who are blind and foolish pastors, and who are true and good ones. For whatsoever work is not directed to the sole end, either of keeping under the body, or of doing service to our neighbour—provided he require nothing contrary to the will of God—is no good or Christian work. Hence I greatly fear that at this day few or no colleges, monasteries, altars, or ecclesiastical functions are Christian ones; and the same may be said of fasts and special prayers to certain Saints. I fear that in all these nothing is being sought but what is already ours; while we fancy that by these things our sins are purged away and salvation is attained, and thus utterly do away with Christian liberty. This comes from ignorance of Christian faith and liberty.

This ignorance, and this crushing of liberty, are diligently promoted by the teaching of very many blind pastors, who stir up and urge the people to a zeal for these things, praising such zeal and puffing up men with their indulgences, but never teaching faith. Now I would advise you, if you have any wish to pray, to fast, or to made foundations in churches, as they call it, to take care not to do so with the object of gaining any advantage, either temporal or eternal. You will thus wrong your faith which alone bestows all things on you, and the increase of which, either by working or by suffering, is alone to be cared for. What you give, give freely and without price, that others may prosper and have increase from you and from your goodness. Thus you will be a truly good man and a Christian. For what do you want with your goods and your works, which are done over and above for the subjection of the body, since you have abundance for yourself through your faith, in which God has given you all things?

We give this rule: the good things which we have from God ought to flow from one to another, and become common to all, so that every one of us may, as it were, put on his neighbour, and so behave towards him as if he were himself in his place. They flowed and do flow from Christ to us; he put us on, and acted for us as if he himself were what we are. From us they flow to those who have need of them; so that my faith and righteousness ought to be laid down before God as a covering and intercession for the sins of my neighbour, which I am to take on myself, and so labour and endure servitude in them, as if they were my own; for thus has Christ done for us. This is true love and the genuine truth of Christian life. But only there is it true and genuine, where there is true and genuine faith. Hence the Apostle attributes to Charity this quality, that she seeketh not her own.

We conclude therefore that a Christian man does not live in himself, but in Christ and in his neighbour, or else is no Christian; in Christ by faith, in his neighbour by love. By faith he is carried upwards above himself to God, and by love he sinks back below himself to his neighbour, still always abiding in God and His love, as Christ says: "Verily I say unto you, hereafter ye shall see heaven open, and the angels of God ascending and descending upon the Son of man." (John i. 51.)

Thus much concerning liberty, which, as you see, is a true and spiritual liberty, making our hearts free from all sins, laws, and commandments; as Paul says: "The law is not made for a righteous man" (1 Tim. i. 9); and one which surpasses every other and outward liberty, as far as heaven is above earth. May Christ make us to understand and preserve this liberty. Amen.

Finally, for the sake of those to whom nothing can be stated so well but that they misunderstand and distort it, we must add a word, in case they can understand even that. There are very many persons, who, when they hear of this liberty of faith, straightway turn it into an occasion of licence. They think that everything is now lawful for them, and do not choose to show themselves free men and Christians in any other way than by their contempt and reprehension of ceremonies, of traditions, of human laws; as if they were Christians merely because they refuse to fast on stated days, or eat flesh when others fast, or omit the customary prayers; scoffing at the precepts of men, but utterly passing over all the rest that belongs to the Christian religion. On the other hand, they are most pertinaciously resisted by those who strive after salvation solely by their observance of and reverence for ceremonies; as if they would be saved merely because they fast on stated days, or abstain from flesh, or make formal prayers; talking loudly of the precepts of the Church and of the Fathers, and not caring a straw about those things which belong to our genuine faith. Both these parties are plainly culpable, in that, while they neglect matters which are of weight and necessary for salvation, they contend noisily about such as are without weight and not necessary.

How much more rightly does the Apostle Paul teach us to walk in the middle path, condemning either extreme, and saying: "Let not him that eateth despise him that eateth not; and let not him which eateth not judge him that eateth." (Rom. xiv. 3.) You see here how the Apostle blames those who, not from religious feeling, but in mere contempt, neglect and rail at ceremonial observances; and teaches them not to despise, since this "knowledge puffeth up." Again he teaches the pertinacious upholders of these things not to judge their opponents. For neither party observes towards the other that charity which edifieth. In this matter we must listen to Scripture, which teaches us to turn aside neither to the right hand nor to the left, but to follow those right precepts of the Lord which rejoice the heart. For just as a man is not righteous, merely because he serves and devotes himself to works and ceremonial rites, so neither will he be accounted righteous, merely because he neglects and despises them.

It is not from works that we are set free by the faith of Christ, but from the belief in works, that is, from foolishly presuming to seek justification through works. Faith redeems our consciences, makes them upright and preserves them, since by it we recognise the truth that justification does not depend on our works, although good works neither can nor ought to be wanting to it; just as we cannot exist without food and drink and all the functions of this mortal body. Still it is not on them that our justification is based, but on faith; and yet they ought not on that account to be despised or neglected. Thus in this world we are compelled by the needs of this bodily life; but we are not hereby justified. "My kingdom is not hence, nor of this world," says Christ; but He does not say: "My kingdom is not here, nor in this world." Paul too says: "Though we walk in the flesh, we do not war after the flesh" (2 Cor. x. 3); and: "The life which I now live in the flesh I live by the faith of the Son of God." (Gal. ii. 20.) Thus our doings, life, and being, in works and ceremonies, are done from the necessities of this life, and with the motive of governing our bodies; but yet we are not justified by these things, but by the faith of the Son of God.

The Christian must therefore walk in the middle path, and set these two classes of men before his eyes. He may meet with hardened and obstinate ceremonialists, who, like deaf adders, refuse to listen to the truth of liberty, and cry up, enjoin, and urge on us their ceremonies, as if they could justify us without faith. Such were the Jews of old, who would not understand, that they might act well. These men we must resist, do just the contrary to what they do, and be bold to give them offence; lest by this impious notion of theirs they should deceive many along with themselves. In the sight of these men it is expedient to eat flesh, to break fasts, and to do in behalf of the liberty of faith things which they hold to be the greatest sins. We must say of them: "Let them alone; they be blind leaders of the blind." (Matt. xv. 14.) In this way Paul also would not have Titus circumcised, though these men urged it; and Christ defended the Apostles, who had plucked ears of corn on the Sabbath day; and many like instances.

Or else we may meet with simple-minded and ignorant persons, weak in the faith, as the Apostle calls them, who are as yet unable to apprehend that liberty of faith, even if willing to do so. These we must spare, lest they should be offended. We must bear with their infirmity, till they shall be more fully instructed. For since these men do not act thus from hardened malice, but only from weakness of faith, therefore, in order to avoid giving them offence, we must keep fasts and do other things which they consider necessary. This is required of us by charity, which injures no one, but serves all men. It is not the fault of these persons that they are weak, but that of their pastors, who by the snares and weapons of their own traditions have brought them into bondage, and wounded their souls, when they ought to have been set free and healed by the teaching of faith and liberty. Thus the Apostle says: "If meat make my brother to offend, I will eat no flesh while the world standeth." (1 Cor. viii. 13.) And again: "I know, and am persuaded by the Lord Jesus, that there is nothing unclean of itself; but to him that esteemeth anything to be unclean, to him it is unclean. It is evil for that man who eateth with offence." (Rom. xiv. 14, 20.)

Thus, though we ought boldly to resist those teachers of tradition, and though those laws of the pontiffs, by which they make aggressions on the people of God, deserve sharp reproof, yet we must spare the timid crowd, who are held captive by the laws of those impious tyrants, till they are set free. Fight vigorously against the wolves, but on behalf of the sheep, not against the sheep. And this you may do by inveighing against the laws and lawgivers, and yet at the same time observing these laws with the weak, lest they be offended; until they shall themselves recognise the tyranny as such, and understand their own liberty. If you wish to use your liberty, do it secretly, as Paul says: "Hast thou faith? have it to thyself before God." (Rom. xiv. 22.) But take care not to use it in the presence of the weak. On the other hand, in the presence of tyrants and obstinate opposers, use your liberty in their despite, and with the utmost pertinacity, that they too may understand that they themselves are tyrants, and their laws useless for justification; nay, that they had no right to establish such laws.

Since, then, we cannot live in this world without ceremonies and works; since the hot and inexperienced period of youth has need of being restrained and protected by such bonds; and since everyone is bound to keep under his own body by attention to these things; therefore the minister of Christ must be prudent and faithful in so ruling and teaching the people of Christ in all these matters that no root of bitterness may spring up among them, and so many be defiled, as Paul warned the Hebrews; that is, that they may not lose the faith, and begin to be defiled by a belief in works, as the means of justification. This is a thing which easily happens, and defiles very many, unless faith be constantly inculcated along with works. It is impossible to avoid this evil, when faith is passed over in silence, and only the ordinances of men are taught, as has been done hitherto by the pestilent, impious, and souldestroying traditions of our pontiffs, and opinions of our theologians. An infinite number of souls have been drawn down to hell by these snares, so that you may recognise the work of Antichrist.

In brief, as poverty is imperilled amid riches, honesty amid business, humility amid honours, abstinence amid feasting, purity amid pleasures, so is justification by faith imperilled among ceremonies. Solomon says: "Can a man take fire in his bosom, and his clothes not be burned?" (Prov. vi. 27.) And yet, as we must live among riches, business, honours, pleasures, feastings, so must we among ceremonies, that is, among perils. Just as infant boys have the greatest need of being cherished in the bosoms and by the care of girls, that they may not die; and yet, when they are grown, there is peril to their salvation in living among girls; so inexperienced and fervid young men require to be kept in and restrained by the barriers of ceremonies, even were they of iron, lest their weak mind should rush headlong into vice. And yet it would be death to them to persevere in believing that they can be justified by these things. They must rather be taught that they have been thus imprisoned, not with the purpose of their being justified or gaining merit in this way, but in order that they might avoid wrong doing, and be more easily instructed in that righteousness which is by faith; a thing which the headlong character of youth would not bear, unless it were put under restraint.

Hence in the Christian life ceremonies are to be no otherwise looked upon than builders and workmen look upon those preparations for building or working which are not made with any view of being permanent or anything in themselves, but only because without them there could be no building and no work. When the structure is completed, they are laid aside. Here you see that we do not contemn these preparations, but set the highest value on them; a belief in them we do contemn, because no one thinks that they constitute a real and permanent structure. If any one were so manifestly out of his senses as to have no other object in life but that of setting up these preparations with all possible expense, diligence, and perseverance, while he never thought of the structure itself, but pleased himself and made his boast of these useless preparations and props; should we not all pity his madness, and think that, at the cost thus thrown away, some great building might have been raised?

Thus too we do not contemn works and ceremonies; nay, we set the highest value on them; but we contemn the belief in works, which no one should consider to constitute true righteousness; as do those hypocrites who employ and throw away their whole life in the pursuit of works, and yet never attain to that for the sake of which the works are done. As the Apostle says, they are "ever learning, and never able to come to the knowledge of the truth." (2 Tim. iii. 7). They appear to wish to build, they make preparations, and yet they never do build; and thus they continue in a show of godliness, but never attain to its power.

Meanwhile they please themselves with this zealous pursuit, and even dare to judge all others, whom they do not see adorned with such a glittering display of works; while, if they had been imbued with faith, they might have done great things for their own and others' salvation, at the same cost which they now waste in abuse of the gifts of God. But since human nature and natural reason, as they call it, are naturally superstitious, and quick to believe that justification can be attained by any laws or works proposed to them; and since nature is also exercised and confirmed in the same view by the practice of all earthly lawgivers, she can never, of her own power, free herself from this bondage to works, and come to a recognition of the liberty of faith.

We have therefore need to pray that God will lead us, and make us taught of God, that is, ready to learn from God; and will Himself, as He has promised, write His law in

124

our hearts; otherwise there is no hope for us. For unless He himself teach us inwardly this wisdom hidden in a mystery, nature cannot but condemn it and judge it to be heretical. She takes offence at it and it seems folly to her; just as we see that it happened of old in the case of the prophets and apostles; and just as blind and impious pontiffs, with their flatterers, do now in my case and that of those who are like me; upon whom, together with ourselves, may God at length have mercy, and lift up the light of His countenance upon them, that we may know His way upon earth and His saving health among all nations, Who is blessed for evermore. Amen. In the year of the Lord MDXX.

III. ON THE BABYLONISH CAPTIVITY OF THE CHURCH

Jesus.

Martin Luther, of the Order of St. Augustine, salutes his friend Hermann Tulichius.

Whether I will or not, I am compelled to become more learned day by day, since so many great masters vie with each other in urging me on and giving me practice. I wrote about indulgences two years ago, but now I extremely regret having published that book. At that time I was still involved in a great and superstitious respect for the tyranny of Rome, which led me to judge that indulgences were not to be totally rejected, seeing them, as I did, to be approved by so general a consent among men. And no wonder, for at that time it was I alone who was rolling this stone. Afterwards, however, with the kind aid of Sylvester and the friars, who supported indulgences so strenuously, I perceived that they were nothing but mere impostures of the flatterers of Rome, whereby to make away with the faith of God and the money of men. And I wish I could prevail upon the booksellers, and persuade all who have read them, to burn the whole of my writings on indulgences, and in place of all I have written about them to adopt this proposition: Indulgences are wicked devices of the flatterers of Rome.

After this, Eccius and Emser, with their fellow-conspirators, began to instruct me concerning the primacy of the Pope. Here too, not to be ungrateful to such learned men, I must confess that their works helped me on greatly; for, while I had denied that the Papacy had any divine right, I still admitted that it had a human right. But after hearing and reading the super-subtle subtleties of those coxcombs, by which they so ingeniously set up their idol—my mind being not entirely unteachable in such matters—I now know and am sure that the Papacy is the kingdom of Babylon, and the power of Nimrod the mighty hunter. Here moreover, that all may go prosperously with my friends, I entreat the booksellers, and entreat my readers, to burn all that I have published on this subject, and to hold to the following proposition:

The Papacy is the mighty hunting of the Bishop of Rome.

This is proved from the reasonings of Eccius, of Emser, and of the Leipzig lecturer on the Bible.

At the present time they are playing at schooling me concerning communion in both kinds, and some other subjects of the greatest importance. I must take pains not to listen in vain to these philosophical guides of mine. A certain Italian friar of Cremona has written a "Revocation of Martin Luther to the Holy See"—that is to say, not that I revoke, as the words imply, but that he revokes me. This is the sort of Latin that the Italians nowadays are beginning to write. Another friar, a German of Leipzig, Lecturer, as you know, on the whole canon of the Bible, has written against me concerning the Sacrament in both kinds, and is about, as I hear, to do still greater and wonderful wonders. The Italian indeed has cautiously concealed his name; perhaps alarmed by the examples of Cajetan and Sylvester. The man of Leipzig, however, as befits a vigorous and fierce German, has set forth in a number of verses on his title-page, his name, his life, his sanctity, his learning, his office, his glory, his honour, almost his very shoe-lasts. From him no doubt I shall learn not a little, since he writes a letter of dedication to the very Son of God; so familiar are these saints with Christ, who reigns in heaven. In short, three magpies seem to be addressing me, one, a Latin one, well; another, a Greek one, still better; the third, a Hebrew one, best of all. What do you think I have to do now, my dear Hermann, but to prick up my ears? The matter is handled at Leipzig by the Observants of the Holy Cross.

Hitherto I have foolishly thought that it would be an excellent thing, if it were determined by a General Council, that both kinds in the Sacrament should be administered to the laity. To correct this opinion, this more than most learned friar says that it was neither commanded nor decreed, whether by Christ or by the Apostles, that both kinds should be administered to the laity; and that it has therefore been left to the judgment of the Church, which we are bound to obey, what should be done or left undone on this point. Thus speaks he. You ask, perhaps, what craze has possession of the man, or against whom he is writing; since I did not condemn the use of one kind, and did leave it to the judgment of the Church to ordain the use of both kinds. And this he himself endeavours to assert, with the object of combating me by this very argument. I reply, that this kind of argument is a familiar one with all who write against Luther; namely, either to assert the very thing which they attack, or to set up a figment that they may attack it. Thus did Sylvester, Eccius, Emser, the men of Cologne too, and those of Louvain. If this friar had gone back from their spirit, he would not have written against Luther.

A greater piece of good fortune, however, has befallen this man than any of the others. Whereas he intended to prove that the use of one kind had neither been commanded nor decreed, but left to the decision of the Church, he brings forward Scriptures to prove that, by the command of Christ, the use of one kind was ordained for the laity. Thus it is true, according to this new interpreter of Scripture, that the use of one kind was not commanded, and at the same time was commanded, by Christ. You know how specially those logicians of Leipzig employ this new kind of argument. Does not Emser also, after having professed in his former book to speak fairly about me, and after having been convicted by me of the foulest envy and of base falsehoods, confess, when about to confute me in his later book, that both were true, and that he had written of me in both an unfair and a fair spirit? A good man indeed, as you know!

But listen to our specious advocate of one species, in whose mind the decision of the Church and the command of Christ are the same thing; and again the command of Christ and the absence of his command are the same thing. With what dexterity he proves that only one kind should be granted to the laity, by the command of Christ, that is, by the decision of the Church! He marks it with capital letters in this way, "AN INFALLIBLE FOUNDATION." Next he handles with incredible wisdom the sixth chapter of the Gospel of St. John, in which Christ speaks of the bread of heaven and the bread of life, which is Himself. These words this most learned man not only misapplies to the Sacrament of the Altar, but goes farther, and, because Christ said: "I am the living bread," and not: "I am the living cup," he concludes that in that passage the sacrament in only one kind was appointed for the laity. But the words that follow: "My flesh is meat indeed, and my blood is drink indeed;" and again, "Unless ye eat the flesh of the Son of Man and drink his blood"—since it was evident to this friar's brains that they tell irrefutably in favour of reception in both kinds, and against that in one kind—he evades very happily and learnedly in this way: "That Christ meant nothing else by these words, than that he who should receive one kind, should receive under this both the body and the blood." This he lays down as his infallible foundation of a structure so worthy of holy and heavenly reverence.

Learn now, along with me, from this man, that in the sixth chapter of St. John Christ commands reception in one kind, but in such a manner that this commanding means leaving the matter to the decision of the Church; and further, that Christ in the same chapter speaks of the laity only, not of the presbyters. For to us this living bread from heaven, that is, the sacrament in one kind, does not belong, but perchance the bread of death from hell. Now what is to be done with the deacons and sub-deacons? As they are neither laymen nor priests, they ought, on this distinguished authority, to use neither one nor both kinds. You understand, my dear Tulichius, this new and *observant* manner of handling Scripture. But you must also learn this, that Christ, in the sixth chapter of St. John, is speaking of the sacrament of the Eucharist; though He Himself teaches us that He is speaking of faith in the incarnate word, by saying: "This is the work of God, that ye believe in him whom He hath sent." But this Leipzig professor of the Bible must be permitted to prove whatever he pleases out of any passage of Scripture he pleases. For he is an Anaxagorean, nay, an Aristotelian theologian, to whom names and words when transposed mean the same things and everything. Throughout his whole book he so fits together the testimonies of Scripture, that, if he wishes to prove that Christ is in the sacrament, he ventures to begin thus: "The Lesson of the book of the Revelation of the blessed John." And as suitably as this would be said, so suitably does he say everything, and thinks, like a wise man, to adorn his ravings by the number of passages he brings forward.

I pass over the rest, that I may not quite kill you with the dregs of this most offensive drain. Lastly he adduces Paul (1 Cor. xi.), who says that he had received from the Lord and had delivered to the Corinthians the use both of the bread and of the cup. Here again, as everywhere else, our advocate of one species handles the Scriptures admirably, and teaches that in that passage Paul permitted—not "delivered"—the use of both kinds. Do you ask how he proves it? Out of his own head, as in the case of the sixth chapter of John; for it does not become this lecturer to give a reason for what he says, since he is one of those whose proofs and teachings all come from their own visions. Here then we are taught that the Apostle in that passage did not write to the whole church of Corinth, but only to the laity, and that therefore he gave no permission to the priests, but that they were deprived of the whole sacrament; and next, that, by a new rule of grammar, "I have received from the Lord" means the same thing as "It has been permitted by the Lord;" and "I delivered to you" the same thing as "I permitted to you." I beg you especially to note this. For it follows hence that not only the Church, but every worthless fellow anywhere will be at liberty, under the teaching of this master, to turn into permissions the whole body of the commandments, institutions, and ordinances of Christ and the Apostles.

I see that this man is possessed by an angel of Satan, and that those who act in collusion with him are seeking to obtain a name in the world through me, as being worthy to contend with Luther. But this hope of theirs shall be disappointed, and, in my contempt for them, I shall leave them for ever unnamed, and shall content myself with this one answer to the whole of their books. If they are worthy that Christ should bring them back to a sound mind, I pray him to do so in his mercy. If they are not worthy of this, then I pray that they may never cease to write such books, and that the enemies of the truth may not be permitted to read any others. It is a common and true saying: "This I know for certain, that if I fight with filth, whether I conquer or am conquered, I am sure to be defiled." In the next place, as I see that they have plenty of leisure and of paper, I will take care that they shall have abundant matter for writing, and will keep in advance of them, so that while they, in the boastfulness of victory, are triumphing over some one heresy of mine, as it seems to them, I shall meanwhile be setting up a new one. For I too am desirous that these illustrious leaders in war should be adorned with many titles of honour. And so, while they are murmuring that I approve of communion in both kinds, and are most successfully engaged on this very important subject, so worthy of themselves, I shall go farther, and shall now endeavour to show that all who deny to the laity communion in both kinds are acting impiously. To do this the more conveniently, I shall make a first essay on the bondage of the Church of Rome; with the intention of saying very much more in its own proper time, when those most learned papists shall have got the better of this book.

This, moreover, I do in order that no pious reader who may meet with my book may be disgusted at the dross I have handled, and have reason to complain that he finds nothing to read which can cultivate or instruct his mind, or at least give occasion for instructive reflection. You know how dissatisfied my friends are that I should occupy myself with the paltry twistings of these men. They say that the very reading of their books is an ample confutation of them, but that from me they look for better things, which Satan is trying to hinder by means of these men. I have determined to follow the advice of my friends, and to leave the business of wrangling and inveighing to those hornets.

Of the Italian friar of Cremona I shall say nothing. He is a simple and unlearned man, who is endeavouring to bring me back by some thongs of rhetoric to the Holy See, from which I am not conscious of having ever withdrawn, nor has any one proved that I have. His principal argument in some ridiculous passages is, that I ought to be moved for the sake of my profession, and of the transfer of the imperial power to the Germans. He seems indeed altogether to have meant not so much to urge my return as to write the praises of the French and of the Roman pontiff, and he must be allowed to testify his obsequiousness to them by this little work, such as it is. He neither deserves to be handled severely, since he does not seem to be actuated by any malice, nor to be learnedly confuted, since through pure ignorance and inexperience he trifles with the whole subject.

To begin. I must deny that there are seven Sacraments, and must lay it down, for the time being, that there are only three, baptism, penance, and the bread, and that by the Court of Rome all these have been brought into miserable bondage, and the Church despoiled of all her liberty. And yet, if I were to speak according to the usage of Scripture, I should hold that there was only one sacrament, and three sacramental signs. I shall speak on this point more at length at the proper time; but now I speak of the sacrament of the bread, the first of all sacraments.

I shall say then what advance I have made as the result of my meditations in the ministry of this sacrament. For at the time when I published a discourse on the Eucharist I was still involved in the common custom, and did not trouble myself either about the rightful or the wrongful power of the Pope. But now that I have been called forth and become practised in argument, nay, have been dragged by force into this arena, I shall speak out freely what I think. Let all the papists laugh or lament against me alone.

In the first place, the sixth chapter of John must be set aside altogether, as not saying a single syllable about the sacrament; not only because the sacrament had not yet been instituted, but much more because the very sequence of the discourse and of its statements shows clearly that Christ was speaking—as I have said before—of faith in the incarnate Word. For He says: "My words, they are spirit and they are life;" showing that He was speaking of that spiritual eating, wherewith he who eats, lives; while the Jews understood Him to speak of a carnal eating, and therefore raised a dispute. But no eating gives life, except the eating of faith, for this is the really spiritual and living eating; as Augustine says: "Why dost thou get ready thy stomach and thy teeth? Believe, and thou hast eaten." A sacramental eating does not give life, for many eat unworthily, so that Christ cannot be understood to have spoken of the sacrament in this passage.

There are certainly some who have misapplied these words to the sacrament, as did the writer of the decretals some time ago, and many others. It is one thing, however, to misapply the Scriptures, and another to take them in their legitimate sense; otherwise when Christ says: "Except ye eat my flesh, and drink my blood, ye have no life in you," He would be condemning all infants, all the sick, all the absent, and all who were hindered in whatever manner from a sacramental eating, however eminent their faith, if in these words He had meant to enjoin a sacramental eating. Thus Augustine, in his second book against Julianus, proves from Innocentius that even infants, without receiving the sacrament, eat the flesh and drink the blood of Christ; that is, partake in the same faith as the Church. Let this then be considered as settled, that the sixth chapter of John has nothing to do with the matter. For which reason I have written elsewhere that the Bohemians could not rightfully depend upon this passage in their defence of reception in both kinds.

CONCERNING THE LORD'S SUPPER

There are two passages which treat in the clearest manner of this subject, and at which we shall look,—the statements in the Gospels respecting the Lord's Supper, and the words of Paul. (1 Cor. xi.) Matthew, Mark, and Luke agree that Christ gave the whole sacrament to all His disciples; and that Paul taught both parts of it is so certain, that no one has yet been shameless enough to assert the contrary. Add to this, that according to the relation of Matthew, Christ did not say concerning the bread, "Eat ye all of this," but did say concerning the cup, "Drink ye all of this." Mark also does not say, "they all ate," but "they all drank of it." Each writer attaches the mark of universality to the cup, not to the bread; as if the Spirit foresaw the schism that should come, and should forbid to some that communion in the cup which Christ would have common to all. How furiously would they rave against us, if they had found the word "all" applied to the bread, and not to the cup. They would leave us no way of escape, would clamour us down, pronounce us heretics, condemn us as schismatics. But when the word stands on our side against them, they allow themselves to be bound by no laws of logic, these men of freest will, while they change, and change again, and throw into utter confusion even the things which are of God.

But suppose me to be standing on the other side and questioning my lords the papists. In the Supper of the Lord, the whole sacrament, or the sacrament in both kinds, was either given to the presbyters alone, or at the same time to the laity. If to the presbyters alone (for thus they will have it to be), then it is in no wise lawful that any kind should be given to the laity; for it ought not to be rashly given to any, to whom

Christ did not give it at the first institution. Otherwise, if we allow one of Christ's institutions to be changed, we make the whole body of His laws of no effect; and any man may venture to say that he is bound by no law or institution of Christ. For in dealing with Scripture one special exception does away with any general statement. If on the other hand it was given to the laity as well, it inevitably follows, that reception in both kinds ought not to be denied to the laity; and in denying it to them when they seek it, we act impiously, and contrary to the deed, example, and institution of Christ.

I confess that I have been unable to resist this reasoning, and have neither read, heard of, nor discovered anything to be said on the other side, while the words and example of Christ stand unshaken, who says—not by way of permission, but of commandment— "Drink ye all of this." For if all are to drink of it, and this cannot be understood as said to the presbyters alone, then it is certainly an impious deed to debar the laity from it when they seek it, were it even an angel from heaven who did so. For what they say of its being left to the decision of the Church which kind should be administered, is said without rational ground, is alleged without authority, and is as easily contemned as proved; nor can it avail against an adversary who opposes to us the word and deed of Christ, and whose blows must therefore be returned with the word of Christ; and this we have not on our side.

If, however, either kind can be denied to the laity, then by the same decision of the Church a part of baptism or of penance might be taken from them, since in each case the reason of the matter and the power are alike. Therefore as the whole of baptism and the whole of absolution are to be granted to all the laity, so is the whole sacrament of the bread, if they seek it. I am much astonished, however, at their assertion that it is wholly unlawful, under pain of mortal sin, for presbyters to receive only one kind in the mass; and this for no other reason than that (as they all unanimously say) the two kinds form one full sacrament, which ought not to be divided. Let them tell me, then, why it is lawful to divide it in the case of the laity, and why they alone should not be granted the entire sacrament. Do they not admit, on their own showing, that either both kinds ought to be granted to the laity, or that it is no lawful sacrament which is granted to them under one kind? How can the one kind be a full sacrament in the case of the laity, and not a full one in the case of the presbyters? Why do they vaunt the decision of the Church and the power of the Pope in this matter? The words of God and the testimonies of truth cannot thus be done away with.

It follows further that, if the Church can take from the laity the one kind, the wine, she can also take from them the other kind, the bread, and thus might take from the laity the whole Sacrament of the Altar, and deprive the institution of Christ of all effect in their case. But, I ask, by what authority? If, however, she cannot take away the bread, or both kinds, neither can she the wine. Nor can any possible argument on this point be brought against an opponent, since the Church must necessarily have the same power in regard to either kind as in regard to both kinds; if she has it not as regards both kinds, she has it not as regards either. I should like to hear what the flatterers of Rome may choose to say on this point.

But what strikes me most forcibly of all, and thoroughly convinces me, is that saying of Christ: "This is my blood, which is shed for you and for many, for the remission of sins." Here you see most clearly that the blood is given to all for whose sins it is shed. Now who will dare to say that it was not shed for the laity? Do you not see who it is that He addresses as He gives the cup? Does He not give it to all? Does He not say that it was shed for all? "For you," He says. Let us grant that these are priests. "And for many," He continues. These cannot be priests; and yet He says: "Drink ye all of it." I also could easily trifle on this point, and turn the words of Christ into a mockery by my words, as that trifler my opponent does. But those who rest upon the Scriptures in arguing against us, must be refuted by the Scriptures. These are the reasons which have kept me from condemning the Bohemians, who, whether they be good or bad men, certainly have the words and deeds of Christ on their side, while we have neither, but only that idle device of men: "The Church hath thus ordered it;" while it was not the Church, but the tyrants of the churches, without the consent of the Church, that is, of the people of God, who have thus ordered it.

Now where, I ask, is the necessity, where is the religious obligation, where is the use, of denying to the laity reception in both kinds, that is, the visible sign, when all men grant them the reality of the sacrament without the sign? If they grant the reality, which is the greater, why do they not grant the sign, which is the less? For in every sacrament the sign, in so far as it is a sign, is incomparably less than the reality itself. What then, I ask, should hinder the granting of the lesser thing, when the greater is granted; unless indeed, as it seems to me, this has happened by the permission of God in His anger, to be the occasion of a schism in the Church; and to show that, having long ago lost the reality of the sacrament, we are fighting on behalf of the sign, which is the lesser thing, against the reality, which is the greatest and only important thing; just as some persons fight on behalf of ceremonies against charity. This monstrous perversion appears to have begun at the same time at which we began in our folly to set Christian charity at nought for the sake of worldly riches, that God might show by this terrible proof that we think signs of greater consequence than the realities themselves. What perversity it would be, if you were to concede that the faith of baptism is granted to one seeking baptism, and yet deny him the sign of that very faith, namely, water.

Last of all stand the irrefutable words of Paul, which must close every mouth (1 Cor. xi.): "I have received of the Lord that which also I delivered unto you." He does not say, as this friar falsely asserts out of his own head, "I permitted to you." Nor is it true that he granted the Corinthians reception in both kinds on account of the contentions among them. In the first place, as the text itself shows, the contention was not about the reception in both kinds, but about the contemptuousness of the rich and the envy of the poor, as is clear from the text, which says: "One is hungry and another is drunken," and, "Ye shame them that have not." Then too he is not speaking of what he delivered as if it were for the first time. He does not say: "I receive from the Lord and I deliver to you," but "I have received and I have delivered," namely, at the beginning of his preaching, long before this contention arose, thus signifying that he had delivered to them the reception in both kinds. This "delivering" means "enjoining," as he elsewhere uses the same word. Thus the smoke clouds of assertion which this friar heaps together concerning permission, without Scripture, without reason, and without cause, go for nothing. His opponents do not ask what his dreams are, but what the judgment of Scripture is on these points; and out of it he can produce not a tittle in support of his dream, while they can bring forward so many thunderbolts in defence of their belief.

Rise up then in one body, all ye flatterers of the Pope, be active, defend yourselves from the charge of impiety, tyranny, and treason against the Gospel, and wrongful calumniation of your brethren, ye who proclaim as heretics those who cannot approve of the mere dreams of your brains, in opposition to such plain and powerful Scriptures. If either of the two are to be called heretics and schismatics, it is not the Bohemians, not the Greeks, since they take their stand on the Gospels; but you Romans who are heretics and impious schismatics, you who presume upon your own figments alone, against the manifest teaching of the Scriptures of God.

But what can be more ridiculous, or more worthy of the head of this friar, than to say that the Apostle wrote thus and gave this permission to a particular church, that of Corinth, but not to the universal Church? Whence does he prove this? Out of his usual store—his own impious head. When the universal Church takes this epistle as addressed to itself, reads it, and follows it in every respect, why not in this part of it? If we admit that any one epistle of Paul, or one passage in any one epistle, does not concern the universal Church, we do away with the whole authority of Paul. The Corinthians might say that what he taught concerning faith, in writing to the Romans, did not concern them. What could be more blasphemous or more mad than this mad idea? Far be it from us to imagine that there can be one tittle in the whole of Paul, which the whole of the universal Church ought not to imitate and keep. Not thus thought the Fathers, nor any until these perilous times, in which Paul foretold that there should be blasphemers, blind and senseless men; among whom this friar is one, or even the foremost.

But let us grant this intolerably wild assertion. If Paul gave permission to a particular church, then, on your own showing, the Greeks and the Bohemians are acting rightly, for they are particular churches, and therefore it is enough that they are not acting against the teaching of Paul, who at least gives them permission. Furthermore, Paul had not power to permit of anything contrary to the institution of Christ. Therefore, on behalf of the Greeks and the Bohemians, I set up these sayings of Christ and of Paul against thee, Rome, and all thy flatterers; nor canst thou show that power has been given thee to change these things by one hair's breadth; much less to accuse others of heresy, because they disregard thy presumptuous pretensions. It is thou who deservest to be accused of impiety and tyranny.

We also read the words of Cyprian, who by himself is powerful enough to stand against all the Romanists, and who testifies in his discourse concerning the lapsed in the fifth book, that it had been the custom in that church for both kinds to be administered to laymen and even to children; yea, for the body of the Lord to be given into their hands; as he shows by many instances. Among other things he thus reproves some of the people: "And because he does not immediately receive the body of the Lord with unclean hands, or drink the blood of the Lord with polluted mouth, he is angry with the priests as sacrilegious." You see that he is here speaking of certain sacrilegious laymen, who wished to receive from the priests the body and the blood. Have you here, wretched flatterer, anything to gabble? Say that this holy martyr, this teacher of the Church, so highly endowed with the apostolic spirit, was a heretic, and availed himself of a permission in his particular church!

He relates in the same place an incident which had occurred in his own sight and presence, when he writes in the plainest terms that as deacon he had given the cup to an infant girl, and when the child struggled against it, had even poured the blood of the Lord into its mouth. We read the same thing of St. Donatus, whose broken cup how dully does this wretched flatterer try to get rid of. "I read," he says, "that the cup was broken, I do not read that the blood was given." What wonder that he who perceives in the Holy Scriptures what he wills to perceive, should also read in historical narratives what he wills to read! But can he in this way at all establish the power of the Church to decide, or can he thus confute heretics? But enough said on this subject; for I did not begin this treatise in order to answer one who is unworthy of an answer, but in order to lay open the truth of the matter.

I conclude, then, that to deny reception in both kinds to the laity is an act of impiety and tyranny, and one not in the power of any angel, much less of any Pope or Council whatever. Nor do I care for the Council of Constance, for, if its authority is to prevail, why should not also that of the Council of Basle, which decreed on the other hand that the Bohemians should be allowed to receive in both kinds? a point which was carried there after long discussion, as the extant annals and documents of that Council prove. This fact that ignorant flatterer brings forward on behalf of his own dreams, so wisely does he handle the whole matter.

The first bondage, then, of this sacrament is as regards its substance or completeness, which the tyranny of Rome has wrested from us. Not that they sin against Christ, who use one kind only, since Christ has not commanded the use of any, but has left it to the choice of each individual, saying: "This do ye, as oft as ye shall do it, in remembrance of me;" but they sin who forbid that both kinds should be given to those who desire to use this freedom of choice, and the fault is not in the laity, but in the priests. The sacrament does not belong to the priests, but to all; nor are the priests lords, but servants, whose duty it is to give both kinds to those who seek them, as often as they seek them. If they have snatched this right from the laity, and forcibly denied it to them, they are tyrants, and the laity are free from blame, whether they go without one or both kinds; for meanwhile they will be saved by their faith, and by their desire for a complete sacrament. So too the ministers themselves are bound to grant baptism and absolution to him who seeks them; if they do not grant them, the seeker has the full merit of his own faith, while they will be accused before Christ as wicked servants. Thus of old the holy Fathers in the desert passed many years without communicating in either kind of the sacrament.

I am not, therefore, advocating the seizing by force on both kinds, as if we were of necessity commanded and compelled to receive them, but I am instructing the conscience, that every man may endure the tyranny of Rome, knowing that he has been forcibly deprived of his right in the sacrament on account of his sins. This only I would have, that none should justify the tyranny of Rome, as if she had done right in denying one kind to the laity, but that we should abhor it, and withhold our consent from it, though we may bear it, just as if we were in bondage with the Turk, where we should not be at liberty to use either kind. For this reason I have said that it would be a fine thing, in my opinion, if this bondage were done away with by the decree of a general council, and Christian liberty restored to us out of the hands of the tyrant of Rome; and if to each man were left his own free choice about seeking and using it, as it is left in the case of baptism and penance. Now, however, by the same tyranny, he compels one kind to be received year by year; so extinct is the liberty granted us by Christ, and such are the deserts of our impious ingratitude.

The other bondage of the same sacrament is a milder one, inasmuch as it regards the conscience, but one which it is by far the most perilous of all things to touch, much more to condemn. Here I shall be a Wickliffite, and a heretic under six hundred names. What then? Since the Bishop of Rome has ceased to be a bishop and has become a tyrant, I fear absolutely none of his decrees, since I know that neither he, nor even a general council, has power to establish new articles of the faith.

Formerly, when I was imbibing the scholastic theology, my lord the Cardinal of Cambray gave me occasion for reflection, by arguing most acutely, in the fourth book of the Sentences, that it would be much more probable, and that fewer superfluous miracles would have to be introduced, if real bread and real wine, and not only their accidents, were understood to be upon the altar, unless the Church had determined the contrary.

Afterwards, when I saw what the church was, which had thus determined, namely, the Thomistic, that is, the Aristotelian Church, I became bolder, and whereas I had been before in great straits of doubt, I now at length established my conscience in the former opinion, namely, that there were real bread and real wine, in which were the real flesh and real blood of Christ, in no other manner and in no less degree than the other party assert them to be under the accidents. And this I did, because I saw that the opinions of the Thomists, whether approved by the Pope or by a council, remained opinions, and did not become articles of the faith, even were an angel from heaven to decree otherwise. For that which is asserted without the support of the Scriptures, or of an approved revelation, it is permitted to hold as an opinion, but it is not necessary to believe. Now this opinion of Thomas is so vague, and so unsupported by the Scriptures, or by reason, that he seems to me to have known neither his philosophy nor his logic. For Aristotle speaks of accidents and subject very differently from St. Thomas; and it seems to me that we ought to be sorry for so great a man, when we see him striving, not only to draw his opinions on matters of faith from Aristotle, but to establish them upon an authority whom he did not understand; a most unfortunate structure raised on a most unfortunate foundation.

I quite consent then that whoever chooses to hold either opinion should do so. My only object now is to remove scruples of conscience, so that no man may fear being guilty of heresy, if he believes that real bread and real wine are present on the altar. Let him know that he is at liberty, without peril to his salvation, to imagine, think, or believe in either of the two ways, since here there is no necessity of faith. In the first place, I will not listen to those, or make the slightest account of them, who will cry out that this doctrine is Wickliffite, Hussite, heretical, and opposed to the decisions of the Church. None will do this but those whom I have convicted of being themselves in many ways heretical, in the matter of indulgences, of free will and the grace of God, of good works and sins, etc. If Wickliff was once a heretic, they are themselves ten times heretics, and it is an excellent thing to be blamed and accused by heretics and perverse sophists, since to please them would be the height of impiety. Besides, they can give no other proof of their own opinions, nor have they any other way of disproving the contrary ones, than by saying: "This is Wickliffite, Hussite, heretical." This feeble argument, and no other, is always at the tip of their tongue; and if you ask for Scripture authority, they say: "This is our opinion, and the Church has decided it thus." To such an extent do men who are reprobate concerning the faith, and unworthy of belief, dare to propose to us their own fancies, under the authority of the Church, as articles of the faith.

There is, however, very much to be said for my opinion; in the first place this—that no violence ought to be done to the words of God, neither by man, nor by angel, but that, as far as possible, they ought to be kept to their simplest meaning, and not to be taken, unless the circumstances manifestly compel us to do so, out of their grammatical and proper signification, that we may not give our adversaries any opportunity of evading the teaching of the whole Scriptures. For this reason the ideas of Origen were rightly rejected, when, in contempt of the plain grammatical meaning, he turned the trees, and all other objects described as existing in Paradise, into allegories; since hence it might be inferred that trees were not created by God. So in the present case, since the Evangelists write clearly that Christ took bread and blessed it, and since the book of Acts and the Apostle Paul also call it bread, real bread and real wine must be understood, just as the cup was real. For even these men do not say that the cup is transubstantiated. Since then it is not necessary to lay it down that a transubstantiation is effected by the operation of divine power, it must be held as a figment of human opinion; for it rests on no support of

Scripture or of reason. It is forcing on us a novel and absurd usage of words, to take bread as meaning the form or accidents of bread, and wine as the form or accidents of wine. Why do they not take all other things as forms or accidents? Even if everything else were consistent with this idea, it would not be lawful thus to enfeeble the word of God, and to deprive it so unjustly of its proper meaning.

The Church, however, kept the right faith for more than twelve centuries, nor did the holy Fathers ever or anywhere make mention of this transubstantiation (a portentous word and dream indeed), until the counterfeit Aristotelian philosophy began to make its inroads on the Church within these last three hundred years, during which many other erroneous conclusions have also been arrived at, such as:—that the Divine essence is neither generated nor generates; that the soul is the substantial form of the human body; and other like assertions, which are made absolutely without reason or cause, as the Cardinal of Cambray himself confesses.

They will say, perhaps, that we shall be in peril of idolatry if we do not admit that bread and wine are not really there. This is truly ridiculous, for the laity have never learnt the subtle philosophical distinction between substance and accidents; nor, if they were taught it, could they understand it; and there is the same peril, if we keep the accidents, which they see, as in the case of the substance, which they do not see. For if it is not the accidents which they adore, but Christ concealed under them, why should they adore the substance, which they do not see?

But why should not Christ be able to include His body within the substance of bread, as well as within the accidents? Fire and iron, two different substances, are so mingled in redhot iron, that every part of it is both fire and iron. Why may not the glorious body of Christ much more be in every part of the substance of the bread?

Christ is believed to have been born of the inviolate womb of his mother. In this case too let them say that the flesh of the Virgin was for a time annihilated; or, as they will have it to be more suitably expressed, transubstantiated, that Christ might be enwrapped in its accidents, and at length come forth through its accidents. The same will have to be said respecting the closed door and the closed entrance of the tomb, through both of which He entered, and went out without injury to them. But hence has sprung that Babylon of a philosophy concerning continuous quantity, distinct from substance, till things have come to such a point, that they themselves do not know what are accidents, and what is substance. For who has ever proved to a certainty that heat and cold, colour, light, weight, and form are accidents? Lastly they have been driven to pretend that God creates a new substance additional to those accidents on the altar, on account of the saying of Aristotle, that the essence of an accident is to be in something; and have been led to an infinity of monstrous ideas, from all of which they would be free, if they simply allowed the bread on the altar to be real bread. I rejoice greatly, that at least among the common people there remains a simple faith in this sacrament. They neither understand nor argue whether there are accidents in it or substance, but believe with simple faith that the body and blood of Christ are truly contained in it, leaving to these men of leisure the task of arguing as to what it contains.

But perhaps they will say that we are taught by Aristotle that we must take the subject and predicate of an affirmative proposition to signify the same thing; or, to quote the words of that monster himself in the 6th book of his Metaphysics, "An affirmative proposition requires the composition of the extremes;" which they explain as their signifying the same thing. Thus in the words, "This is my body," they say that we cannot take the subject to signify the bread, but the body of Christ.

What shall we say to this? Whereas we are making Aristotle and human teachings the censors of such sublime and divine matters, why do we not rather cast away these curious enquiries; and simply adhere to the words of Christ, willing to be ignorant of what is done in this sacrament, and content to know that the real body of Christ is present in it by virtue of the words of consecration? Is it necessary to comprehend altogether the manner of the Divine working?

But what do they say to Aristotle, who applies the term "subject" to all the categories of accidents, although he takes the substance to be the first subject? Thus, in his opinion, "this white," "this great," "this something," are subjects, because something is predicated of them. If this is true, and if it is necessary to lay down a doctrine of transubstantiation in order that it may not be asserted of the bread that it is the body of Christ; why, I ask, is not a doctrine of transaccidentation also laid down, that it may not be affirmed of an accident that it is the body of Christ? For the same danger remains, if we regard "this white thing," or "this round thing" as the subject. On whatever principle transubstantiation is taught, on the same ought transaccidentation to be taught, on account of the two terms of the proposition, as is alleged, signifying the same thing.

If, however, by a high effort of understanding, you make abstraction of the accident, and refuse to regard it as signified by the subject in saying: "This is my body," why can you not as easily rise above the substance of the bread, and refuse to let it be understood as signified by the subject; so that "this is my body" may be true in the substance no less than in the accident? Especially so since this is a divine work of almighty power, which can operate to the same extent and in the same way in the substance, as it can in the accident.

But, not to philosophize too far, does not Christ appear to have met these curious enquiries in a striking manner, when He said concerning the wine, not, "*Hoc est sanguis meus*," but "*Hic est sanguis meus*." He speaks much more clearly still when He brings in the mention of the cup, saying: "This cup is the New Testament in my blood." (1 Cor. xi.) Does He not seem to have meant to keep us within the bounds of simple faith, just so far as to believe that His blood is in the cup? If, for my part, I cannot understand how the bread can be the body of Christ, I will bring my understanding into captivity to the obedience of Christ, and firmly believe, in simple adherence to His word, not only that the body of Christ is in the bread, but that the bread is the body of Christ. For so shall I be kept safe by his words, where it is said: "Jesus took bread, and blessed it, and brake it, and said, Take, eat, this (that is, this bread, which He had taken and broken) is my body." Paul also says: "The bread which we break, is it not the communion of the body of Christ?" He does not say that the communion is in the bread, but that the bread itself is the communion of the body of Christ. What if philosophy does not understand these things? The Holy Spirit is greater than Aristotle. Does it even understand the transubstantiation which these men speak of, seeing that they themselves confess that all philosophy breaks down on this point? The reason why, in the Greek and Latin, the pronoun *this* is referred to the body, is that the genders are alike; but in the Hebrew, where there is no neuter gender, it is referred to the bread; so that we might properly say: "This (bread) is my body." Both the usage of language and common sense prove that the subject points to the bread, and not to the body, when He says, *Hoc est corpus meum*, that is, this bread is my body.

As then the case is with Christ Himself, so is it also with the sacrament. For it is not necessary to the bodily indwelling of the Godhead that the human nature should be transubstantiated, that so the Godhead may be contained beneath the accidents of the human nature. But each nature is entire, and we can say with truth: This man is God; this God is man. Though philosophy does not receive this, yet faith receives it, and greater is the authority of the word of God, than the capacity of our intellect. Thus too in the sacrament, it is not necessary to the presence of the real body and real blood, that the bread and wine should be transubstantiated, so that Christ may be contained beneath the accidents; but while both bread and wine continue there, it can be said with truth, "this bread is my body, this wine is my blood," and conversely. Thus will I understand this matter in honour of the holy words of God, which I will not allow to have violence done them by the petty reasonings of men, or to be distorted into meanings alien to them. I give leave, however, to others to follow the other opinion, which is distinctly laid down in the decretal, provided only (as I have said) they do not press us to accept their opinions as articles of faith.

The third bondage of this same sacrament is that abuse of it—and by far the most impious—by which it has come about that at this day there is no belief in the Church more generally received or more firmly held than that the mass is a good work and a sacrifice. This abuse has brought in an infinite flood of other abuses, until faith in the sacrament has been utterly lost, and they have made this divine sacrament a mere subject of traffic, huckstering, and money-getting contracts. Hence communions, brotherhoods, suffrages, merits, anniversaries, memorials, and other things of that kind are bought and sold in the Church, and made the subjects of bargains and agreements; and the entire maintenance of priests and monks depends upon these things.

I am entering on an arduous task, and it may perhaps be impossible to uproot an abuse which, strengthened by the practice of so many ages, and approved by universal consent, has fixed itself so firmly among us, that the greater part of the books which have influence at the present day must needs be done away with, and almost the entire aspect of the churches be changed, and a totally different kind of ceremonies be brought in, or rather, brought back. But my Christ lives, and we must take heed to the word of God with greater care, than to all the intellects of men and angels. I will perform my part, will bring forth the subject into the light, and will impart the truth freely and ungrudgingly as I have received it. For the rest, let every one look to his own salvation; I will strive, as in the presence of Christ my judge, that no man may be able to throw upon me the blame of his own unbelief and ignorance of the truth.

Concerning the Sacrament of the Altar. To begin,—if we wish to attain safely and prosperously to the true and free knowledge of this sacrament, we must take the utmost care to put aside all that has been added by the zeal or the notions of men to the primitive and simple institution; such as vestments, ornaments, hymns, prayers, musical instruments, lamps, and all the pomp of visible things; and must turn our eyes and our attention only to the pure institution of Christ; and set nothing else before us but those very words of Christ, with which He instituted and perfected that sacrament, and committed it to us. In that word, and absolutely in nothing else, lies the whole force, nature, and substance of the mass. All the rest are human notions, accessory to the word of Christ; and the mass can perfectly well subsist and be kept up without them. Now the words in which Christ instituted this sacrament are as follows:—While they were at supper Jesus took bread, and blessed it, and brake it, and gave it to His disciples, and said: "Take, eat; this is my body which is given for you." And He took the cup, and gave thanks, and gave it to them, saying: "Drink ye all of this; this cup is the New Testament in my blood, which is shed for you and for many for the remission of sins; do this in remembrance of me."

These words the Apostle Paul (1 Cor. xi.) also delivers to us and explains at greater length. On these we must rest, and build ourselves up as on a firm rock, unless we wish to be carried about with every wind of doctrine, as we have hitherto been, through the impious teachings of men who pervert the truth. For in these words nothing has been omitted which pertains to the completeness, use, and profit of this sacrament; and nothing laid down which it is superfluous or unnecessary for us to know. He who passes over these words in his meditations or teachings concerning the mass will teach monstrous impieties; as has been done by those who have made an opus *operatum* and a sacrifice of it.

Let this then stand as a first and infallible truth, that the mass or Sacrament of the Altar is the testament of Christ, which He left behind Him at His death, distributing an inheritance to those who believe in Him. For such are His words: "This cup is the new testament in my blood." Let this truth, I say, stand as an immovable foundation, on which we shall erect all our arguments. You will see how we shall thus overthrow all the impious attacks of men on this sweetest sacrament. The truthful Christ, then, says with truth, that this is the new testament in His blood, shed for us. It is not without cause that I urge this; the matter is no small one, but must be received into the depths of our minds.

If then we enquire what a testament is, we shall also learn what the mass is; what are its uses, advantages, abuses. A testament is certainly a promise made by a man about to die, by which he assigns his inheritance and appoints heirs. Thus the idea of a testament implies, first, the death of the testator, and secondly, the promise of the inheritance, and the appointment of an heir. In this way Paul (Rom. iv.; Gal. iii., iv.; Heb. ix.) speaks at some length of testaments. We also see this clearly in those words of Christ. Christ testifies of His own death, when He says: "This is my body which is given; this is my blood which is shed." He assigns and points out the inheritance, when He says: "For the remission of sins." And He appoints heirs when He says: "For you and for many;" that is, for those who accept and believe the promise of the testator; for it is faith which makes us heirs, as we shall see.

You see then that the mass—as we call it—is a promise of the remission of sins, made to us by God; and such a promise as has been confirmed by the death of the Son of God. For a promise and a testament only differ in this, that a testament implies the death of the promiser. A testator is a promiser who is about to die; and a promiser is, so to speak, a testator who is about to live. This testament of Christ was prefigured in all the promises of God from the beginning of the world; yea! whatsoever value the ancient promises had, lay in that new promise which was about to be made in Christ, and on which they depended. Hence the words, "agreement, covenant, testament of the Lord," are constantly employed in the Scriptures; and by these it was implied that God was about to die. "For where a testament is, there must also of necessity be the death of the testator." (Heb. ix. 16.) God having made a testament, it was necessary that He should die. Now He could not die, unless He became a man; and thus in this one word "testament" the incarnation and the death of Christ are both comprehended.

From all this it is now self-evident what is the use, and what the abuse, of the mass; what is a worthy or an unworthy preparation for it. If the mass is a promise, as we have said, we can approach to it by no works, no strength, no merits, but by faith alone. For where we have the word of God who promises, there we must have faith on the part of man who accepts; and it is thus clear that the beginning of our salvation is faith, depending on the word of a promising God, who, independently of any efforts of ours, prevents us by His free and undeserved mercy, and holds out to us the word of His promise. "He sent His word and healed them." (Ps. cvii. 20.) He did not receive our works and so save us. First of all comes the word of God; this is followed by faith, and faith by love, which in its turn does every good work, because it worketh no evil, yea, it is the fulfilling of the law. There is no other way in which man can meet or deal with God but by faith. It is not man by any works of his, but God, who by His own promise is the author of salvation; so that everything depends, is contained, and preserved in the word of His power, by which He begot us, that we might be a kind of first-fruits of His creation.

Thus, when Adam was to be raised up after the fall, God gave him a promise, saying to the serpent: "I will place enmity between thee and the woman, and between thy seed and her seed; she shall bruise thy head, and thou shalt bruise her heel." In this word of promise, Adam with his posterity was, as it were, borne in the bosom of God, and preserved by faith in Him; waiting patiently for the woman who should bruise the head of the serpent, as God had promised. In this faith and waiting he died; not knowing when and how the promise would be accomplished, but not doubting that it would be accomplished. For such a promise, being the truth of God, preserves even in hell those who believe and wait for it. This promise was followed by another, made to Noah; the bow in the cloud being given as a sign of the covenant, believing in which he and his posterity found God propitious. After this, God promised to Abraham that in his seed all the kindreds of the earth should be blessed. This is that bosom of Abraham into which his posterity have been received. Lastly to Moses, and to the children of Israel, especially to David, God gave a most distinct promise of Christ; and thus at length revealed what had been the meaning of the promise made to them of old time.

Thus we come to the most perfect promise of all, that of the new Testament, in which life and salvation are freely promised in plain words, and are bestowed on those who believe the promise. Christ conspicuously distinguishes this testament from the old one, by calling it the "New Testament." The old testament given by Moses was a promise, not of remission of sins, nor of eternal blessings, but of temporal ones, namely, those of the land of Canaan; and by it no one could be renewed in spirit, and fitted to receive a heavenly inheritance. Hence it was necessary that, as a figure of Christ, an unreasoning lamb should be slain, in the blood of which the same testament was confirmed; thus, as is the blood, so is the testament; as is the victim, so is the promise. Now Christ says, "The new testament in my blood," not in another's, but in His own blood, by which grace is promised through the Spirit for the remission of sins, that we may receive the inheritance.

The mass then, as regards its substance, is properly nothing else than the aforesaid words of Christ, "Take, eat," etc. He seems to say:—"Behold, O man, sinner and condemned as thou art, out of the pure and free love with which I love thee, according to the will of the Father of mercies, I promise to thee in these words, antecedently to any merits or prayers of thine, remission of all thy sins, and eternal life. That thou mayest be most certain of this, my irrevocable promise, I will confirm it by my very death; I will give my body and shed my blood, and will leave both to thee, as a sign and memorial of this very promise. As often as thou shalt receive them, remember me; declare and praise my love and bounty to thee; and give thanks."

From this you see that nothing else is required for a worthy reception of the mass than faith, resting with confidence on this promise, believing Christ to be truthful in these words of His, and not doubting that these immeasurable blessings have been bestowed upon us. On this faith a spontaneous and most sweet affection of the heart will speedily follow, by which the spirit of the man is enlarged and enriched; that is, love, bestowed through the Holy Spirit on believers in Christ. Thus the believer is carried away to Christ, that bounteous and beneficent testator, and becomes altogether another and a new man. Who would not weep tears of delight, nay, almost die for joy in Christ, if he believed with unhesitating faith that this inestimable promise of Christ belongs to him? How can he fail to love such a benefactor, who of His own accord offers, promises, and gives the greatest riches and an eternal inheritance to an unworthy sinner, who has deserved very different treatment?

Our one great misery is this, that while we have many masses in the world, few or none of us recognise, consider, or apprehend the rich promises set before us in them. Now in the mass the one thing that demands our greatest, nay, our sole attention, is to keep these words and promises of Christ, which indeed constitute the mass itself, constantly before our eyes; that we should meditate on and digest them, and exercise, nourish, increase, and strengthen our faith in them by this daily commemoration. This is what Christ commands when He says, "Do this in remembrance of me." It is the work of an evangelist faithfully to present and commend that promise to the people and to call forth faith in it on their part. As it is—to say nothing of the impious fables of those who teach human traditions in the place of this great promise—how many are there who know that the mass is a promise of Christ? Even if they teach these words of Christ, they do not teach them as conveying a promise or a testament, and therefore call forth no faith in them.

It is a deplorable thing in our present bondage, that nowadays the utmost care is taken that no layman should hear those words of Christ, as if they were too sacred to be committed to the common people. We priests are so mad that we arrogate to ourselves alone the right of secretly uttering the words of consecration—as they are called; and that in a way which is unprofitable even to ourselves, since we never look at them as promises or a testament for the increase of faith. Under the influence of some superstitious and impious notion we do reverence to these words instead of believing them. In this our misery Satan so works among us that, while he has left nothing of the mass to the Church, he yet takes care that every corner of the earth shall be full of masses, that is, of abuses and mockeries of the testament of God; and that the world shall be more and more heavily loaded with the gravest sins of idolatry, to increase its greater damnation. For what more grievous sin of idolatry can there be, than to abuse the promises of God by our perverse notions, and either neglect or extinguish all faith in them.

God (as I have said) never has dealt, or does deal, with men otherwise than by the word of promise. Again, we can never deal with God otherwise than by faith in the word of His promise. He takes no heed of our works, and has no need of them,—though it is by these we deal with other men and with ourselves;—but He does require to be esteemed by us truthful in His promises, and to be patiently considered as such, and thus worshipped in faith, hope, and love. And thus it is that He is glorified in us, when we receive and hold every blessing not by our own efforts, but from His mercy, promise, and gift. This is that true worship and service of God, which we are bound to render in the mass. But when the words of the promise are not delivered to us, what exercise of faith can there be? And without faith who can hope? who can love? without faith, hope, and love, what service can there be? There is no doubt therefore that, at the present day, the whole body of priests and monks, with their bishops and all their superiors, are idolaters, and living in a most perilous state, through their ignorance, abuse, and mockery of the mass, or sacrament, or promise of God.

It is easy for any one to understand that two things are necessary at the same time, the promise and faith. Without a promise we have nothing to believe; while without faith the promise is useless, since it is through faith that it is established and fulfilled. Whence we easily conclude that the mass, being nothing else than a promise, can be approached and partaken of by faith alone; without which whatever prayers, preparations, works, signs, or gestures are practised, are rather provocations to impiety than acts of piety. It constantly happens that when men have given their attention to all these things they imagine that they are approaching the altar lawfully; and yet, in reality, could never be more unfit to approach it, because of the unbelief which they bring with them. What a number of sacrificing priests you may daily see everywhere, who if they have committed some trifling error, by unsuitable vestments, or unwashed hands, or by some hesitation in the prayers, are wretched, and think themselves guilty of an immense crime! Meanwhile, as for the mass itself, that is, the divine promise, they neither heed nor believe it; yea, are utterly unconscious of its existence. O, unworthy religion of our age, the most impious and ungrateful of all ages!

There is then no worthy preparation for the mass, or rightful use of it, except faith, by which it is believed in as a divine promise. Wherefore let him who is about to approach the altar, or to receive the sacrament, take care not to appear before the Lord his God empty. Now he will be empty, if he has not faith in the mass, or New Testament; and what more grievous impiety can he commit against the truth of God than by this unbelief? As far as in him lies, he makes God a liar, and renders His promises idle. It will be safest then to go to the mass in no other spirit than that in which thou wouldst go to hear any other promise of God; that is, to be prepared, not to do many works, and bring many gifts, but to believe and receive all that is promised thee in that ordinance, or is declared to thee through the ministry of the priest as promised. Unless thou comest in this spirit, beware of drawing near; for thou wilt surely draw near unto judgment.

I have rightly said then, that the whole virtue of the mass consists in those words of Christ, in which He testifies that remission is granted to all who believe that His body is given and His blood shed for them. There is nothing then more necessary for those who are about to hear mass than to meditate earnestly and with full faith on the very words of Christ; for unless they do this, all else is done in vain. It is certainly true that God has ever been wont, in all His promises, to give some sign, token, or memorial of His promise; that it might be kept more faithfully and tell more strongly on men's minds. Thus when He promised to Noah that the earth should not be destroyed by another deluge, He gave His bow in the cloud, and said that He would thus remember His covenant. To Abraham, when He promised that his seed should inherit the earth, He gave circumcision as a seal of the righteousness which is by faith. Thus to Gideon He gave the dry and the dewy fleece, to confirm His promise of victory over the Midianites. Thus to Ahaz He gave a sign through Isaiah, to confirm his faith in the promise of victory over the kings of Syria and Samaria. We read in the Scriptures of many such signs of the promises of God.

So too in the mass, that first of all promises, He gave a sign in memory of so great a promise, namely, His own body and His own blood in the bread and wine, saying, "Do this in remembrance of me." Thus in baptism He adds to the words of the promise the sign of immersion in water. Whence we see that in every promise of God two things are set before us, the word and the sign. The word we are to understand as being the testament, and the sign as being the sacrament; thus, in the mass, the word of Christ is the testament, the bread and wine are the sacrament. And as there is greater power in the word than in the sign, so is there greater power in the testament than in the sacrament. A man can have and use the word or testament without the sign or sacrament. "Believe," saith Augustine, "and thou hast eaten;" but in what do we believe except in the word of Him who promises? Thus I can have the mass daily, nay hourly; since, as often as I will, I can set before myself the words of Christ, and nourish and strengthen my faith in them; and this is in very truth the spiritual eating and drinking.

Here we see how much the theologians of the Sentences have done for us in this matter. In the first place, not one of them handles that which is the sum and substance of the whole, namely, the testament and word of promise; and thus they do away with faith and the whole virtue of the mass. In the next place, the other part of it, namely, the sign or sacrament, is all that they deal with; but they do not teach faith even in this, but their own preparations, *opera operata*, participations and fruits of the mass. At length they have reached the very depth of error, and have involved themselves in an infinity of metaphysical triflings concerning transubstantiation and other points; so that they have done away with all faith, and with the knowledge and true use as well of the testament as of the sacrament; and have caused the people of Christ—as the prophet says—to forget their God for many days. But do thou leave others to recount the various fruits of hearing mass, and apply thy mind to saying and believing with the prophet, that God has prepared a table before thee in the presence of thine enemies—a table at which thy faith may feed and grow strong. Now it is only on the word of the divine promise that thy faith can feed; for man shall not live by bread alone, but by every word that proceedeth out of the mouth of God. (Matt. iv. 4.) Wherefore, in the mass, thou must look above all things most closely to the word of promise as to a most sumptuous banquet, full of every kind of food and holy nourishment for thy soul; this thou must esteem above all things; in this thou must place all thy trust, and cleave firmly to it, even in the midst of death and all thy sins. If thou dost this, thou wilt possess not only those drops as it were and littlenesses of the fruits of the mass, which some have superstitiously invented, but the main fount of life itself, namely, that faith in the word from which every good thing flows; as Christ said, "He that believeth on me, out of his belly shall flow rivers of living water." (John vii. 38); and again, "Whosoever drinketh of the water that I shall give him shall never thirst; but the water that I shall give him, shall be in him a well of water springing up into everlasting life." (John iv. 14.)

There are two difficulties which are wont to beset us, and prevent our receiving the benefits of the mass. The one is, that we are sinners and unworthy, from our utter vileness, of such great blessings. The other is—even if we were worthy—the very greatness of the blessings themselves, which are such that weak nature cannot dare to seek or hope for them. Who would not be struck in the first place with amazement rather than with the desire for the remission of sins and eternal life, if he rightly estimates the greatness of the blessings which come through these—namely, the having God as his Father, and being a child of God, and heir of all good things? To meet this double weakness of nature, thou must take hold of the word of Christ, and fix thine eyes much more strongly on it, than on these cogitations of thine own infirmity. For the works of the Lord are great, and He is mighty to give, beyond all that we can seek or comprehend. Indeed, unless His works surpassed our worthiness, our capacity, our whole comprehension, they would not be divine. Thus too Christ encourages us, saying: "Fear not, little flock; for it is your Father's good pleasure to give you the kingdom." (Luke xii. 32.) This incomprehensible exuberance of God's mercy, poured out on us through Christ, makes us, in our turn, to love Him above all things, to cast ourselves upon Him with the most perfect trust, to despise all things, and be ready to suffer all things for Him. Hence this sacrament has been rightly called the fountain of love.

Here we may draw an example from human affairs. If some very rich lord were to bequeath a thousand pieces of gold to any beggar, or even to an unworthy and bad servant, such a one would certainly demand and receive them confidently, without regard either to his own unworthiness or to the greatness of the legacy. If any one were to set these before him as objections, what do you think he would reply? He would certainly answer: "What is that to you? It is not by my deserving, nor by any right of my own, that I receive what I do receive. I know that I am unworthy of it, and that I am receiving much more than I deserve; nay, I have deserved the very contrary. But what I claim, I claim by right of a testament, and of the goodness of another; if it was not an unworthy act to leave such a legacy to me who am so unworthy, why should my unworthiness make me hesitate to accept it? Nay, the more unworthy I am, the more readily do I embrace this free favour from another." With such reasonings we must arm our own consciences against all their scruples and anxieties, that we may hold this promise of Christ with unhesitating faith. We must give the utmost heed not to approach in any confidence in our own confessions, prayers, and preparations; we must despair of all these and come in a lofty confidence in the promise of Christ—since it is the word of promise which alone must reign here—and in pure faith, which is the one and sole sufficient preparation.

We see from all this, how great the wrath of God has been which has permitted our impious teachers to conceal from us the words of this testament, and thus, as far as in them lay, to extinguish faith itself. It is self-evident what must necessarily follow this extinction of faith, namely, the most impious superstitions about works. For when faith perishes and the word of faith is silent, then straightway works, and traditions of works, rise up in its place. By these we have been removed from our own land, as into bondage at Babylon, and all that was dear to us has been taken from us. Even thus it has befallen us with the mass, which, through the teaching of wicked men, has been changed into a good work, which they call *opus operatum*, and by which they imagine that they are all powerful with God. Hence they have gone to the extreme of madness; and, having first falsely affirmed that the mass is of avail through the force of the opus operatum, they have gone on to say, that even if it be hurtful to him who offers it impiously, yet it is none the less useful to others. On this basis they have established their applications, participations, fraternities, anniversaries, and an infinity of lucrative and gainful business of that kind.

You will scarcely be able to stand against these errors, many and strong as they are, and deeply as they have penetrated, unless you fix what has been said firmly in your memory, and give the most stedfast heed to the true nature of the mass. You have heard that the mass is nothing else than the divine promise or testament of Christ, commended to us by the sacrament of His body and blood. If this is true, you will see that it cannot in any way be a work, nor can any work be performed in it, nor can it be handled in any way but by faith alone. Now faith is not a work, but the mistress and life of all works. Is there any man so senseless as to call a promise he has received, or a legacy that has been bestowed on him, a good work done on his part towards the testator? What heir is there, who thinks that he is doing a service to his father when he receives the testamentary documents along with the inheritance bequeathed to him? Whence then this impious rashness of ours, that we come to receive the testament of God as if we were doing a good work towards Him? Is not such ignorance of that testament, and such a state of bondage of that great sacrament, a grief beyond all tears? Where we ought to be grateful for blessings bestowed on us, we come in our pride to give what we ought to receive, and make a mockery, with unheard-of perversity, of the mercy of the Giver. We give to Him as a work of ours what we receive as a gift from Him; and we thus make the testator no longer the bestower of His good gifts on us, but the receiver of ours. Alas for such impiety!

Who has ever been so senseless as to consider baptism a good work? What candidate for baptism has ever believed he was doing a work which he might offer to God on behalf of himself and others? If then in one sacrament and testament there is no good work communicable to others, neither can there be any in the mass, which is itself nothing but a testament and a sacrament. Hence it is a manifest and impious error, to offer or apply the mass for sins, for satisfactions, for the dead, or for any necessities of our own or of others. The evident truth of this statement you will easily understand, if you keep closely to the fact, that the mass is a divine promise, which can profit no one, be applied to no one, be communicated to no one, except to the believer himself; and that solely by his own faith. Who can possibly receive or apply for another a promise of God, which requires faith on the part of each individual? Can I give another man the promise of God, if he does not believe it? or can I believe for another man? or can I make another believe? Yet all this I must be able to do if I can apply and communicate the mass to others; for there are in the mass only these two things, God's promise, and man's faith which receives that promise. If I can do all this, I can also hear and believe the gospel on behalf of other men, I can be baptized for another man, I can be absolved from sin for another man, I can partake of the Sacrament of the Altar for another man; nay, to go through the whole list of their sacraments, I can also marry for another man, be ordained priest for another man, be confirmed for another man, receive extreme unction for another man.

Why did not Abraham believe on behalf of all the Jews? Why was every individual Jew required to exercise faith in the same promise which Abraham believed? Let us keep to this impregnable truth:—where there is a divine promise, there every man stands for himself; individual faith is required; every man shall give account for himself, and shall bear his own burdens; as Christ says: "He that believeth and is baptized shall be saved; but he that believeth not shall be damned." (Mark xvi. 16.) Thus every man can make the mass useful only to himself, by his own faith, and can by no means communicate it to others; just as a priest cannot administer a sacrament to any man on behalf of another, but administers the same sacrament to each individual separately. The priests in their work of consecration and administration act as ministers for us; not that we offer up any good work through them, or communicate actively; but by their means we receive the promise and its sign, and communicate passively. This idea continues among the laity; for they are not said to do a good work, but to receive a gift. But the priests have gone after their own impieties and have made it a good work that they communicate and make an offering out of the sacrament and testament of God, whereas they ought to have received it as a good gift.

But you will say: "What? will you ever overthrow the practices and opinions which, for so many centuries, have rooted themselves in all the churches and monasteries; and all that superstructure of anniversaries, suffrages, applications, and communications, which they have established upon the mass, and from which they have drawn the amplest revenues?" I reply: It is this which has compelled me to write concerning the bondage of the Church. For the venerable testament of God has been brought into a profane servitude to gain, through the opinions and traditions of impious men, who have passed over the Word of God, and have set before us the imaginations of their own hearts, and thus have led the world astray. What have I to do with the number or the greatness of those who are in error? Truth is stronger than all. If you can deny that Christ teaches that the mass is a testament and a sacrament, I am ready to justify those men. Again, if you can say that the man who receives the benefit of a testament, or who uses for this purpose the sacrament of promise, is doing a good work, I am ready and willing to condemn all that I have said. But since neither is possible, why hesitate to despise the crowd which hastens to do evil, whilst you give glory to God and confess His truth, namely, that all priests are perversely mistaken, who look on the mass as a work by which they may aid their own necessities, or those of others, whether dead or alive? My statements, I know, are unheard of and astounding. But if you look into the true nature of the mass, you will see that I speak the truth. These errors have proceeded from that over-security, which has kept us from perceiving that the wrath of God was coming upon us.

This I readily admit, that the prayers which we pour forth in the presence of God, when we meet to partake of the mass, are good works or benefits, which we mutually impart, apply, and communicate, and offer up for one another; as the Apostle James teaches us to pray for one another that we may be saved. Paul also exhorts that supplications, prayers, intercessions, and giving of thanks, be made for all men; for kings, and for all that are in authority. (1 Tim. ii. 1, 2.) These things are not the mass, but works of the mass;—if, indeed, we can call the prayers of our hearts and our lips works—because they spring from the existence and growth of faith in the sacrament. The mass or promise of God is not completed by our prayers, but only by our faith; and in faith we pray and do other good works. But what priest sacrifices with the intention and idea of only offering up prayers? They all imagine that they are offering Christ himself to God the Father as an all-sufficient victim; and that they are doing a good work on behalf of all men, who, as they allege, will profit by it. They trust in the *opus operatum*, and do not attribute the effect to prayer. Thus, by a gradual growth of error, they attribute to the sacrament the benefit which springs from prayer; and they offer to God what they ought to receive as a gift from Him.

We must therefore make a clear distinction between the testament and sacrament itself, and the prayers which we offer at the same time. And not only so, but we must understand that those prayers are of no value at all, either to him who offers them, or to those for whom they are offered, unless the testament has been first received by faith, so that the prayer may be that of faith, which alone is heard, as the Apostle James teaches us. So widely does prayer differ from the mass. I can pray for as many persons as I will; but no one receives the mass unless he believes for himself; and that only so far as he believes; nor can it be given either to God or to men, but it is God alone who by the ministry of the priest gives it to men, and they receive it by faith alone, without any works or merits. No one would be so audaciously foolish as to say that, when a poor and needy man comes to receive a benefit from the hand of a rich man, he is doing a good work. Now the mass is the benefit of a divine promise, held forth to all men by the hand of the priest. It is certain, therefore, that the mass is not a work communicable to others, but the object of each man's individual faith, which is thus to be nourished and strengthened.

We must also get rid of another scandal, which is a much greater and a very specious one; that is, that the mass is universally believed to be a sacrifice offered to God. With this opinion the words of the canon of the mass appear to agree, such as—"These gifts; these offerings; these holy sacrifices;" and again, "this oblation." There is also a very distinct prayer that the sacrifice may be accepted like the sacrifice of Abel. Hence Christ is called the victim of the altar. To this we must add the sayings of the holy Fathers, a great number of authorities, and the usage that has been constantly observed throughout the world.

To all these difficulties, which beset us so pertinaciously, we must oppose with the utmost constancy the words and example of Christ. Unless we hold the mass to be the promise or testament of Christ, according to the plain meaning of the words, we lose all the gospel and our whole comfort. Let us allow nothing to prevail against those words, even if an angel from heaven taught us otherwise. Now in these words there is nothing about a work or sacrifice. Again, we have the example of Christ on our side. When Christ instituted this sacrament and established this testament in the Last Supper, he did not offer himself to God the Father, or accomplish any work on behalf of others, but, as he sat at the table, he declared the same testament to each individual present and bestowed on each the sign of it. Now the more any mass resembles and is akin to that first mass of all which Christ celebrated at the Last Supper, the more Christian it is. But that mass of Christ was most simple; without any display of vestments, gestures, hymns, and other ceremonies; so that if it had been necessary that it should be offered as a sacrifice, His institution of it would not have been complete.

Not that any one ought rashly to blame the universal Church, which has adorned and extended the mass with many other rites and ceremonies; but we desire that no one should be so deceived by showy ceremonies, or so perplexed by the amount of external display, as to lose the simplicity of the mass, and in fact pay honour to some kind of transubstantiation; as will happen if we pass by the simple substance of the mass, and fix our minds on the manifold accidents of its outward show. For whatever has been added to the mass beyond the word and example of Christ, is one of its accidents; and none of these ought we to consider in any other light than we now consider monstrances—as they are called—and altar cloths, within which the host is contained. It is a contradiction in terms that the mass should be a sacrifice; since we receive the mass, but give a sacrifice. Now the same thing cannot be received and offered at the same time, nor can it be at once given and accepted by the same person. This is as certain as that prayer and the thing prayed for cannot be the same; nor can it be the same thing to pray and to receive what we pray for.

What shall we say then to the canon of the mass and the authority of the Fathers? First of all I reply:—If there were nothing to be said, it would be safer to deny their authority altogether, than to grant that the mass is a work or a sacrifice, and thus to deny the word of Christ and to overthrow faith and the mass together. However, that we may keep the Fathers too, we will explain (1 Cor. xi.) that the believers in Christ, when they met to celebrate the mass, were accustomed to bring with them portions of food and drink, called "collects," which were distributed among the poor, according to the example of the Apostles (Acts iv.), and from which were taken the bread and wine consecrated for the sacrament. Since all these gifts were sanctified by the word and prayer after the Hebrew rite, in accordance with which they were lifted on high, as we read in Moses, the words and the practice of elevation, or of offering, continued in the Church long after the custom had died out of collecting and bringing together the gifts which were offered or elevated. Thus Hezekiah (Isaiah xxxvii. 4) bids Isaiah to lift his prayer for the remnant that is left. Again, the Psalmist says: "Lift up your hands to the holy place;" and—"To thee will I lift up my hands;" and again—"That men pray everywhere, lifting up holy hands." (1 Tim. ii. 8.) Hence the expressions "sacrifice" or "oblation" ought to be referred, not to the sacrament and testament, but to the "collects" themselves. Hence too the word collect has remained in use for the prayers said in the mass.

For the same reason the priest elevates the bread and the cup as soon as he has consecrated them; but the proof that he is not therein offering anything to God is that in no single word does he make mention of a victim or an oblation. This too is a remnant of the Hebrew rite, according to which it was customary to elevate the gifts which, after being received with giving of thanks, were brought back to God. Or it may be considered as an admonition to us, to call forth our faith in that testament which Christ on that occasion brought forward and set before us; and also as a display of its sign. The oblation of the bread properly corresponds to the words: "This is my body;" and Christ, as it were, addresses us bystanders by this very sign. Thus too the oblation of the cup properly corresponds to these words: "This cup is the New Testament in my blood." The priest ought to call forth our faith by the very rite of elevation. And as he openly elevates the sign or sacrament in our sight, so I wish that he also pronounced the word or testament with loud and clear voice in our hearing; and that in the language of every nation, that our faith might be more efficaciously exercised. Why should it be lawful to perform mass in Greek, and Latin, and Hebrew, and not also in German, or in any other language?

Wherefore, in this abandoned and most perilous age, let the priests who sacrifice take heed in the first place that those words of the major and minor canon, with the collects, which speak only too plainly of a sacrifice, are to be applied, not to the sacrament, but either to the consecration of the bread and wine themselves, or to their own prayers. For the bread and wine are presented beforehand to receive a blessing, that they may be sanctified by the word and prayer. But after being blessed and consecrated, they are no longer offered, but are received as a gift from God. And in this matter let the priest consider that the gospel is to be preferred to all canons and collects composed by men; but the gospel, as we have seen, does not allow the mass to be a sacrifice.

In the next place, when the priest is performing mass publicly, let him understand that he is only receiving and giving to others the communion in the mass; and let him beware of offering up at the same moment his prayers for himself and others, lest he should seem to be presuming to offer the mass. The priest also who is saying a private mass must consider himself as administering the communion to himself. A private mass is not at all different from, nor more efficient than, the simple reception of the communion by any layman from the hand of the priest, except for the prayers, and that the priest consecrates and administers it to himself. In the matter itself of the mass and the sacrament, we are all equal, priests and laymen.

Even if he is requested by others to do so, let him beware of celebrating votive masses—as they are called—and of receiving any payment for the mass, or presuming to offer any votive sacrifice; but let him carefully refer all this to the prayers which he offers, whether for the dead or the living. Let him think thus:—I will go and receive the sacrament for myself alone, but while I receive it I will pray for this or that person, and thus, for purposes of food and clothing, receive payment for my prayers, and not for the mass. Nor let it shake thee in this view, though the whole world is of the contrary opinion and practice. Thou hast the most certain authority of the gospel, and relying on this, thou mayest easily contemn the ideas and opinions of men. If however, in despite of what I say, thou wilt persist in offering the mass, and not thy prayers only, then know that I have faithfully warned thee, and that I shall stand clear in the day of judgment, whilst thou wilt bear thine own sin. I have said what I was bound to say to thee, as a brother to a brother, for thy salvation; it will be to thy profit if thou take heed to my words, to thy hurt if thou neglect them. And if there are some who will condemn these statements of mine, I reply in the words of Paul: "Evil men and seducers shall wax worse and worse, deceiving, and being deceived." (2 Tim. iii. 13.)

Hence any one may easily understand that often-quoted passage from Gregory, in which he says that a mass celebrated by a bad priest is not to be considered of less value than one by a good priest, and that one celebrated by St. Peter would not have been better than one celebrated by the traitor Judas. Under cover of this saying some try to shelter their own impiety, and have drawn a distinction between the opus operatum and the opus operans; that they might continue secure in their evil living, and yet pretend to be benefactors to others. Gregory indeed speaks the truth, but these men pervert his meaning. It is most true that the testament and sacrament are not less effectively given and received at the hands of wicked priests than at those of the most holy. Who doubts that the gospel may be preached by wicked men? Now the mass is a part of the gospel; nay, the very sum and compendium of the gospel. For what is the whole gospel but the good news of the remission of sins? Now all that can be said in the most ample and copious words concerning the remission of sins and the mercy of God, is all briefly comprehended in the word of the testament. Hence also sermons to the people ought to be nothing else but expositions of the mass, that is, the setting forth of the divine promise of this testament. This would be to teach faith, and truly to edify the Church. But those who now expound the mass make a sport and mockery of the subject by figures of speech derived from human ceremonies.

As therefore a wicked man can baptize, that is, can apply the word of promise and the sign of water to the person baptized, so can he also apply and minister the promise of this sacrament to those who partake of it, and partake himself with them, as the traitor Judas did in the supper of the Lord. Still the sacrament and testament remains always the same; it performs in the believer its own proper work, in the unbeliever it performs a work foreign to itself. But in the matter of oblations the case is quite different; for since it is not the mass but prayers which are offered to God, it is evident that the oblations of a wicked priest are of no value. As Gregory himself says, when we employ an unworthy person as an advocate, the mind of the judge is prejudiced against us. We must not therefore confound these two things, the mass and prayer, sacrament and work, testament and sacrifice. The one comes from God to us through the ministry of the priest, and requires faith on our part; the other goes forth from our faith to God through the priest, and requires that He should hear us; the one comes down, the other goes upwards. The one therefore does not necessarily require that the minister should be worthy and pious, but the other does require it, because God does not hear sinners. He knows how to do us good by means of wicked men, but He does not accept the works of any wicked man, as He showed in the case of Cain. It is written: "The sacrifice of the wicked is an abomination to the Lord." (Prov. xv. 8); and again: "Whatsoever is not of faith is sin." (Rom. xiv. 23.)

We shall now make an end of this first part of the subject, but I am ready to produce further arguments when any one comes forward to attack these. From all that has been said we see for whom the mass was intended, and who are worthy partakers of it; namely, those alone who have sad, afflicted, disturbed, confused, and erring consciences. For since the word of the divine promise in this sacrament holds forth to us remission of sins, any man may safely draw near to it who is harassed either by remorse for sin, or by temptation to sin. This testament of Christ is the one medicine for past, present, and future sins; provided thou cleavest to it with unhesitating faith, and believest that that which is signified by the words of the testament is freely given to thee. If thou dost not so believe, then nowhere, never, by no works, by no efforts, wilt thou be able to appease thy conscience. For faith is the sole peace of conscience, and unbelief the sole disturber of conscience.

CONCERNING THE SACRAMENT OF BAPTISM

Blessed be the God and Father of our Lord Jesus Christ, who according to the riches of His mercy has at least preserved this one sacrament in His Church uninjured and uncontaminated by the devices of men, and has made it free to all nations and to men of every class. He has not suffered it to be overwhelmed with the foul and impious monstrosities of avarice and superstition; doubtless having this purpose, that He would have little children, incapable of avarice and superstition, to be initiated into this sacrament, and to be sanctified by perfectly simple faith in His word. To such, even at the present day, baptism is of the highest advantage. If this sacrament had been intended to be given to adults and those of full age, it seems as if it could have hardly preserved its efficacy and its glory, in the presence of that tyranny of avarice and superstition which has supplanted all divine ordinances among us. In this case too, no doubt, fleshly wisdom would have invented its preparations, its worthinesses, its reservations, its restrictions, and other like nets for catching money; so that the water of baptism would be sold no cheaper than parchments are now.

Yet, though Satan has not been able to extinguish the virtue of baptism in the case of little children, still he has had power to extinguish it in all adults; so that there is scarcely any one nowadays who remembers that he has been baptized, much less glories in it; so many other ways having been found of obtaining remission of sins and going to heaven. Occasion has been afforded to these opinions by that perilous saying of St. Jerome, either misstated or misunderstood, in which he calls penitence the second plank of safety after shipwreck; as if baptism were not penitence. Hence, when men have fallen into sin, they despair of the first plank, or the ship, as being no longer of any use, and begin to trust and depend only on the second plank, that is, on penitence. Thence have sprung those infinite loads of vows, religious dedications, works, satisfactions, pilgrimages, indulgences, and systems; and from them those oceans of books and of human questionings, opinions, and traditions, which the whole world nowadays cannot contain. Thus this tyranny possesses the Church of God in an incomparably worse form than it ever possessed the synagogue, or any nation under heaven.

It was the duty of Bishops to remove all these abuses, and to make every effort to recall Christians to the simplicity of baptism; that so they might understand their own position, and what as Christians they ought to do. But the one business of Bishops at the present day is to lead the people as far as possible away from baptism and to plunge them all under the deluge of their own tyranny; and thus, as the prophet says, to make the people of Christ forget Him for ever. Oh wretched men who are called by the name of Bishops! they not only do nothing and know nothing which Bishops ought, but they are even ignorant what they ought to know and do. They fulfil the words of Isaiah: "His watchmen are blind; they are all ignorant; they are shepherds that cannot understand; they all look to their own way, every one for his gain, from his quarter." (Is. lvi. 10, 11.)

The first thing then we have to notice in baptism is the divine promise, which says: He who believes and is baptized shall be saved. This promise is to be infinitely preferred to the whole display of works, vows, religious orders, and whatever has been introduced by the invention of man. On this promise depends our whole salvation, and we must take heed to exercise faith in it, not doubting at all that we are saved, since we have been baptized. Unless this faith exists and is applied, baptism profits us nothing; nay, it is hurtful to us, not only at the time when it is received, but in the whole course of our after life. For unbelief of this kind charges the divine promise with falsehood; and to do this is the greatest of all sins. If we attempt this exercise of faith, we shall soon see how difficult a thing it is to believe this divine promise. For human weakness, conscious of its own sinfulness, finds it the most difficult thing in the world to believe that it is saved, or can be saved; and yet, unless it believes this, it cannot be saved, because it does not believe the divine truth which promises salvation.

This doctrine ought to have been studiously inculcated upon the people by preaching; this promise ought to have been perpetually reiterated; men ought to have been constantly reminded of their baptism; faith ought to have been called forth and nourished. When this divine promise has been once conferred upon us, its truth continues even to the hour of our death; and thus our faith in it ought never to be relaxed, but ought to be nourished and strengthened even till we die, by a perpetual recollection of the promise made to us in baptism. Thus, when we rise out of our sins and exercise penitence, we are simply reverting to the efficacy of baptism and to faith in it, whence we had fallen; and we return to the promise then made to us, but which we had abandoned through our sin. For the truth of the promise once made always abides, and is ready to stretch out the hand and receive us when we return. This, unless I mistake, is the meaning of that obscure saying, that baptism is the first of sacraments and the foundation of them all, without which we can possess none of the others.

Thus it will be of no little profit to a penitent, first of all to recall to mind his own baptism, and to remember with confidence that divine promise which he had deserted; rejoicing that he is still in a fortress of safety, in that he has been baptized; and detesting his own wicked ingratitude in having fallen away from the faith and truth of baptism. His heart will be marvellously comforted, and encouraged to hope for mercy, if he fixes his eyes upon that divine promise once made to him, which could not lie, and which still continues entire, unchanged, and unchangeable by any sins of his; as Paul says: "If we believe not, yet He abideth faithful; He cannot deny Himself." (2 Tim. ii. 13.) This truth of God will preserve him; and even if all other hopes perish, this, if he believes it, will not fail him. Through this truth he will have something to oppose to the insolent adversary; he will have a barrier to throw in the way of the sins which disturb his conscience; he will have an answer to the dread of death and judgment; finally, he will have a consolation under every kind of temptation, in being able to say: God is faithful to His promise; and in baptism I received the sign of that promise. If God is for me, who can be against me?

If the children of Israel, when returning to God in repentance, first of all called to mind their exodus from Egypt, and in remembrance of this turned back to God, who had brought them out—a remembrance which is so often inculcated on them by Moses, and referred to by David—how much more ought we to remember our exodus from Egypt, and in remembrance of it to return to Him who brought us out through the washing of the new birth. Now this we can do most advantageously of all in the sacrament of the bread and wine. So of old these three sacraments, penitence, baptism, and the bread, were often combined in the same act of worship; and the one added strength to the other. Thus we read of a certain holy virgin who, whenever she was tempted, relied on her baptism only for defence, saying, in the briefest words: "I am a Christian." The enemy forthwith felt the efficacy of baptism, and of the faith which depended on the truth of a promising God, and fled from her.

We see then how rich a Christian, or baptized man, is; since, even if he would, he cannot lose his salvation by any sins however great, unless he refuses to believe; for no sins whatever can condemn him, but unbelief alone. All other sins, if faith in the divine promise made to the baptized man stands firm or is restored, are swallowed up in a moment through that same faith; yea, through the truth of God, because He cannot deny Himself, if thou confess Him, and cleave believingly to His promise. Whereas contrition, and confession of sins, and satisfaction for sins, and every effort that can be devised by men, will desert thee at thy need, and will make thee more miserable than ever, if thou forgettest this divine truth and puffest thyself up with such things as these. For whatever work is wrought apart from faith in the truth of God is vanity and vexation of spirit.

We also see how perilous and false an idea it is that penitence is a second plank of refuge after shipwreck; and how pernicious an error it is to suppose that the virtue of baptism has been brought to an end by sin, and that this ship has been dashed to pieces. That ship remains one, solid, and indestructible, and can never be broken up into different planks. In it all are conveyed who are carried to the port of salvation, since it is the truth of God giving promises in the sacraments. What certainly does happen is that many rashly leap out of the ship into the sea and perish; these are they who abandon faith in the promise and rush headlong into sin. But the ship itself abides, and passes on safely in its course; and any man who, by the grace of God, returns to the ship, will be borne on to life, not on a plank, but on the solid ship itself. Such a man is he who returns by faith to the fixed and abiding promise of God. Thus Peter charges those who sin with having forgotten that they were purged from their old sins (2 Peter i. 9); doubtless meaning to reprove their ingratitude for the baptism they had received, and the impiety of their unbelief.

What profit then is there in writing so much about baptism, and yet not teaching faith in the promise? All the sacraments were instituted for the purpose of nourishing faith, and yet so far are they from attaining this object, that men are even found impious enough to assert that a man ought not to be sure of the remission of sins, or of the grace of the sacraments. By this impious doctrine they deprive the whole world of its senses, and utterly extinguish, or at least bring into bondage that sacrament of baptism, in which the first glory of our conscience stands. Meanwhile they senselessly persecute wretched souls with their contritions, their anxious confessions, their circumstances, satisfactions, works, and an infinity of such trifles. Let us then read with caution, or rather despise the Master of Sentences (Book iv.) with all his followers; who, when they write their best, write only about the matter and form of the sacraments, and so handle only the dead and perishing letter of those sacraments, while they do not even touch upon their spirit, life, and use; that is, the truth of the divine promise, and faith on our part.

See then that thou be not deceived by the display of works, and by the fallacies of human traditions, and so wrong the truth of God and thy own faith. If thou wilt be saved, thou must begin by faith in the sacraments, without any works. Thy faith will be followed by these very works, but thou must not hold faith cheap, for it is itself the most excellent and most difficult of all works, and by it alone thou wilt be saved, even if thou wert compelled to be destitute of all other works. For it is a work of God, not of man, as Paul teaches. All other works He performs with us, and by us; this one work He performs in us and without us.

From what has been said we may clearly distinguish the difference between man the minister and God the Author of baptism. Man baptizes and does not baptize; he baptizes, because he performs the work of dipping the baptized person; he does not baptize, because in this work he does not act upon his own authority, but in the place of God. Hence we ought to receive baptism from the hand of man just as if Christ Himself, nay, God Himself, were baptizing us with His own hands. For it is not a man's baptism, but that of Christ and God; though we receive it by the hand of a man. Even so any other creature which we enjoy through the hand of another is really only God's. Beware then of making any such distinction in baptism, as to attribute the outward rite to man, and the inward blessing to God. Attribute both of them to God alone, and consider the person of him who confers baptism in no other light than as the vicarious instrument of God, by means of which the Lord sitting in heaven dips thee in the water with His own hands, and promises thee remission of sins upon earth, speaking to thee with the voice of a man through the mouth of His minister.

The very words of the minister tell thee this, when he says: "I baptize thee in the name of the Father, and of the Son, and of the Holy Spirit. Amen." He does not say: "I baptize thee in my name;" but says, as it were: "What I do, I do not by my own authority, but in the place and in the name of God; and thou must look upon it as if the Lord Himself did it in visible shape. The Author and the minister are different, but the work of both is the same; nay, rather it is that of the Author alone through my ministry." In my judgment the expression, "In the name," relates to the person of the Author, so that not only is the name of the Lord brought forward and invoked in the doing of the work, but the work itself is performed, as being that of another, in the name and in the place of another. By the like figure Christ says: "Many shall come in my name." (Matt. xxiv. 5.) And again: "By whom we have received grace and apostleship, for obedience to the faith among all nations, for his name." (Rom. i. 5.)

I most gladly adopt this view; because it is a thing most full of consolation, and an effective aid to faith, to know that we have been baptized, not by a man, but by the very Trinity Itself through a man, who acts towards us in Its name. This brings to an end that idle contention which is carried on about the "form" of baptism—as they call the words themselves—the Greeks saying: "Let the servant of Christ be baptized;" the Latins: "I baptize." Others also, in their pedantic trifling, condemn the use of the expression: "I baptize thee in the name of Jesus Christ"—though it is certain that the Apostles baptized in this form, as we read in the Acts of the Apostles—and will have it that no other form is valid than the following: "I baptize thee in the name of the Father, and of the Son, and of the Holy Spirit. Amen." But they strive in vain; they prove nothing; they only bring forward their own dreams. In whatever manner baptism is administered, provided it is administered, not in the name of a man, but in the name of the Lord, it truly saves us. Nay, I have no doubt that if a man received baptism in the name of the Lord, even from a wicked minister who did not give it in the name of the Lord, he would still be truly baptized in the name of the Lord. For the efficacy of baptism depends not so much on the faith of him who confers it, as of him who receives it. Thus we read an instance of a certain player who was baptized in jest. These and similar narrow questions and disputes have been raised for us by those who attribute nothing to faith, and everything to works and ceremonies. On the contrary, we owe nothing to ceremonies, and everything to faith alone, which makes us free in spirit from all these scruples and fancies.

Another thing which belongs to baptism is the sign or sacrament, which is that dipping into water whence it takes its name. For in Greek to baptize signifies to dip, and baptism is a dipping. We have said already that, side by side with the divine promises, signs also are given us, to represent by a figure the meaning of the words of the promise; or, as the moderns say, the sacrament has an effectual significance. What that significance is we shall see. Very many have thought that in the word and the water there is some occult spiritual virtue, which works the grace of God in the soul of the recipient. Others deny this, and declare that there is no virtue in the sacraments, but that grace is given by God alone, who, according to His covenant, is present at the sacraments instituted by Himself. All however agree in this, that the sacraments are effectual signs of grace. They are led to this conclusion by this one argument, that it does not otherwise appear what pre-eminence the sacraments of the new law would have over those of the old, if they were only signs. Hence they have been driven to attribute such efficacy to the sacraments of the new law, that they have stated them to be profitable even to those who are in mortal sin; and have declared that neither faith nor grace are requisite, but that it is sufficient that we do not place any impediment in the way, that is, any actual purpose of sinning afresh.

We must carefully avoid and fly from these doctrines, for they are impious and unbelieving, repugnant to faith and to the nature of the sacraments. It is a mistake to suppose that the sacraments of the new law differ from the sacraments of the old law as regards the efficacy of their significance. Both are on an equality in their significance; for the same God who now saves us by baptism and the bread, saved Abel by his sacrifice, Noah by the Ark, Abraham by circumcision, and all the other Patriarchs by their own proper signs. There is no difference then between a sacrament of the old and of the new law, as regards their significance; provided we understand by the old law all the dealings of God with the Patriarchs and other Fathers in the time of the law. For those signs which were given to the Patriarchs and Fathers are completely distinct from the legal figures which Moses instituted in his law; such as the rites of the priesthood, in relation to vestments, vessels, food, houses, and the like. These are as different as possible, not only from the sacraments of the new law, but also from those signs which God gave from time to time to the Fathers who lived under the law; such as that given to Gideon in the fleece, to Manoah in his sacrifice; such also as that which Isaiah offered to Ahaz. In all these cases alike, some promise was given which required faith in God.

In this then the figures of the law differ from signs new or old, that the figures of the law have no word of promise annexed to them, requiring faith, and therefore are not signs of justification, inasmuch as they are not sacraments of faith, which alone justify, but only sacraments of works. Their whole force and nature lay in works, not in faith; for he who did them fulfilled them, even if his work was without faith. Now our signs or sacraments and those of the Fathers have annexed to them a word of promise, which requires faith, and can be fulfilled by no other work. Thus they are signs or sacraments of justification, because they are sacraments of justifying faith and not of works; so that their whole efficacy lies in faith itself, not in working. He who believes them fulfils them, even though he do no work. Hence the saying: It is not the sacrament, but faith in the sacrament which justifies. Thus circumcision did not justify Abraham and his seed; and yet the Apostle calls it a seal of the righteousness of faith, because faith in that promise with which circumcision was connected did justify, and fulfilled the meaning of circumcision. Faith was that circumcision of the heart in spirit, which was figured by the circumcision of the flesh in the letter. Thus it was evidently not the sacrifice of Abel which justified him, but the faith by which he offered himself entirely to God; of which faith the outward sacrifice was a figure.

Thus it is not baptism which justifies any man, or is of any advantage; but faith in that word of promise to which baptism is added; for this justifies, and fulfils the meaning of baptism. For faith is the submerging of the old man, and the emerging of the new man. Hence it cannot be that the new sacraments differ from the ancient sacraments, for they both alike have divine promises and the same spirit of faith; but they differ incomparably from the ancient *figures*, on account of the word of promise, which is the sole and most effective means of difference. Thus at the present day the pomp of vestments, localities, meats, and an infinite variety of ceremonies, doubtless figure excellent works to be fulfilled in the spirit; and yet, since no word of divine promise is connected with them, they can in no way be compared with the signs of baptism and the bread. Nor can they justify men nor profit them in any way, since their fulfilment lies in the very practice or performance of them without faith; for when they are done or performed, they are fulfilled. Thus the Apostle speaks of those things, "which all are to perish with the using; after the commandments and doctrines of men." (Col. ii. 22.) Now the sacraments are not fulfilled by being done, but by being believed.

Thus it cannot be true that there is inherent in the Sacraments a power effectual to produce justification, or that they are efficacious signs of grace. These things are said in ignorance of the divine promise and to the great detriment of faith; unless indeed we call them efficacious in this sense, that, if along with them there be unhesitating faith, they do confer grace most certainly and most effectually. But that it is not this kind of efficacy which those writers attribute to them is evident from this, that they assert them to be profitable to all men, even the wicked and unbelieving, provided they put no obstacle in the way; as if unbelief itself were not the most persistent of all obstacles, and the most hostile to grace. Thus they have endeavoured to make out of the sacrament a precept, and out of faith a work. For if a sacrament confers grace on me, merely because I receive it, then it is certainly by my own work and not by faith that I obtain grace; nor do I apprehend any promise in the sacrament, but only a sign instituted and commanded by God. It is evident from this how utterly the sacraments are misunderstood by these theologians of the Sentences, inasmuch as they make no account either of faith or of the promise in the sacraments, but cleave only to the sign and the use of the sign, and carry us away from faith to works, from the word to the sign. Thus, as I have said, they have not only brought the sacraments into bondage, but, as far as in them lay, have entirely done away with them.

Let us then open our eyes, and learn to look more to the word than the sign, more to faith than to the work or use of the sign; and let us understand that wherever there is a divine promise, there faith is required; and that both of these are so necessary that neither can be of any effect without the other. We can neither believe unless we have a promise, nor is the promise effectual unless it is believed; while if these two act reciprocally, they produce a real and sure efficacy in the sacraments. Hence to seek efficacy in the sacrament independently of the promise and of faith is to strive in vain and to fall into condemnation. Thus Christ says: "He that believeth and is baptized shall be saved, but he that believeth not shall be damned." (Mark xvi. 16.) Thus He shows that in the sacrament faith is so necessary that it can save us even without the sacrament; and on this account when He says: "He that believeth not," He does not add: "and is not baptized."

Baptism then signifies two things, death and resurrection; that is, full and complete justification. When the minister dips the child into the water, this signifies death; when he draws him out again, this signifies life. Thus Paul explains the matter: "Therefore we are buried with him by baptism into death; that like as Christ was raised up from the dead by the glory of the Father, even so we also should walk in newness of life." (Rom. vi. 4.) This death and resurrection we call a new creation, a regeneration, and a spiritual birth; and these words are not only to be understood allegorically, as they are by many, of the death of sin and the life of grace, but of a real death and resurrection. For baptism has no fictitious meaning, nor does sin die or grace rise fully within us, until the body of sin which we bear in this life is destroyed; for, as the Apostle says, as long as we are in the flesh, the desires of the flesh work in us and are worked upon. Hence when we begin to believe, we begin at the same time to die to this world, and to live to God in a future life; so that faith is truly a death and resurrection; that is, that spiritual baptism in which we are submerged and emerge.

When then the washing away of sins is attributed to baptism, it is rightly so attributed; but the meaning of the phrase is too slight and weak to fully express baptism, which is rather a symbol of death and resurrection. For this reason I could wish that the baptized should be totally immersed, according to the meaning of the word and the signification of the mystery; not that I think it necessary to do so, but that it would be well that so complete and perfect a thing as baptism should have its sign also in completeness and perfection, even as it was doubtless instituted by Christ. For a sinner needs not so much to be washed as to die, that he may be altogether renewed into another creature, and that there may thus be a correspondence in him to the death and resurrection of Christ along with whom he dies and rises again in baptism. For though we may say that Christ was washed from His mortality when He died and rose again, yet it is a weaker expression than if we said that He was totally changed and renewed; and so there is more intensity in saying that death and resurrection to eternal life are signified to us by baptism, than that we are washed from sin.

Here again we see that the sacrament of baptism, even in respect to the sign, is not the mere business of a moment, but has a lasting character. For though the transaction itself passes quickly, the thing signified by it lasts even until death, yea, till the resurrection at the last day. For as long as we live we are always doing that which is signified by baptism; that is, we are dying and rising again. We are dying, I say, not only in our affections and spiritually, by renouncing the sins and vanities of the world, but in very deed we are beginning to leave this bodily life and to apprehend the future life, so that there is a real (as they call it) and also a bodily passing out of this world to the Father.

We must therefore keep clear of the error of those who have reduced the effect of baptism to such small and slender dimensions that, while they say that grace is infused by it, they assert that this grace is afterwards, so to speak, effused by sin; and that we must then go to heaven by some other way, as if baptism had now became absolutely useless. Do not thou judge thus, but understand that the significance of baptism is such that thou mayest live and die in it; and that neither by penitence nor by any other way canst thou do aught but return to the effect of baptism, and do afresh what thou wert baptized in order to do, and what thy baptism signified. Baptism never loses its effect, unless in desperation thou refuse to return to salvation. Thou mayst wander away for a time from the sign, but the sign does not on that account lose its effect. Thus thou hast been baptized once for all sacramentally, but thou needest continually to be baptized by faith, and must continually die and continually live. Baptism hath swallowed up thy whole body and given it forth again; and so the substance of baptism ought to swallow up thy whole life, in body and in soul, and to give it back in the last day, clothed in the robe of brightness and immortality. Thus we are never without the sign as well as the substance of baptism; nay, we ought to be continually baptized more and more, until we fulfil the whole meaning of the sign at the last day.

We see then that whatever we do in this life tending to the mortifying of the flesh and the vivifying of the spirit is connected with baptism; and that the sooner we are set free from this life, the more speedily we fulfil the meaning of our baptism; and the greater the sufferings we endure, the more happily do we answer the purpose of baptism. The Church was at its happiest in those days when martyrs were daily put to death and counted as sheep for the slaughter; for then the virtue of baptism reigned in the Church with full power, though now we have quite lost sight of it for the multitude of human works and doctrine. The whole life which we live ought to be a baptism, and to fulfil the sign or sacrament of baptism; since we have been set free from all other things and given up to baptism alone, that is, to death and resurrection.

To whom can we assign the blame that this glorious liberty of ours and this knowledge of baptism are nowadays in bondage, except only to the tyranny of the Roman Pontiff? He most of all men, as becomes a chief shepherd, ought to have been the preacher and the asserter of this liberty and this knowledge; as Paul says: "Let a man so account of us, as of the ministers of Christ, and stewards of the mysteries of God." (1 Cor. iv. 1.) But his sole object is to oppress us by his decrees and laws, and to ensnare us into bondage to his tyrannical power. Not to speak of the impious and damnable way in which the Pope fails to teach these mysteries, by what right, I ask, has he established laws over us? Who has given him authority to bring into bondage this liberty of ours, given us by baptism? One purpose, as I have said, we ought to carry out in our whole lives, namely, to be baptized, that is, to be mortified, and to live by faith in Christ. This faith alone ought to have been taught, above all by the chief shepherd. But now not a word is said about faith, but the Church is crushed by an infinite number of laws concerning works and ceremonies; the virtue and knowledge of baptism are taken away; the faith of Christ is hindered.

I say then, neither Pope, nor bishop, nor any man whatever has the right of making one syllable binding on a Christian man, unless it is done with his own consent. Whatever is done otherwise is done in a spirit of tyranny; and thus the prayers, fastings, almsgiving, and whatever else the Pope ordains and requires in the whole body of his decrees, which are as many as they are iniquitous, he has absolutely no right to require and ordain; and he sins against the liberty of the Church as often as he attempts anything of the kind. Hence it has come to pass that while the churchmen of the present day are strenuous defenders of church liberty, that is, of wood, stone, fields, and money (for in this day things ecclesiastical are synonymous with things spiritual), they yet, by their false teaching, not only bring into bondage the true liberty of the Church, but utterly destroy it; yea, more than the Turk himself could; contrary to the mind of the Apostle, who says: "Be not ye the servants of men." (1 Cor. vii. 23.) We are indeed made servants of men, when we are subjected to their tyrannical ordinances and laws.

This wicked and flagitious tyranny is aided by the disciples of the Pope, who distort and pervert to this end the saying of Christ: "He who heareth you heareth me." They swell out these words into a support for their own traditions; whereas this saying was addressed by Christ to the Apostles when they were going forth to preach the gospel, and therefore ought to be understood as referring to the gospel alone. These men, however, leave the gospel out of sight, and make this saying fit in with their own inventions. Christ says: "My sheep hear my voice, but they know not the voice of strangers." For this cause the gospel was bequeathed to us, that the pontiffs might utter the voice of Christ; but they utter their own voice, and are determined to be heard. The Apostle also says of himself that he was not sent to baptize, but to preach the gospel; and thus no man is bound to receive the traditions of the pontiff, or to listen to him, except when he teaches the gospel and Christ; and he himself ought to teach nothing but the freest faith. Since, however, Christ says: "he who hears you hears me," why does not the Pope also hear others? Christ did not say to Peter alone: "he who hears thee." Lastly, where there is true faith, there must also of necessity be the word of faith. Why then does not the unbelieving Pope listen to his believing servant who has the word of faith? Blindness, blindness reigns among the pontiffs.

Others however, far more shamelessly, arrogate to the Pope the power of making laws; arguing from the words: "Whatsoever thou shalt bind on earth shall be bound in heaven; and whatsoever thou shalt loose on earth shall be loosed in heaven." (Matt. xvi. 19.) Christ is speaking there of the binding and loosing of sins, not of bringing the whole Church into bondage and making laws to oppress it. Thus the papal tyranny acts in all things on its own false maxims; while it forcibly wrests and perverts the words of God. I admit indeed that Christians must endure this accursed tyranny, as they would any other violence inflicted on them by the world, according to the saying of Christ: "Whosoever shall smite thee on thy right cheek, turn to him the other also." (Matt. v. 39.) But I complain of this, that wicked pontiffs boast that they have a rightful power to act thus, and pretend that in this Babylon of theirs they are providing for the interests of Christendom; an idea which they have persuaded all men to adopt. If they did these things in conscious and avowed impiety and tyranny, or if it were simple violence that we endured, we might meanwhile quietly reckon up the advantages thus afforded us for the mortification of this life and the fulfilment of baptism, and should retain the full right of glorying in conscience at the wrong done us. As it is, they desire so to ensnare our consciences in the matter of liberty that we should believe all that they do to be well done, and should think it unlawful to blame or complain of their iniquitous actions. Being wolves, they wish to appear shepherds; being antichrists, they wish to be honoured like Christ.

I cry aloud on behalf of liberty and conscience, and I proclaim with confidence that no kind of law can with any justice be imposed on Christians, whether by men or by angels, except so far as they themselves will; for we are free from all. If such laws are imposed on us, we ought so to endure them as still to preserve the consciousness of our liberty. We ought to know and stedfastly to protest that a wrong is being done to that liberty, though we may bear and even glory in that wrong; taking care neither to justify the tyrant nor to murmur against the tyranny. "Who is he that will harm you, if ye be followers of that which is good?" (1 Peter iii. 13.) All things work together for good to the elect of God. Since, however, there are but few who understand the glory of baptism and the happiness of Christian liberty, or who can understand them for the tyranny of the Pope—I for my part will set free my own mind and deliver my conscience, by declaring aloud to the Pope and to all papists, that, unless they shall throw aside all their laws and traditions, and restore liberty to the churches of Christ, and cause that liberty to be taught, they are guilty of the death of all the souls which are perishing in this wretched bondage, and that the papacy is in truth nothing else than the kingdom of Babylon and of very Antichrist. For who is the man of sin and the son of perdition, but he who by his teaching and his ordinances increases the sin and perdition of souls in the Church; while he yet sits in the Church as if he were God? All these conditions have now for many ages been fulfilled by the papal tyranny. It has extinguished faith, darkened the sacraments, crushed the gospel; while it has enjoined and multiplied without end its own laws, which are not only wicked and sacrilegious, but also most unlearned and barbarous.

Behold then the wretchedness of our bondage. "How doth the city sit solitary, that was full of people! How is she become as a widow! She that was great among the nations, and princess among the provinces, how is she become tributary! Among all her lovers she hath none to comfort her; all her friends have dealt treacherously with her." (Lam. i. 1, 2.) There are at this day so many ordinances, so many rites, so many parties, so many professions, so many works to occupy the minds of Christians, that they forget their baptism. For this multitude of locusts, caterpillars, and cankerworms, no man is able to remember that he was baptized, or what it was that he obtained in baptism. We ought to have been like babes when they are baptized, who, being preoccupied by no zeal and by no works, are free for all things, at rest and safe in the glory of their baptism alone. We also ourselves are babes in Christ, unremittingly baptized.

In opposition to what I have said, an argument will perhaps be drawn from the baptism of infants, who cannot receive the promise of God, or have faith in their baptism; and it will be said that therefore either faith is not requisite, or infants are baptized in vain. To this I reply, what all men say, that infants are aided by the faith of others, namely, that of those who bring them to baptism. For as the word of God, when it is preached, is powerful enough to change the heart of a wicked man, which is not less devoid of sense and feeling than any infant, so through the prayers of the Church which brings the child in faith, to which prayers all things are possible, the infant is changed, cleansed, and renewed by faith infused into it. Nor should I doubt that even a wicked adult, if the Church were to bring him forward and pray for him, might undergo a change in any of the sacraments; just as we read in the gospel that the paralytic man was healed by the faith of others. In this sense too I should readily admit that the sacraments of the new law are effectual for the bestowal of grace, not only on those who do not place any obstacle in the way, but on the most obstinate of those who do. What difficulty cannot the faith of the Church and the prayer of faith remove, when Stephen is believed to have converted the Apostle Paul by this power? But in these cases the sacraments do what they do, not by their own virtue, but by that of faith; without which, as I have said, they have no effect at all.

A question has been raised whether a child yet unborn, but of which only a hand or a foot appears, can be baptized. On this point I would give no hasty judgment, and I confess my own ignorance. Nor do I know whether the reason on which they base their opinion is sufficient, namely, that the whole soul exists in every part of the body; for it is not the soul, but the body, which is outwardly baptized. On the other hand, I cannot pronounce that, as some assert, he who has not yet been born, cannot be born again; though it is a very strong argument. I leave this question to the decision of the Spirit, and meanwhile would have every man to be fully persuaded in his own mind.

I will add one thing, of which I wish I could persuade every one; that is, that all vows, whether those of religious orders, or of pilgrimages, or of works of any kind, should be entirely done away with, or at least avoided, and that we should remain in the liberty of baptism, full as it is of religious observances and of good works. It is impossible to express to what an extent this far too much extolled belief in vows detracts from baptism, and obscures the knowledge of Christian liberty; not to mention the unspeakable and infinite danger to souls which is daily increased by this immoderate passion for vows, and thoughtless rashness in making them. Oh ye most wicked Bishops and most unhappy pastors, who slumber at your ease and disport yourselves with your own desires, while ye have no pity for the grievous and perilous affliction of Joseph!

It would be well either to do away by a general edict with all vows, especially those which are perpetual, and to recall all men to their baptismal vows, or at least to admonish all to take no vow rashly; and not only to invite no vows, but to place delays and difficulties in the way of their being taken. We make an ample vow at baptism, a greater one than we can fulfil; and we shall have enough to do if we give all our efforts to this alone. But now we compass sea and land to make many proselytes; we fill the world with priests, monks, and nuns; and we imprison all these in perpetual vows. We shall find those who will argue on this point, and lay it down that works performed under the sanction of a vow are better than those performed independently of vows, and will be preferred in heaven and meet with far higher reward. Blind and impious Pharisees! who measure righteousness and holiness by the greatness and number of works, or by some other quality in them; while in God's sight they are measured by faith alone; since in His sight there is no difference between works, except so far as there is a difference in faith.

By this inflated talk wicked men create a great opinion of their own inventions, and puff up human works, in order to allure the senseless multitude, who are easily led by a specious show of works; to the great ruin of faith, forgetfulness of baptism, and injury to Christian liberty. As a vow is a sort of law and requires a work, it follows that, as vows are multiplied, so laws and works are multiplied; and by the multiplication of these, faith is extinguished, and the liberty of baptism is brought into bondage. Not content with these impious allurements, others go further, and assert that entrance into a religious order is like a new baptism, which may be successively renewed, as often as the purpose of a religious life is renewed. Thus these devotees attribute to themselves alone righteousness, salvation, and glory, and leave to the baptized absolutely no room for comparison with them. The Roman pontiff, that fountain and author of all superstitions, confirms, approves, and embellishes these ideas by grandly worded bulls and indulgences; while no one thinks baptism worthy even of mention. By these showy displays they drive the easily led people of Christ into whatever whirlpools of error they will; so that, unthankful for their baptism, they imagine that they can do better by their works than others by their faith.

Wherefore God also, who is froward with the froward, resolving to avenge Himself on the pride and unthankfulness of these devotees, causes them either to fail in keeping their vows, or to keep them with great labour and to continue immersed in them, never becoming acquainted with the grace of faith and of baptism. As their spirit is not right with God, He permits them to continue to the end in their hypocrisy, and to become at length a laughing-stock to the whole world, always following after righteousness, and never attaining to it; so that they fulfil that saying: "Their land also is full of idols." (Is. ii. 8.)

I should certainly not forbid or object to any vow which a man may make of his own private choice. I do not wish altogether to condemn or depreciate vows; but my advice would be altogether against the public establishment or confirmation of any such mode of life. It is enough that every man should be at liberty to make private vows at his own peril; but that a public system of living under the constraint of vows should be inculcated, I consider to be a thing pernicious to the Church and to all simple souls. In the first place, it is not a little repugnant to the Christian life, inasmuch as a vow is a kind of ceremonial law, and a matter of human tradition or invention; from all which the Church has been set free by baptism, since the Christian is bound by no law, except that of God. Moreover there is no example of it in the Scriptures, especially of the vow of perpetual chastity, obedience, and poverty. Now a vow of which we have no example in the Scriptures is a perilous one, which ought to be urged upon no man, much less be established as a common and public mode of life; even if every individual must be allowed to venture upon it at his own peril, if he will. There are some works which are wrought by the Spirit in but few, and these ought by no means to be brought forward as an example, or as a manner of life.

I greatly fear, however, that these systems of living under vows in the religious, are of the number of those things of which the Apostle foretold: "Speaking lies in hypocrisy; forbidding to marry, and commanding to abstain from meats, which God hath created to be received with thanksgiving." (1 Tim. iv. 2, 3.) Let no one cite against me the example of St. Bernard, St. Francis, St. Dominic, and such like authors or supporters of religious orders. God is terrible and wonderful in His dealings with the children of men. He could preserve Daniel, Ananias, Azarias, and Misael holy, even as ministers of the kingdom of Babylon, that is, in the very midst of wickedness; He may also have sanctified the men of whom I have spoken in their perilous mode of life, and have guided them by the special working of His Spirit; while yet He would not have this made an example for other men. It is certain that not one of these men was saved by his vows or his religious order, but by faith alone, by which all men are saved, but to which these showy servitudes of vows are especially hostile.

In this matter let every man be fully persuaded in his own mind. I shall carry out my undertaking, and speak on behalf of the liberty of the Church and of the glory of baptism; and I shall state for the general benefit what I have learnt under the teaching of the Spirit. And first I counsel those who are in high places in the Church to do away with all those vows and the practice of living under vows, or, at the least, not to approve or extol them. If they will not do this, then I earnestly advise all who desire to make their salvation the safer—particularly growing youths and young men—to keep aloof from all vows, especially from such as are extensive and life-long. I give this advice in the first place because this mode of life, as I have already said, has no evidence or example in the Scriptures, but rests only on the bulls of the pontiffs, who are but men; and secondly, because it tends to lead men into hypocrisy through its singularity and showy appearance, whence arise pride and contempt of the ordinary Christian life. If there were no other cause for doing away with these vows, this one by itself would have weight enough, that by them faith and baptism are depreciated, and works are magnified. Now these cannot be magnified without ruinous consequences, for among many thousands there is scarcely one who does not look more to his works as a member of a religious order, than to faith; and under this delusion they claim superiority over each other as being stricter or laxer, as they call it.

Hence I advise no man, yea, I dissuade every man from entering into the priesthood or any religious order, unless he be so fortified with knowledge as to understand that, however sacred and lofty may be the works of priests or of the religious orders, they differ not at all in the sight of God from the works of a husbandman labouring in his field, or of a woman attending to her household affairs, but that in His eyes all things are measured by faith alone; as it is written: "In all thy work believe with the faith of thy soul, for this is the keeping of the commandments of God." (Eccles. xxxii. 23.) Nay, it very often happens that the common work of a servant or a handmaiden is more acceptable to God than all the fastings and works of a monk or a priest, when they are done without faith. Since, then, it is likely that at the present day vows only tend to increase men's pride and presumption in their own works, it is to be feared that there is nowhere less of faith and of the Church than in priests, monks, and bishops; and that these very men are really Gentiles and hypocrites, who consider themselves to be the Church, or the very heart of the Church, spiritual persons, and rulers of the Church, when they are very far indeed from being so. These are really the people of the captivity, among whom all the free gifts bestowed in baptism have been brought into bondage; while the poor and slender remnant of the people of the land appear vile in their eyes.

From this we perceive two conspicuous errors on the part of the Roman Pontiff. The first is, that he gives dispensations in the matter of vows, and does this as if he alone possessed authority beyond all other Christians. So far does the rashness and audacity of wicked men extend. If a vow can be dispensed with, any brother can dispense for his neighbour, or even for himself. If he cannot grant such dispensations, neither has the Pope any right to do so. Whence has he this authority? From the keys? They are common to all, and only have power over sins. But since the Pope himself confesses that vows have a divine right, why does he cheat and ruin wretched souls by giving dispensations in a matter of divine right, which admits of no dispensation? He prates of the redemption of vows, and declares that he has power to change vows, just as under the law of old the first-born of an ass was exchanged for a lamb; as if a vow, which requires to be fulfilled everywhere and constantly, were the same thing with the first-born of an ass; or as if, because God in His own law ordered an ass to be exchanged for a lamb, therefore the Pope, who is but a man, had the same power with respect to a law which is not his, but God's. It was not a pope who made this decretal, but an ass which had been exchanged for a pope, so utterly mad and impious was he.

The Pope commits a second great error again, in decreeing that the bond of marriage may be broken through, if one of the parties, even against the will of the other, desires to enter a monastery, provided the marriage has not yet been consummated. What devil inspires this portentous decree of the Pope? God commands men to keep faith and observe truth towards one another, and that every man should bring gifts out of his own substance; for He hates robbery for burnt-offering, as He declares by the mouth of Isaiah. Now husband and wife owe fidelity to each other by their compact, a fidelity which can be dissolved by no law. Neither can say: "I belong to myself," or can do without robbery whatever is done against the will of the other. Else why not also have a rule that a man who is in debt, if he enter into a religious order, shall be freed from his debts, and be at liberty to deny his bond? Ye blind! ye blind! Which is greater—good faith, which is a command of God, or a vow, invented and chosen by men? Art thou a shepherd of souls, O Pope? Are ye doctors of sacred theology, who teach in this way? Why do ye teach thus? Because ye extol a vow as being a better work than marriage; but it is not faith, which itself alone can magnify anything, that ye magnify, but works, which in the sight of God are nothing, or at least all equal as concerns their merit.

I cannot doubt then that from such vows as it is right to make, neither men nor angels can give a dispensation. But I have not been able to convince myself that all the vows made in these days fall under the head of rightful vows; such as that ridiculous piece of folly, when parents devote their child yet unborn, or an infant, to a life of religion or to perpetual chastity. Nay it is certain that this is no rightful vow; it appears to be a mockery of God, since the parents vow what it is in no wise in their power to perform. I come now to members of the religious orders. The more I think of their three vows, the less I understand them, and the more I wonder how the exaction of such vows has grown upon us. Still less do I understand at what period of life such vows can be taken, so as to be legitimate and valid. In this all are agreed, that such vows, taken before the age of puberty, are not valid. And yet in this matter they deceive a great number of youths, who know as little of their own age as of what it is they are vowing. The age of puberty is not looked to when the vows are taken, but consent is supposed to follow afterwards, and the professed are held in bondage and devoured by dreadful scruples of conscience; as if a vow in itself void could become valid by the progress of time.

To me it seems folly that any limit to a legitimate vow should be laid down by others, who cannot lay one down in their own case. Nor do I see why a vow made in a man's eighteenth year should be valid, but not if made in his tenth or twelfth year. It is not enough to say that in his eighteenth year a man feels the impulses of the flesh. What if he scarcely feels them in his twentieth or thirtieth year; or feels them more strongly in his thirtieth year than in his twentieth? Why, again, is not a similar limitation placed on the vows of poverty and obedience? What time shall we assign for a man to feel himself avaricious or proud, when even the most spiritually minded men have a difficulty in detecting these affections in themselves? There will never be any sure and legitimate vow, until we shall have become thoroughly spiritual, and so have no need of vows. We see then that vows are most uncertain and perilous things. It would be a salutary course to leave this lofty manner of living under vows free to the spirit alone, as it was of old, and by no means to convert it into a perpetual mode of life. We have now, however, said enough on the subject of baptism and liberty. The time will perhaps come for treating more fully of vows, and in truth they greatly need to be treated of.

CONCERNING THE SACRAMENT OF PENANCE

In this third part I shall speak of the sacrament of penance. By the tracts and disputations which I have published on this subject I have given offence to very many, and have amply expressed my own opinions. I must now briefly repeat these statements, in order to unveil the tyranny which attacks us on this point as unsparingly as in the sacrament of the bread. In these two sacraments gain and lucre find a place, and therefore the avarice of the shepherds has raged to an incredible extent against the sheep of Christ; while even baptism, as we have seen in speaking of vows, has been sadly obscured among adults, that the purposes of avarice might be served.

The first and capital evil connected with this sacrament is, that they have totally done away with the sacrament itself, leaving not even a vestige of it. Whereas this, like the other two sacraments, consists of the word of the divine promise on one side and of our faith on the other, they have overthrown both of these. They have adapted to the purposes of their own tyranny Christ's word of promise, when He says: "Whatsoever thou shalt bind on earth shall be bound in heaven: and whatsoever thou shalt loose on earth shall be loosed in heaven" (Matt. xvi. 19); and: "Whatsoever ye shall bind on earth shall be bound in heaven: and whatsoever ye shall loose on earth shall be loosed in heaven" (Matt. xviii. 18); and again: "Whose soever sins ye remit, they are remitted unto them; and whose soever sins ye retain, they are retained." (John xx. 23.) These words are meant to call forth the faith of penitents, that they may seek and obtain remission of their sins. But these men, in all their books, writings, and discourses, have not made it their object to explain to Christians the promise conveyed in these words, and to show them what they ought to believe, and how much consolation they might have, but to establish in the utmost length, breadth and depth their own powerful and violent tyranny. At last some have even begun to give orders to the angels in heaven, and to boast, with an incredible frenzy of impiety, that they have received the right to rule in heaven and on earth, and have the power of binding even in heaven. Thus they say not a word about the saving faith of the people, but talk largely of the tyrannical power of the pontiffs; whereas Christ's words do not deal at all with power, but entirely with faith.

It was not principalities, powers, and dominions that Christ instituted in His Church, but a ministry, as we learn from the words of the Apostle: "Let a man so account of us, as of the ministers of Christ, and stewards of the mysteries of God." (1 Cor. iv. 1.) When Christ said: "Whosoever believeth and is baptized shall be saved," He meant to call forth faith on the part of those seeking baptism; so that, on the strength of this word of promise, a man might be sure that, if he believed and were baptized, he would obtain salvation. No sort of power is here bestowed on His servants, but only the ministry of baptism is committed to them. In the same way, when Christ says: "Whatsoever ye shall bind," etc., He means to call forth the faith of the penitent, so that, on the strength of this word of promise, he may be sure that, if he believes and is absolved, he will be truly absolved in heaven. Evidently nothing is said here of power, but it is the ministry of absolution which is spoken of. It is strange enough that these blind and arrogant men have not arrogated to themselves some tyrannical power from the terms of the baptismal promise. If not, why have they presumed to do so from the promise connected with penitence? In both cases there is an equal ministry, a like promise, and the same character in the sacrament; and it cannot be denied that, if we do not owe baptism to Peter alone, it is a piece of impious tyranny to claim the power of the keys for the Pope alone.

Thus also when Christ says: "Take, eat, this is my body which is given for you; this is the cup in my blood," He means to call forth faith in those who eat, that their conscience may be strengthened by faith in these words, and that they may feel sure that, when they believe eat, they receive remission of sins. There is nothing here which speaks of power, but only of a ministry. The promise of Baptism has remained with us, at least in the case of infants, but the promise of the Bread and the Cup has been destroyed, or brought into servitude to avarice, and faith has been turned into a work and a testament into a sacrifice. Thus also the promise of Penance has been perverted into a most violent tyranny, and into the establishment of a dominion that is more than temporal.

Not content with this, our Babylon has so utterly done away with faith as to declare with shameless front that it is not necessary in this sacrament; nay, in her antichristian wickedness, she pronounces it a heresy to assert the necessity of faith. What more is there that that tyranny could do, and has not done? Verily "by the rivers of Babylon, there we sat down; yea, we wept, when we remembered Zion. We hanged our harps upon the willows in the midst thereof." (Psalm cxxxvii. 1, 2.) May the Lord curse the barren willows of those rivers! Amen. The promise and faith having been blotted out and overthrown, let us see what they have substituted for them. They have divided penitence into three parts, contrition, confession, and satisfaction; but in doing this they have taken away all that was good in each of these, and have set up in each their own tyranny and caprice.

In the first place, they have so taught contrition as to make it prior to faith in the promise, and far better as not being a work of faith, but a merit; nay, they make no mention of faith. They stick fast in works and in examples taken from the Scriptures, where we read of many who obtained pardon through humility and contrition of heart, but they never think of the faith which wrought this contrition and sorrow of heart; as it is written concerning the Ninevites: "The people of Nineveh believed God, and proclaimed a fast, and put on sackcloth." (Jonah iii. 5.) These men, worse and more audacious than the Ninevites, have invented a certain "attrition," which, by the virtue of the keys (of which they are ignorant), may become contrition; and this they bestow on the wicked and unbelieving, and thus do away entirely with contrition. O unendurable wrath of God, that such things should be taught in the Church of Christ! So it is that, having got rid of faith and its work, we walk heedlessly in the doctrines and opinions of men, or ratherperish in them. A contrite heart is a great matter indeed, and can only proceed from an earnest faith in the Divine promises and threats—a faith which, contemplating the unshakeable truth of God, makes the conscience to tremble, terrifies and bruises it, and, when it is thus contrite, raises it up again, consoles, and preserves it. Thus, the truth of the threatening is the cause of contrition, and the truth of the promise is the cause of consolation, when they are believed; and by this faith a man merits remission of sins. Therefore faith above all things ought to be taught and called forth; when faith is produced, contrition and consolation will follow of their own accord by an inevitable consequence.

Hence, although there is something in the teaching of those who assert that contrition is to be brought about by the collection—as they call it—and contemplation of our own sins, still theirs is a perilous and perverse doctrine, because they do not first teach the origin and cause of contrition, namely, the unshakeable truth of the Divine threatenings and promises, in order to call forth faith; that so men might understand that they ought to look with much more earnest attention to the truth of God, by which to be humbled and raised up again, than to the multitude of their own sins, which, if they be looked at apart from the truth of God, are more likely to renew and increase the desire for sin, than to produce contrition. I say nothing of that insurmountable chaos of labour which they impose upon us, namely, that we are to frame a contrition for all our sins, for this is impossible. We can know but a small part of our sins; indeed even our good works will be found to be sins; as it is written: "Enter not into judgment with thy servant: for in thy sight shall no man living be justified." (Psalm cxliii. 2.) It is enough that we sorrow for those sins which vex our conscience at the present moment, and which are easily recognised by an effort of our memory. He who is thus disposed will without doubt be ready to feel sorrow and fear on account of all his sins, and will feel sorrow and fear when in future they are revealed to him.

Beware then of trusting in thine own contrition, or attributing remission of sins to thy own sorrow. It is not because of these that God looks on thee with favour, but because of the faith with which thou hast believed His threatenings and promises, and which has wrought that sorrow in thee. Therefore whatever good there is in penitence is due, not to the diligence with which we reckon up our sins, but to the truth of God and to our faith. All other things are works and fruits which follow of their own accord, and which do not make a man good, but are done by a man who has been made good by his faith in the truth of God. Thus it is written: "Because he was wroth, there went up a smoke in his presence." (Psalm xviii. 8.) The terror of the threatening comes first, which devours the wicked; but faith, accepting the threatening, sends forth contrition as a cloud of smoke.

Contrition, though it has been completely exposed to wicked and pestilent doctrines, has yet given less occasion to tyranny and the love of gain. But confession and satisfaction have been turned into the most noted workshops for lucre and ambition. To speak first of confession. There is no doubt that confession of sins is necessary, and is commanded by God. "They were baptized of John in Jordan, confessing their sins." (Matt. iii. 6.) "If we confess our sins, he is faithful and just to forgive us our sins. If we say that we have not sinned, we make him a liar, and his word is not in us." (1 John i. 9, 10.) If the saints must not deny their sin, how much more ought those who are guilty of great or public offences to confess them. But the most effective proof of the institution of confession is given when Christ tells us that an offending brother must be told of his fault, brought before the Church, accused, and finally, if he neglect to hear the Church, excommunicated. He "hears" when he yields to reproof, and acknowledges and confesses his sin.

The secret confession, however, which is now practised, though it cannot be proved from Scripture, is in my opinion highly satisfactory, and useful or even necessary. I could not wish it not to exist; nay, I rejoice that it does exist in the Church of Christ, for it is the one great remedy for afflicted consciences; when, after laying open our conscience to a brother, and unveiling all the evil which lay hid there, we receive from the mouth of that brother the word of consolation sent forth from God; receiving which by faith we find peace in a sense of the mercy of God, who speaks to us through our brother. What I protest against is the conversion of this institution of confession into a means of tyranny and extortion by the bishops. They reserve certain cases to themselves as secret, and then order them to be revealed to confessors named by themselves, and thus vex the consciences of men; filling the office of bishop, but utterly neglecting the real duties of a bishop, which are, to preach the gospel and to minister to the poor. Nay, these impious tyrants principally reserve to themselves the cases which are of less consequence, while they leave the greater ones everywhere to the common herd of priests,—cases such as the ridiculous inventions of the bull "In Cœna Domini." That their wicked perverseness may be yet more manifest, they do not reserve those things which are offences against the worship of God, against faith, and against the chief commandments, but even approve and teach them; such as those journeyings hither and thither on pilgrimage, the perverted worship of saints, the lying legends of saints, the confidence in and practice of works and ceremonies; by all which things the faith of God is extinguished, and idolatry is nourished, as it is at this day. The pontiffs we have nowadays are such as those whom Jeroboam established at Dan and Beersheba as ministers of the golden calves—men who are ignorant of the law of God, of faith, and of all that concerns the feeding of the sheep of Christ, and who only thrust their own inventions upon the people by terror and power.

Although I exhort men to endure the violence of these reservers, even as Christ bids us to endure all the tyrannical conduct of men, and teaches us to obey such extortioners; still I neither admit nor believe that they have any right of reservation. By no jot or tittle can they prove this; while I can prove the contrary. In the first place, if, in speaking of public offences, Christ says that we have gained our brother, if he hears us when told of his fault, and that he is not to be brought before the Church, unless he has refused to hear us, and that offences may thus be set right between brethren; how much more true will it be concerning private offences, that the sin is taken away, when brother has voluntarily confessed it to brother, so that he need not bring it before the Church, that is, before a prelate or priest, as these men say in their foolish interpretation. In support of my opinion we have again the authority of Christ, when he says in the same passage: "Whatsoever ye shall bind on earth shall be bound in heaven; and whatsoever ye shall loose on earth shall be loosed in heaven." (Matt. xviii. 18.) This saying is addressed to all Christians and to every Christian. Once more he says to the same effect: "Again I say unto you, that if two of you shall agree on earth as touching anything that they shall ask, it shall be done for them of my Father which is in heaven." (Matt. xviii. 19.) Now a brother, laying open his secret sins to a brother and seeking pardon, certainly agrees on earth with that brother in the truth, which is Christ. In confirmation of what he had said before, Christ says still more clearly in the same passage: "Where two or three are gathered together in my name, there am I in the midst of them." (Matt. xviii. 20.)

From all this I do not hesitate to say that whosoever voluntarily confesses his sins privately, in the presence of any brother, or, when told of his faults, asks pardon and amends his life, is absolved from his secret sins, since Christ has manifestly bestowed the power of absolution on every believer in Him, with whatever violence the pontiffs may rage against this truth. Add also this little argument, that, if any reservation of hidden sins were valid, and there could be no salvation unless they were remitted, the greatest hindrance to salvation would lie in those things which I have mentioned above—even those good works and idolatries which we are taught at the present day by the pontiffs. While, if these most weighty matters are not a hindrance, with how much less reason are those lighter offences so foolishly reserved! It is by the ignorance and blindness of the pastors that these portents are wrought in the Church. Wherefore I would warn these princes of Babylon and bishops of Beth-aven to abstain from reserving cases of any kind whatever, but to allow the freest permission to hear confessions of secret sins to all brethren and sisters; so that the sinner may reveal his sin to whom he will, with the object of seeking pardon and consolation, that is, the word of Christ uttered by the mouth of his neighbour. They effect nothing by their rash presumption, but to ensnare needlessly the consciences of the weak, to establish their own wicked tyranny, and to feed their own avarice on the sins and perdition of their brethren. Thus they stain their hands with the blood of souls, and children are devoured by their parents, and Ephraim devours Judah, and Syria Israel, as Isaiah says.

To these evils they have added circumstances—mothers, daughters, sisters, relatives, branches, fruits of sins, all devised at complete leisure by the most subtle of men, who have set up, even in the matter of sins, a sort of tree of consanguinity and affinity. So fertile of results are ignorance and impiety; for these devices of some worthless fellow have passed into public law, as has happened in many other cases. So vigilantly do the shepherds watch over the Church of Christ, that whatever dreams of superstition or of new works these senseless devotees indulge, they forthwith bring forward, and dress them up with indulgences, and fortify them with bulls. So far are they from prohibiting these things, and protecting the simplicity of faith and liberty for the people of God; for what has liberty to do with the tyranny of Babylon?

I should advise the total neglect of all that concerns circumstances. Among Christians there is but one circumstance, and that is, that a brother has sinned. No character is to be compared to Christian brotherhood; nor has the observation of places, times, days, and persons, or any other such superstitious exaggeration, any effect but to magnify things which are nothing, at the expense of those things which are everything. As if there could be anything greater or more weighty than the glory of Christian brotherhood, they so tie us down to places and days and persons, that the name of brother is held cheap, and instead of being freemen we are slaves in bondage—we to whom all days, places, persons, and all other outward things, are equal.

How unworthily they have treated the matter of satisfaction. I have abundantly shown in the case of indulgences. They have abused it notably, to the destruction of Christians in body and in soul. In the first place, they have so taught it that the people have not understood the real meaning of satisfaction, which is a change of life. Furthermore, they so urge it and represent it as necessary, that they leave no room for faith in Christ; but men's consciences are most wretchedly tortured by scruples on this point. One runs hither, another thither; one to Rome, another into a convent, another to some other place; one scourges himself with rods, another destroys his body with vigils and fasting; while all, under one general delusion, say: Here is Christ, or there; and imagine that the kingdom of God, which is really within us, will come with observation. These monstrous evils we owe to thee, See of Rome, and to thy homicidal laws and rites, by which thou hast brought the world to such a point of ruin, that they think they can make satisfaction to God for their sins by works, while it is only by the faith of a contrite heart that He is satisfied. This faith thou not only compellest to silence in the midst of these tumults, but strivest to destroy, only in order that thy avarice, that insatiable leech, may have some to whom to cry: Bring, bring; and may make a traffic of sins.

Some have even proceeded to such a length in framing engines of despair for souls, as to lay it down that all sins, the satisfaction enjoined for which has been neglected, must be gone over afresh in confession. What will not such men dare, men born for this end, to bring everything ten times over into bondage? Moreover, I should like to know how many people there are who are fully persuaded that they are in a state of salvation, and are making satisfaction for their sins, when they murmur over the prayers enjoined by the priest with their lips alone, and meanwhile do not even think of any amendment of life. They believe that by one moment of contrition and confession their whole life is changed, and that there remains merit enough over and above to make satisfaction for their past sins. How should they know better, when they are taught nothing better? There is not a thought here of mortification of the flesh; the example of Christ goes for nothing; who, when he absolved the woman taken in adultery, said to her: "Go, and sin no more;" thereby laying on her the cross of mortification of the flesh. No slight occasion has been given to these perverted ideas by our absolving sinners before they have completed their satisfaction; whence it comes that they are more anxious about completing their satisfaction, which is a thing that lasts, than about contrition, which they think has been gone through in the act of confession. On the contrary, absolution ought to follow the completion of satisfaction, as it did in the primitive Church, whence it happened that, the work being over, they were afterwards more exercised in faith and newness of life. On this subject, however, it must suffice to have repeated so far what I have said at greater length in writing on indulgences. Let it also suffice for the present to have said this much in the whole respecting these three sacraments, which are treated of and not treated of in so many mischievous books of Sentences and of law. It remains for me to say a few words about the remaining sacraments also, that I may not appear to have rejected them without sufficient reason.

OF CONFIRMATION

It is surprising that it should have entered any one's mind to make a Sacrament of Confirmation out of that laying on of hands which Christ applied to little children, and by which the apostles bestowed the Holy Spirit, ordained presbyters, and healed the sick; as the Apostle writes to Timothy: "Lay hands suddenly on no man." (1 Tim. v. 22.) Why not also make a confirmation out of the sacrament of bread, because it is written: "And when he had received meat, he was strengthened" (Acts ix. 19); or again: "Bread which strengtheneth man's heart?" (Ps. civ. 15.) Thus confirmation would include three sacraments, of bread, of orders, and of confirmation itself. But if whatever the apostles did is a sacrament, why has not preaching rather been made into a sacrament?

I do not say this, because I condemn the seven sacraments, but because I deny that they can be proved from the Scriptures. I wish there were in the Church such a laying on of hands as there was in the time of the Apostles, whether we chose to call it confirmation or healing. As it is, however, none of it remains, except so much as we have ourselves invented in order to regulate the duties of the bishops, that they may not be entirely without work in the Church. For when they had left the sacraments which involved labour, along with the word, to their inferiors, as being beneath their attention (on the ground, forsooth, that whatever institutions the Divine majesty has set up must needs be an object of contempt to men), it was but right that we should invent some easy duty, not too troublesome for the daintiness of these great heroes, and by no means commit it to inferiors, as if it were of little importance. What human wisdom has ordained ought to be honoured by men. Thus, such as the priests are, such should be the ministry and office which they hold. For what is a bishop who does not preach the gospel, or attend to the cure of souls, but an idol in the world, having the name and form of a bishop?

At present, however, we are enquiring into the sacraments of divine institution; and I can find no reason for reckoning confirmation among these. To constitute a sacrament we require in the very first place a word of divine promise, on which faith may exercise itself. But we do not read that Christ ever gave any promise respecting confirmation, although he himself laid hands upon many, and although he mentions among the signs that should follow them that believe: "They shall lay hands on the sick, and they shall recover." (Mark xvi. 18.) No one, however, has interpreted these words of a sacrament, or could do so. It is enough then to consider confirmation as a rite or ceremony of the Church; of like nature to those other ceremonies by which water and other things are consecrated. For if every other creature is sanctified by the word and prayer, why may not man much more be sanctified by the same means, even though they cannot be called sacraments of faith, inasmuch as they contain no divine promise? Neither do these work salvation; while sacraments save those who believe in the divine promise.

OF MATRIMONY

It is not only without any warrant of Scripture that matrimony is considered a sacrament, but it has been turned into a mere mockery by the very same traditions which vaunt it as a sacrament. Let us look a little into this. I have said that in every sacrament there is contained a word of divine promise, which must be believed in by him who receives the sign; and that the sign alone cannot constitute a sacrament. Now we nowhere read that he who marries a wife will receive any grace from God; neither is there in matrimony any sign of divine institution, nor do we anywhere read that it was appointed of God to be a sign of anything; although it is true that all visible transactions may be understood as figures and allegorical representations of invisible things. But figures and allegories are not sacraments, in the sense in which we are speaking of sacraments.

Furthermore, since matrimony has existed from the beginning of the world, and still continues even among unbelievers, there are no reasons why it should be called a sacrament of the new law, and of the Church alone. The marriages of the patriarchs were not less marriages than ours, nor are those of unbelievers less real than those of believers; and yet no one calls them a sacrament. Moreover there are among believers wicked husbands and wives, worse than any Gentiles. Why should we then say there is a sacrament here, and not among the Gentiles? Shall we so trifle with baptism and the Church as to say, like those who rave about the temporal power existing only in the Church, that matrimony is a sacrament only in the Church? Such assertions are childish and ridiculous, and by them we expose our ignorance and rashness to the laughter of unbelievers.

It will be asked however: Does not the Apostle say that "they two shall be one flesh," and that "this is a great sacrament;" and will you contradict the plain words of the Apostle? I reply that this argument is a very dull one, and proceeds from a careless and thoughtless reading of the original. Throughout the holy Scriptures this word *"sacramentum,"* has not the meaning in which we employ it, but an opposite one. For it everywhere signifies, not the sign of a sacred thing, but a sacred thing which is secret and hidden. Thus Paul says: "Let a man so account of us, as of the ministers of Christ, and stewards of the mysteries (that is, sacraments) of God." (1 Cor. iv. 1.) Where we use the Latin term "sacrament," in Greek the word "mystery" is employed; and thus in Greek the words of the Apostle are: "They two shall be one flesh; this is a great mystery." This ambiguity has led men to consider marriage as a sacrament of the new law, which they would have been far from doing, if they had read the word "mystery," as it is in the Greek.

Thus the Apostle calls Christ himself a "sacrament," saying: "And without controversy great is the sacrament (that is, mystery) of godliness. God was manifest in the flesh, justified in the spirit, seen of angels, preached unto the Gentiles, believed on in the world, received up into glory." (1 Tim. iii. 16.) Why have they not deduced from this an eighth sacrament of the new law, under such clear authority from Paul? Or, if they restrained themselves in this case, where they might so suitably have been copious in the invention of sacraments, why are they so lavish of them in the other? It is because they have been misled by their ignorance as well of things as of words; they have been caught by the mere sound of the words and by their own fancies. Having once, on human authority, taken a sacrament to be a sign, they have proceeded, without any judgment or scruple, to make the word mean a sign, wherever they have met with it in the sacred writings. Just as they have imported other meanings of words and human habits of speech into the sacred writings, and transformed these into dreams of their own, making anything out of anything. Hence their constant senseless use of the words: good works, bad works, sin, grace, righteousness, virtue, and almost all the most important words and things. They use all these at their own discretion, founded on the writings of men, to the ruin of the truth of God and of our salvation.

Thus sacrament and mystery, in Paul's meaning, are the very wisdom of the Spirit, hidden in a mystery, as he says: "Which none of the princes of this world knew; for had they known it, they would not have crucified the Lord of glory." (1 Cor. ii. 8.) There remains to this day this folly, this stone of stumbling and rock of offence, this sign which shall be spoken against. Paul calls preachers the stewards of these mysteries, because they preach Christ, the power and wisdom of God; but so preach him that unless men believe, they cannot understand. Thus a sacrament means a mystery and a hidden thing, which is made known by words, but is received by faith of heart. Such is the passage of which we are speaking at present: "They two shall be one flesh; this is a great mystery." These men think that this was said concerning matrimony; but Paul brings in these words in speaking of Christ and the Church, and explains his meaning clearly by saying: "I speak concerning Christ and the Church." See how well Paul and these men agree! Paul says that he is setting forth a great mystery concerning Christ and the Church; while they set it forth as concerning male and female. If men may thus indulge their own caprices in interpreting the sacred writings, what wonder if anything can be found in them, were it even a hundred sacraments?

Christ then and the Church are a mystery, that is, a great and hidden thing, which may indeed and ought to be figured by matrimony, as in a sort of real allegory; but it does not follow that matrimony ought to be called a sacrament. The heavens figuratively represent the apostles; the sun Christ; the waters nations; but these things are not therefore sacraments; for in all these cases the institution is wanting and the divine promise; and these it is which make a sacrament complete. Hence Paul is either, of his own spirit, applying to Christ the words used in Genesis concerning matrimony, or else he teaches that, in their general sense, the spiritual marriage of Christ is also there declared, saying: "Even as the Lord cherisheth the Church; for we are members of his body, of his flesh, and of his bones. For this cause shall a man leave his father and mother, and shall be joined unto his wife, and they two shall be one flesh. This is a great mystery, but I speak concerning Christ and the Church." (Eph. v. 29–32.) We see that he means this whole text to be understood as spoken by him about Christ. He purposely warns the reader to understand the "Sacrament" as in Christ and the Church, not in matrimony.

I admit, indeed, that even under the old law, nay, from the beginning of the world, there was a sacrament of penitence; but the new promise of penitence and the gift of the keys are peculiar to the new law. As we have baptism in the place of circumcision, so we now have the keys in the place of sacrifices or other signs of penitence. I have said above that, at different times, the same God has given different promises and different signs for the remission of sins and the salvation of men, while yet it is the same grace that all have received. As it is written: "We, having the same spirit of faith, believe, and therefore speak." (2 Cor. iv. 13.) "Our fathers did all eat the same spiritual meat, and did all drink the same spiritual drink; for they drank of that spiritual rock that followed them, and that rock was Christ." (1 Cor. x. 3, 4.) "These all died in faith, not having received the promises; God having provided some better thing for us, that they without us should not be made perfect." (Heb. xi. 13, 40.) For Christ himself, the same yesterday, and to-day, and for ever, is the head of his Church from the beginning even to the end of the world. There are then different signs, but the faith of all believers is the same; since without faith it is impossible to please God, and by it Abel pleased Him.

Let then matrimony be a figure of Christ and the Church, not however a sacrament divinely instituted, but one invented in the Church by men led astray by their ignorance alike of things and of words. So far as this invention is not injurious to the faith, it must be borne with in charity; just as many other devices of human weakness and ignorance are borne with in the Church, so long as they are not injurious to faith and to the sacred writings. But we are now contending for the firmness and purity of faith and of Scripture; lest, if we affirm anything to be contained in the sacred writings and in the articles of our faith, and it is afterwards proved not to be so contained, we should expose our faith to mockery, be found ignorant of our own special business, cause scandal to our adversaries and to the weak, and fail to exalt the authority of holy Scripture. For we must make the widest possible distinction between those things which have been delivered to us from God in the sacred writings, and those which have been invented in the Church by men, of however eminent authority from their holiness and their learning.

Thus far I have spoken of matrimony itself. But what shall we say of those impious human laws by which this divinely appointed manner of life has been entangled and tossed up and down? Good God! it is horrible to look upon the temerity of the tyrants of Rome, who thus, according to their own caprices, at one time annul marriages and at another time enforce them. Is the human race given over to their caprice for nothing but to be mocked and abused in every way, and that these men may do what they please with it for the sake of their own fatal gains?

There is a book in general circulation and held in no slight esteem, which has been confusedly put together out of all the dregs and filth of human traditions, and entitled the Angelic Summary; while it is really a more than diabolical summary. In this book, among an infinite number of monstrous statements, by which confessors are supposed to be instructed, while they are in truth most ruinously confused, eighteen impediments to matrimony are enumerated. If we look at these with the just and free eye of faith, we shall see that the writer is of the number of those of whom the Apostle foretold that they should "give heed to seducing spirits and doctrines of devils; speaking lies in hypocrisy; forbidding to marry." (1 Tim. iv. 1–3.) What is forbidding to marry, if this is not forbidding it—to invent so many impediments, and to set so many snares, that marriages cannot be contracted, or, if they are contracted, must be dissolved? Who has given this power to men? Granted that such men have been holy and led by a pious zeal; why does the holiness of another encroach upon my liberty? Why does the zeal of another bring me into bondage? Let whosoever will be as holy and as zealous as he will, but let him not injure others, or rob me of my liberty.

I rejoice, however, that these disgraceful laws have at length attained the glory they deserve, in that by their aid the men of Rome have nowadays become common traders. And what do they sell? The shame of men and women; a merchandise worthy of these traffickers, who surpass all that is most sordid and disgusting in their avarice and impiety. There is not one of those impediments, which cannot be removed at the intercession of Mammon; so that these laws seem to have been made for no other purpose than to be nets for money and snares for souls in the hands of those greedy and rapacious Nimrods; and in order that we might see in the holy place, in the Church of God, the abomination of the public sale of the shame and ignominy of both sexes. A business worthy of our pontiffs, and fit to be carried on by men who, with the utmost disgrace and baseness, are given over to a reprobate mind, instead of that ministry of the gospel which, in their avarice and ambition, they despise.

But what am I to say or do? If I were to enter upon every particular, this treatise would extend beyond all bounds; for the subject is in the utmost confusion, so that no one can tell where he is to begin, how far he is to go, or where he is to stop. This I know, that no commonwealth can be prosperously administered by mere laws. If the magistrate is a wise man, he will govern more happily under the guidance of nature than by any laws; if he is not a wise man, he will effect nothing but mischief by laws, since he will not know how to use them, or to adapt them to the wants of the time. In public matters, therefore, it is of more importance that good and wise men should be at the head of affairs, than that any laws should be passed; for such men will themselves be the best of laws, since they will judge cases of all kinds with energy and justice. If, together with natural wisdom, there be learning in divine things, then it is clearly superfluous and mischievous to have any written laws; and charity above all things has absolutely no need of laws. I say, however, and do all that in me lies, admonishing and entreating all priests and friars, if they see any impediment with which the Pope can dispense, but which is not mentioned in Scripture, to consider all those marriages valid which have been contracted, in whatever way, contrary to ecclesiastical or pontifical laws. Let them arm themselves with the Divine law which says: What God hath joined together, let not man put asunder. The union of husband and wife is one of divine right, and holds good, however much against the laws of men it may have taken place, and the laws of men ought to give place to it, without any scruple. For if a man is to leave his father and mother and cleave to his wife, how much more ought he to tread under foot the frivolous and unjust laws of men, that he may cleave to his wife? If the Pope, or any bishop or official, dissolves any marriage, because it has been contracted contrary to the papal laws, he is an antichrist, does violence to nature, and is guilty of treason against God; because this sentence stands: Whom God hath joined together, let not man put asunder.

Besides this, man has no right to make such laws, and the liberty bestowed on Christians through Christ is above all the laws of men, especially when the divine law comes in, as Christ says: "The Sabbath was made for man, and not man for the Sabbath; therefore the Son of man is Lord also of the Sabbath." (Mark ii. 27–28.) Again, such laws were condemned beforehand by Paul, when he foretold that those should arise who would forbid to marry. Hence in this matter all those rigorous impediments derived from spiritual affinity, or legal relationship and consanguinity, must give way, as far as is permitted by the sacred writings, in which only the second grade of consanguinity is prohibited, as it is written in the book of Leviticus, where twelve persons are prohibited, namely:—mother, step-mother, full sister, half sister by either parent, grand-daughter, father's sister, mother's sister, daughter-in-law, brother's wife, wife's sister, step-daughter, uncle's wife. In these only the first grade of affinity and the second of consanguinity are prohibited, and not even these universally, as is clear when we look carefully at the subject; for the daughter and grand-daughter of a brother and sister are not mentioned as prohibited, though they are in the second grade. Hence, if at any time a marriage has been contracted outside these grades, than which no others have ever been prohibited by God's appointment, it ought by no means to be dissolved on account of any laws of men. Matrimony, being a divine institution, is incomparably above all laws, and therefore it cannot rightfully be broken through for the sake of laws, but rather laws for its sake.

Thus all those fanciful spiritual affinities of father, mother, brother, sister, or child, ought to be utterly done away with in the contracting of matrimony. What but the superstition of man has invented that spiritual relationship? If he who baptizes is not permitted to marry her whom he has baptized, or a godfather his god-daughter, why is a Christian man permitted to marry a Christian woman? Is the relationship established by a ceremony or by the sign of the sacrament stronger than that established by the substance itself of the sacrament? Is not a Christian man the brother of a Christian sister? Is not a baptized man the spiritual brother of a baptized woman? How can we be so senseless? If a man instructs his wife in the gospel and in the faith of Christ, and thus becomes truly her father in Christ, shall it not be lawful for her to continue his wife? Would not Paul have been at liberty to marry a maiden from among those Corinthians, all of whom he declares that he had begotten in Christ? See, then, how Christian liberty has been crushed by the blindness of human superstition!

Much more idle still is the doctrine of legal relationship; and yet they have raised even this above the divine right of matrimony. Nor can I agree to that impediment which they call disparity of religion, and which forbids a man to marry an unbaptized woman, neither simply, nor on condition of converting her to the faith. Who has prohibited this, God or man? Who has given men authority to prohibit marriages of this kind? Verily the spirits that speak lies in hypocrisy, as Paul says; of whom it may be truly said: The wicked have spoken lies to me, but not according to thy law. Patricius, a heathen, married Monica, the mother of St. Augustine, who was a Christian; why should not the same thing be lawful now? A like instance of foolish, nay wicked rigour is the impediment of crime; as when a man marries a woman previously polluted by adultery, or has plotted the death of a woman's husband, that he may be able to marry her. Whence, I ask, a severity on the part of men against men, such as even God has never exacted? Do these men pretend not to know that David, a most holy man, married Bathsheba the wife of Uriah, though both these crimes had been committed; that is, though she had been polluted by adultery and her husband had been murdered? If the divine law did this, why do tyrannical men act thus against their fellow servants?

It is also reckoned as an impediment when there exists what they call a bond; that is, when one person is bound to another by betrothal. In this case they conclude that if either party have subsequently had intercourse with a third, the former betrothal comes to an end. I cannot at all receive this doctrine. In my judgment, a man who has bound himself to one person is no longer at his own disposal, and therefore, under the prohibitions of the divine right, owes himself to the former, though he has not had intercourse with her, even if he have afterwards had intercourse with another. It was not in his power to give what he did not possess; he has deceived her with whom he has had intercourse, and has really committed adultery. That which has led some to think otherwise is that they have looked more to the fleshly union than to the divine command, under which he who has promised fidelity to one person is bound to observe it. He who desires to give, ought to give of that which is his own. God forbid that any man should go beyond or defraud his brother in any matter; for good faith ought to be preserved beyond and above all traditions of all men. Thus I believe that such a man cannot with a safe conscience cohabit with a second woman, and that this impediment ought to be entirely reversed. If a vow of religion deprives a man of his power over himself, why not also a pledge of fidelity given and received; especially since the latter rests on the teaching and fruits of the Spirit (Gal. v.), while the former rests on human choice? And if a wife may return to her husband, notwithstanding any vow of religion she may have made, why should not a betrothed man return to his betrothed, even if connexion with another have followed? We have said, however, above that a man who has pledged his faith to a maiden is not at liberty to make a vow of religion, but is bound to marry her, because he is bound to keep his faith, and is not at liberty to abandon it for the sake of any human tradition, since God commands that it should be kept. Much more will it be his duty to observe his pledge to the first to whom he has given it, because it was only with a deceitful heart that he could give it to a second; and therefore he has not really given it, but has deceived his neighbour, against the law of God. Hence the impediment called that of error takes effect here, and annuls the marriage with the second woman.

The impediment of holy orders is also a mere contrivance of men, especially when they idly assert that even a marriage already contracted is annulled by this cause, always exalting their own traditions above the commands of God. I give no judgment respecting the order of the priesthood, such as it is at the present day; but I see that Paul commands that a bishop should be the husband of one wife, and therefore the marriage of a deacon, of a priest, of a bishop, or of a man in any kind of orders, cannot be annulled; although Paul knew nothing of that kind of priests and those orders which we have at the present day. Perish then these accursed traditions of men, which have come in for no other end than to multiply perils, sins, and evils in the Church! Between a priest and his wife, then, there is a true and inseparable marriage, approved by the divine command. What if wicked men forbid or annul it of their own mere tyranny? Be it that it is unlawful in the sight of men; yet it is lawful in the sight of God, whose commandment, if it be contrary to the commandments of men, is to be preferred.

Just as much a human contrivance is the so-called impediment of public propriety, by which contracted marriages are annulled. I am indignant at the audacious impiety which is so ready to separate what God has joined together. You may recognise Antichrist in this opposition to everything which Christ did or taught. What reason is there, I ask, why, on the death of a betrothed husband before actual marriage, no relative by blood, even to the fourth degree, can marry her who was betrothed to him? This is no vindication of public propriety, but mere ignorance of it. Why among the people of Israel, which possessed the best laws, given by God himself, was there no such vindication of public propriety? On the contrary, by the very command of God, the nearest relative was compelled to marry her who had been left a widow. Ought the people who are in Christian liberty to be burdened with more rigid laws than the people who were in legal bondage? And to make an end of these figments rather than impediments, I will say that at present it is evident to me that there is no impediment which can rightfully annul a marriage already contracted, except physical unfitness for cohabiting with a wife, ignorance of a marriage previously contracted, or a vow of chastity. Concerning such a vow, however, I am so uncertain even to the present moment, that I do not know at what time it ought to be reckoned valid; as I have said above in speaking of baptism. Learn then, in this one matter of matrimony, into what an unhappy and hopeless state of confusion, hindrance, entanglement, and peril all things that are done in the Church have been brought by the pestilent, unlearned, and impious traditions of men! There is no hope of a remedy, unless we can do away once for all with all the laws of all men, call back the gospel of liberty, and judge and rule all things according to it alone. Amen.

It is necessary also to deal with the question of physical incapacity. But be it premised that I desire what I have said about impediments to be understood of marriages already contracted, which ought not to be annulled for any such causes. But with regard to the contracting of matrimony I may briefly repeat what I have said before, that if there be any urgency of youthful love, or any other necessity, on account of which the Pope grants a dispensation, then any brother can also grant a dispensation to his brother, or himself to himself, and thus snatch his wife, in whatever way he can, out of the hands of tyrannical laws. Why is my liberty to be done away with by another man's superstition and ignorance? Or if the Pope gives dispensation for money, why may not I give a dispensation to my brother or to myself for the advantage of my own salvation? Does the Pope establish laws? Let him establish them for himself, but let my liberty be untouched.

The question of divorce is also discussed, whether it be lawful. I, for my part, detest divorce, and even prefer bigamy to it; but whether it be lawful I dare not define. Christ himself, the chief of shepherds, says: "Whosoever shall put away his wife, saving for the cause of fornication, causeth her to commit adultery; and whosoever shall marry her that is divorced committeth adultery." (Matt. v. 32.) Christ therefore permits divorce only in the case of fornication. Hence the Pope must necessarily be wrong, as often as he permits divorce for other reasons, nor ought any man forthwith to consider himself safe, because he has obtained a dispensation by pontifical audacity rather than power. I am more surprised, however, that they compel a man who has been separated from his wife by divorce to remain single, and do not allow him to marry another. For if Christ permits divorce for the cause of fornication, and does not compel any man to remain single, and if Paul bids us rather to marry than to burn, this seems plainly to allow of a man's marrying another in the place of her whom he has put away. I wish that this subject were fully discussed and made clear, that provision might be made for the numberless perils of those who at the present day are compelled to remain single without any fault of their own; that is, whose wives or husbands have fled and deserted their partner, not to return for ten years, or perhaps never. I am distressed and grieved by these cases, which are of daily occurrence, whether this happens by the special malice of Satan, or from our neglect of the word of God.

I cannot by myself establish any rule contrary to the opinion of all; but for my own part, I should exceedingly wish at least to see applied to this subject the words: "But if the unbelieving depart, let him depart. A brother or a sister is not under bondage in such cases" (1 Cor. vii. 15). Here the Apostle permits that the unbelieving one who departs should be let go, and leaves it free to the believer to take another. Why should not the same rule hold good, if a believer, that is, a nominal believer, but in reality just as much an unbeliever, deserts husband or wife, especially if with the intention of never returning? I cannot discover any distinction between the two cases. In my belief, however, if in the Apostle's time the unbeliever who had departed had returned, or had become a believer, or had promised to live with the believing wife, he would not have been received, but would himself have been authorised to marry another woman. Still, I give no definite opinion on these questions, though I greatly wish that a definite rule were laid down, for there is nothing which more harasses me and many others. I would not have any rule on this point laid down by the sole authority of the Pope or the bishops; but if any two learned and good men agreed together in the name of Christ, and pronounced a decision in the spirit of Christ, I should prefer their judgment even to that of councils, such as are assembled nowadays, which are celebrated simply for their number and authority, independently of learning and holiness. I therefore suspend my utterances on this subject, until I can confer with some better judge.

OF ORDERS

Of this sacrament the Church of Christ knows nothing; it was invented by the church of the Pope. It not only has no promise of grace, anywhere declared, but not a word is said about it in the whole of the New Testament. Now it is ridiculous to set up as a sacrament of God that which can nowhere be proved to have been instituted by God. Not that I consider that a rite practised for so many ages is to be condemned; but I would not have human inventions established in sacred things, nor should it be allowed to bring in anything as divinely ordained, which has not been divinely ordained; lest we should be objects of ridicule to our adversaries. We must endeavour that whatever we put forward as an article of the faith should be certain and uncorrupt and established by clear proofs from Scripture; and this we cannot show even in the slightest degree in the case of the present sacrament.

The Church has no power to establish new divine promises of grace, as some senselessly assert, who say that, since the Church is governed by the Holy Spirit, whatever she ordains has no less authority than that which is ordained of God. The Church is born of the word of promise through faith, and is nourished and preserved by the same word; that is, she herself is established by the promises of God, not the promise of God by her. The word of God is incomparably above the Church, and her part is not to establish, ordain, or make anything in it, but only to be established, ordained, and made, as a creature. What man begets his own parent? Who establishes the authority by which he himself exists?

This power the Church certainly has—that she can distinguish the word of God from the words of men. So Augustine confesses that his motive for believing the gospel was the authority of the Church, which declared it to be the gospel. Not that the Church is therefore above the gospel; for, if so, she would also be above God, in whom we believe, since she declares Him to be God; but, as Augustine says elsewhere, the soul is so taken possession of by the truth, that thereby it can judge of all things with the utmost certainty, and yet cannot judge the truth itself, but is compelled by an infallible certainty to say that this is the truth. For example, the mind pronounces with infallible certainty that three and seven are ten, and yet can give no reason why this is true, while it cannot deny that it is true. In fact the mind itself is taken possession of, and, having truth as its judge, is judged rather than judges. Even such a perception is there in the Church, by the illumination of the Spirit, in judging and approving of doctrines; a perception which she cannot demonstrate, but which she holds as most sure. Just as among philosophers no one judges of those conceptions which are common to all, but everyone is judged by them, so is it among us with regard to that spiritual perception which judgeth all things, yet is judged of no man, as the Apostle says.

Let us take it then for certain that the Church cannot promise grace, to do which is the part of God alone, and therefore cannot institute a sacrament. And even, if she had the most complete power to do so, it would not forthwith follow, that orders are a sacrament. For who knows what is that Church which has the Spirit, when only a few bishops and learned men are usually concerned in setting up these laws and institutions? It is possible that these men may not be of the Church, and may all be in error; as councils have very often been in error, especially that of Constance, which has erred the most impiously of all. That only is a proved article of the faith which has been approved by the universal Church, and not by that of Rome alone. I grant therefore that orders may be a sort of church rite, like many others which have been introduced by the Fathers of the Church, such as the consecration of vessels, buildings, vestments, water, salt, candles, herbs, wine, and the like. In all these no one asserts that there is any sacrament, nor is there any promise in them. Thus the anointing of a man's hands, the shaving of his head, and other ceremonies of the kind, do not constitute a sacrament, since nothing is promised by these things, but they are merely employed to prepare men for certain offices, as in the case of vessels or instruments.

But it will be asked: What do you say to Dionysius, who reckons up six sacraments, among which he places Orders, in his Hierarchy of the Church? My answer is: I know that he is the only one of the ancient authorities who is considered as holding seven sacraments, although, by the omission of matrimony, he has only given six. We read nothing at all in the rest of the Fathers about these sacraments, nor did they reckon them under the title of sacrament, when they spoke of these things, for the invention of such sacraments is a modern one. Then too—if I may be rash enough to say so—it is altogether unsatisfactory that so much importance should be attributed to this Dionysius, whoever he was, for there is almost nothing of solid learning in him. By what authority or reason, I ask, does he prove his inventions concerning angels in his Celestial Hierarchy, a book on the study of which curious and superstitious minds have spent so much labour? Are they not all fancies of his own, and very much like dreams, if we read them and judge them freely? In his mystic theology indeed, which is so much cried up by certain very ignorant theologians, he is even very mischievous, and follows Plato rather than Christ, so that I would not have any believing mind bestow even the slightest labour on the study of these books. You will be so far from learning Christ in them that, even if you know Him, you may lose Him. I speak from experience. Let us rather hear Paul, and learn Jesus Christ and Him crucified. For this is the way, the truth, and the life; this is the ladder by which we come to the Father, as it is written: "No man cometh unto the Father, but by Me."

So in his Hierarchy of the Church, what does he do but describe certain ecclesiastical rites, amusing himself with his own allegories, which he does not prove, just as has been done in our time by the writer of the book called the Rationale of Divine things? This pursuit of allegories is only fit for men of idle minds. Could I have any difficulty in amusing myself with allegories about any created thing whatever? Did not Bonaventura apply the liberal arts allegorically to theology? It would give me no trouble to write a better Hierarchy than that of Dionysius, as he knew nothing of popes, cardinals, and archbishops, and made the bishops the highest order. Who, indeed, is there of such slender wits that he cannot venture upon allegory? I would not have a theologian bestow any attention upon allegories, until he is perfectly acquainted with the legitimate and simple meaning of Scripture; otherwise, as it happened to Origen, his theological speculations will not be without danger.

We must not then immediately make a sacrament of anything which Dionysius describes; otherwise why not make a sacrament of the procession which he describes in the same passage, and which continues in use even to the present day? Nay, there will be as many sacraments as there are rites and ceremonies which have grown up in the Church. Resting, however, on this very weak foundation, they have invented and attributed to this sacrament of theirs certain indelible characters, supposed to be impressed on those who receive orders. Whence, I ask, such fancies? By what authority, by what reasoning are they established? Not that we object to their being free to invent, learn, or assert whatever they please; but we also assert our own liberty, and say that they must not arrogate to themselves the right of making articles of the faith out of their own fancies, as they have hitherto had the presumption to do. It is enough that, for the sake of concord, we submit to their rights and inventions, but we will not be compelled to receive them as necessary to salvation, when they are not necessary. Let them lay aside their tyrannical requirements, and we will show a ready compliance with their likings, that so we may live together in mutual peace. For it is a disgraceful, unjust, and slavish thing for a Christian man, who is free, to be subjected to any but heavenly and divine traditions.

After this they bring in their very strongest argument, namely, that Christ said at the last supper: "Do this in remembrance of me." "Behold!" they say, "Christ ordained them as priests." Hence, among other things, they have also asserted that it is to priests alone that both kinds should be administered. In fact they have extracted out of this text whatever they would; like men who claim the right to assert at their own free choice whatsoever they please out of any words of Christ, wherever spoken. But is this to interpret the words of God? Let us reply to them that in these words Christ gives no promise, but only a command that this should be done in remembrance of Him. Why do they not conclude that priests were ordained in that passage also where Christ, in laying upon them the ministry of the word and of baptism, said: "Go ye into all the world, and preach the gospel to every creature, baptizing them in the name of the Father, and of the Son, and of the Holy Ghost"? It is the peculiar office of priests to preach and to baptize. Again, since at the present day it is the very first business of a priest, and, as they say, an indispensable one, to read the canonical Hours; why have they not taken their idea of the sacrament of orders from those words in which Christ commanded His disciples—as he did in many other places, but especially in the garden of Gethsemane—to pray that they might not enter into temptation? Unless indeed they evade the difficulty by saying that it is not commanded to pray, for it suffices to read the canonical Hours; so that this cannot be proved to be a priestly work from any part of Scripture, and that consequently this praying priesthood is not of God; as indeed it is not.

Which of the ancient Fathers has asserted that by these words priests were ordained? Whence then this new interpretation? It is because it has been sought by this device to set up a source of implacable discord, by which clergy and laity might be placed farther asunder than heaven and earth, to the incredible injury of baptismal grace and confusion of evangelical communion. Hence has originated that detestable tyranny of the clergy over the laity, in which, trusting to the corporal unction by which their hands are consecrated, to their tonsure, and to their vestments, they not only set themselves above the body of lay Christians, who have been anointed with the Holy Spirit, but almost look upon them as dogs, unworthy to be numbered in the Church along with themselves. Hence it is that they dare to command, exact, threaten, drive, and oppress, at their will. In fine, the sacrament of orders has been and is a most admirable engine for the establishment of all those monstrous evils which have hitherto been wrought, and are yet being wrought, in the Church. In this way Christian brotherhood has perished; in this way shepherds have been turned into wolves, servants into tyrants, and ecclesiastics into more than earthly beings.

How if they were compelled to admit that we all, so many as have been baptized, are equally priests? We are so in fact, and it is only a ministry which has been entrusted to them, and that with our consent. They would then know that they have no right to exercise command over us, except so far as we voluntarily allow of it. Thus it is said: "Ye are a chosen generation, a royal priesthood, a holy nation." (1 Pet. ii. 9.) Thus all we who are Christians are priests; those whom we call priests are ministers chosen from among us to do all things in our name; and the priesthood is nothing else than a ministry. Thus Paul says: "Let a man so account of us as of the ministers of Christ, and stewards of the mysteries of God." (1 Cor. iv. 1.)

From this it follows that he who does not preach the word, being called to this very office by the Church, is in no way a priest, and that the sacrament of orders can be nothing else than a ceremony for choosing preachers in the Church. This is the description given of a priest: "The priest's lips should keep knowledge, and they should seek the law at his mouth; for he is the messenger of the Lord of hosts." (Malachi ii. 7.) Be sure then that he who is not a messenger of the Lord of hosts, or who is called to anything else than a messengership—if I may so speak—is certainly not a priest; as it is written: "Because thou hast rejected knowledge, I will also reject thee, that thou shalt be no priest to me." (Hosea iv. 6.) They are called pastors because it is their duty to give the people pasture, that is, to teach them. Therefore those who are ordained only for the purpose of reading the canonical Hours and offering up masses are popish priests indeed, but not Christian priests, since they not only do not preach but are not even called to be preachers; nay, it is the very thing intended, that a priesthood of this kind shall stand on a different footing from the office of preacher. Thus they are priests of Hours and missals, that is, a kind of living images, having the name of priests, but very far from being really so; such priests as those whom Jeroboam ordained in Beth-aven, taken from the lowest dregs of the people, and not from the family of Levi.

See then how far the glory of the Church has departed. The whole world is full of priests, bishops, cardinals, and clergy; of whom however, (so far as concerns their official duty) not one preaches—unless he be called afresh to this by another calling besides his sacramental orders—but thinks that he amply fulfils the purposes of that sacrament if he murmurs over, in a vain repetition, the prayers which he has to read, and celebrates masses. Even then, he never prays these very Hours, or, if he does pray, he prays for himself; while, as the very height of perversity, he offers up his masses as a sacrifice, though the mass is really the use of the sacrament. Thus it is clear that those orders by which, as a sacrament, men of this kind are ordained to be clergy, are in truth a mere and entire figment, invented by men who understand nothing of church affairs, of the priesthood, of the ministry of the word, or of the sacraments. Such as is the sacrament, such are the priests it makes. To these errors and blindnesses has been added a greater degree of bondage, in that, in order to separate themselves the more widely from all other Christians, as if these were profane, they have burdened themselves with a most hypocritical celibacy.

It was not enough for their hypocrisy and for the working of this error to prohibit bigamy, that is, the having two wives at the same time, as was done under the law—for we know that that is the meaning of bigamy—but they have interpreted it to be bigamy, if a man marries two virgins in succession, or a widow once. Nay, the most sanctified sanctity of this most sacrosanct sacrament goes so far, that a man cannot even become a priest if he have married a virgin, as long as she is alive as his wife. And, in order to reach the very highest summit of sanctity, a man is kept out of the priesthood, if he have married one who was not a pure virgin, though it were in ignorance and merely by an unfortunate chance. But he may have polluted six hundred harlots, or corrupted any number of matrons or virgins, or even kept many Ganymedes, and it will be no impediment to his becoming a bishop or cardinal, or even Pope. Then the saying of the Apostle: "the husband of one wife," must be interpreted to mean: "the head of one church;" unless that magnificent dispenser the Pope, bribed with money or led by favour—that is to say, moved by pious charity, and urged by anxiety for the welfare of the churches—chooses to unite to one man three, twenty, or a hundred wives, that is, churches.

O pontiffs, worthy of this venerable sacrament of orders! O princes not of the Catholic churches, but of the synagogues of Satan, yea, of very darkness! We may well cry out with Isaiah: "Ye scornful men, that rule this people which is in Jerusalem" (Isaiah xxviii. 14); and with Amos: "Woe to them that are at ease in Zion, and trust in the mountain of Samaria, which are named chief of the nations, to whom the house of Israel came!" (Amos vi. 1.) O what disgrace to the Church of God from these monstrosities of sacerdotalism! Where are there any bishops or priests who know the gospel, not to say preach it? Why then do they boast of their priesthood? why do they wish to be thought holier and better and more powerful than other Christians, whom they call the laity? What unlearned person is not competent to read the Hours? Monks, hermits, and private persons, although laymen, may use the prayers of the Hours. The duty of a priest is to preach, and unless he does so, he is just as much a priest as the picture of a man is a man. Does the ordination of such babbling priests, the consecration of churches and bells, or the confirmation of children, constitute a bishop? Could not any deacon or layman do these things? It is the ministry of the word that makes a priest or a bishop.

Fly then, I counsel you; fly, young men, if ye wish to live in safety; and do not seek admission to these holy rites, unless ye are either willing to preach the gospel, or are able to believe that ye are not made any better than the laity by this sacrament of orders. To read the Hours is nothing. To offer the mass is to receive the sacrament. What then remains in you, which is not to be found in any layman? Your tonsure and your vestments? Wretched priesthood, which consists in tonsure and vestments! Is it the oil poured on your fingers? Every Christian is anointed and sanctified in body and soul with the oil of the Holy Spirit, and formerly was allowed to handle the sacrament no less than the priests now do; although our superstition now imputes it as a great crime to the laity, if they touch even the bare cup, or the corporal; and not even a holy nun is allowed to wash the altar cloths and sacred napkins. When I see how far the sacrosanct sanctity of these orders has already gone, I expect that the time will come when the laity will not even be allowed to touch the altar, except when they offer money. I almost burst with anger when I think of the impious tyrannies of these reckless men, who mock and ruin the liberty and glory of the religion of Christ by such frivolous and puerile triflings.

Let every man then who has learnt that he is a Christian recognise what he is, and be certain that we are all equally priests; that is, that we have the same power in the word, and in any sacrament whatever; although it is not lawful for any one to use this power, except with the consent of the community, or at the call of a superior. For that which belongs to all in common no individual can arrogate to himself, until he be called. And therefore the sacrament of orders, if it is anything, is nothing but a certain rite by which men are called to minister in the Church. Furthermore, the priesthood is properly nothing else than the ministry of the word—I mean the word of the gospel, not of the law. The diaconate is a ministry, not for reading the gospel or the epistle, as the practice is nowadays, but for distributing the wealth of the Church among the poor, that the priests may be relieved of the burden of temporal things, and may give themselves more freely to prayer and to the word. It was for this purpose, as we read in the Acts of the Apostles, that deacons were appointed. Thus he who does not know the gospel, or does not preach it, is not only to priest or bishop, but a kind of pest to the Church, who, under the false title of priest or bishop, as it were in sheep's clothing, hinders the gospel, and acts the part of the wolf in the Church.

Wherefore those priests and bishops with whom the Church is crowded at the present day, unless they work out their salvation on another plan—that is, unless they acknowledge themselves to be neither priests nor bishops, and repent of bearing the name of an office the work of which they either do not know, or cannot fulfil, and thus deplore with prayers and tears the miserable fate of their hypocrisy—are verily the people of eternal perdition, concerning whom the saying will be fulfilled: "My people are gone into captivity, because they have no knowledge; and their honourable men are famished, and their multitude dried up with thirst. Therefore hell hath enlarged herself, and opened her mouth without measure; and their glory, and their multitude, and their pomp, and he that rejoiceth, shall descend into it." (Isaiah v. 13, 14.) O word of dread for our age, in which Christians are swallowed up in such an abyss of evil!

As far then as we are taught from the Scriptures, since what we call the priesthood is a ministry, I do not see at all for what reason a man who has once been made priest cannot become a layman again, since he differs in no wise from a layman, except by his ministerial office. But it is so far from impossible for a man to be set aside from the ministry, that even now this punishment is constantly inflicted on offending priests, who are either suspended for a time, or deprived for ever of their office. For that fiction of an indelible character has long ago become an object of derision. I grant that the Pope may impress this character, though Christ knows nothing of it, and for this very reason the priest thus consecrated is the lifelong servant and bondsman, not of Christ, but of the Pope, as it is at this day. But, unless I deceive myself, if at some future time this sacrament and figment fall to the ground, the Papacy itself will scarcely hold its ground, and we shall recover that joyful liberty in which we shall understand that we are all equal in every right, and shall shake off the yoke of tyranny and know that he who is a Christian has Christ, and he who has Christ has all things that are Christ's, and can do all things—on which I will write more fully and more vigorously when I find that what I have here said displeases my friends the papists.

ON THE SACRAMENT OF EXTREME UNCTION

To this rite of anointing the sick our theologians have made two additions well worthy of themselves. One is, that they call it a sacrament; the other, that they make it extreme, so that it cannot be administered except to those who are in extreme peril of life. Perhaps—as they are keen dialecticians—they have so made it in relation to the first unction of baptism, and the two following ones of confirmation and orders. They have this, it is true, to throw in my teeth, that, on the authority of the Apostle James, there are in this case a promise and a sign, which two things, I have hitherto said, constitute a sacrament. He says: "Is any sick among you? let him call for the elders of the church, and let them pray over him, anointing him with oil in the name of the Lord; and the prayer of faith shall save the sick, and the Lord shall raise him up; and if he have committed sins, they shall be forgiven him." (James v. 14, 15.) Here, they say, is the promise of remission of sins, and the sign of the oil.

I, however, say that if folly has ever been uttered, it has been uttered on this subject. I pass over the fact that many assert, and with great probability, that this epistle was not written by the Apostle James, and is not worthy of the apostolic spirit; although, whosesoever it is, it has obtained authority by usage. Still, even if it were written by the Apostle James, I should say that it was not lawful for an apostle to institute a sacrament by his own authority; that is, to give a divine promise with a sign annexed to it. To do this belonged to Christ alone. Thus Paul says that he had received the sacrament of the Eucharist from the Lord; and that he was sent, not to baptize, but to preach the gospel. Nowhere, however, in the gospel do we read of this sacrament of extreme unction. But let us pass this over, and let us look to the words themselves of the Apostle, or of whoever was the author of this Epistle, and we shall at once see how those men have failed to observe their true meaning, who have thus increased the number of sacraments.

In the first place—if they think the saying of the Apostle true and worthy to be followed, by what authority do they change and resist it? Why do they make an extreme and special unction of that which the Apostle meant to be general? The Apostle did not mean it to be extreme, and to be administered only to those about to die. He says expressly: "Is any sick among you?" He does not say: "Is any dying?" Nor do I care what Dionysius's Ecclesiastical Hierarchy may teach about this; the words of the Apostle are clear, on which he and they alike rest, though they do not follow them. Thus it is evident that, by no authority, but at their own discretion, they have made, out of the ill-understood words of the Apostle, a sacrament and an extreme unction; thus wronging all the other sick, whom they have deprived on their own authority of that benefit of anointing which the Apostle appointed for them.

But it is even a finer argument, that the promise of the Apostle expressly says: "The prayer of faith shall save the sick, and the Lord shall raise him up." The Apostle commands the use of anointing and prayer for the very purpose that the sick man may be healed and raised up, that is, may not die, and that the unction may not be extreme. This is proved by the prayers which are used even at this day during the ceremony of anointing, and in which we ask that the sick man may be restored. They say, on the contrary, that unction should not be administered except to those on the point of departing; that is, that they may not be healed and raised up. If the matter were not so serious, who could refrain from laughing at such fine, apt, and sound comments on the words of the Apostle? Do we not manifestly detect here that sophistical folly which, in many other cases as well as in this, affirms what Scripture denies, and denies what it affirms? Shall we not render thanks to these distinguished teachers of ours? I have said rightly then, that nowhere have they displayed wilder folly than in this instance.

Further—if this unction is a sacrament, it must be beyond doubt an effectual sign (as they say) of that which it seals and promises. Now it promises health and restoration to the sick, as the words plainly show: "The prayer of faith shall save the sick, and the Lord shall raise him up." Who does not see, however, that this promise is seldom, or rather never fulfilled? Scarcely one among a thousand is restored; and even this no one believes to be effected by the sacrament, but by the help of nature or of medicine; while to the sacrament they attribute a contrary effect. What shall we say then? Either the Apostle is deceiving us in this promise, or this unction is not a sacrament; for a sacramental promise is sure, while this in most cases disappoints us. Nay—to recognise another example of the prudence and carefulness of these theologians—they will have it to be extreme unction in order that that promise may not stand; that is, that the sacrament may not be a sacrament. If the unction is extreme, it does not heal, but yields to the sickness; while if it heals, it cannot be extreme. Thus, according to the interpretation of these teachers, James must be understood to have contradicted himself, and to have instituted a sacrament, on purpose not to institute a sacrament; for they will have it to be extreme unction, in order that it may not be true that the sick are healed by it, which is what the Apostle ordained. If this is not madness, what, I ask, is madness?

The words of the Apostle: "Desiring to be teachers of the law; understanding neither what they say, nor whereof they affirm" (1 Tim. i. 7.), apply to these men; with so little judgment do they read and draw conclusions. With the same stupidity they have inferred the doctrine of auricular confession from the words of the Apostle James: "Confess your faults one to another." They do not even observe the command of the Apostle, that the elders of the Church should be called for, and that they should pray over the sick. Scarcely one priest is sent now, though the Apostle would have many to be present, not for the purpose of anointing, but for that of prayer; as he says: "The prayer of faith shall save the sick." Moreover, I am not sure that he means priests to be understood in this case, since he says elders, that is, seniors in age. Now it does not follow that an elder must be a priest or a minister, and we may suspect that the Apostle intended that the sick should be visited by the men of greater age and weightier character in the Church, who should do this as a work of mercy, and heal the sick by the prayer of faith. At the same time it cannot be denied, that of old the churches were ruled by the older men, chosen for this purpose on account of their age and long experience of life, without the ordinations and consecrations now used.

I am therefore of opinion that this is the same anointing as that used by the Apostles, of whom it is written: "They anointed with oil many that were sick, and healed them." (Mark vi. 13.) It was a rite of the primitive Church, long since obsolete, by which they did miracles for the sick; just as Christ says of them that believe: "They shall take up serpents; they shall lay hands on the sick, and they shall recover." (Mark xvi. 18.) It is astonishing that they have not made sacraments out of these words also; since they have a like virtue and promise with those words of James. This pretended extreme unction, then, is not a sacrament, but a counsel of the Apostle James, taken, as I have said, from the Gospel of Mark; and one which any one who will may follow. I do not think that it was applied to all sick persons, for the Church glories in her infirmities, and thinks death a gain; but only to those who bore their sickness impatiently and with little faith, and whom the Lord therefore left, that on them the miraculous power and the efficacy of faith might be conspicuously shown.

James, indeed, has carefully and intentionally provided against this very mistake, in that he connects the promise of healing and of remission of sins, not with the anointing, but with the prayer of faith; for he says: "The prayer of faith shall save the sick, and the Lord shall raise him up; and if he have committed sins, they shall be forgiven him." (James v. 15.) Now a sacrament does not require prayer or faith on the part of him who administers it, for even a wicked man may baptize and consecrate the elements without prayer; but it rests solely on the promise and institution of God, and requires faith on the part of him who receives it. But where is the prayer of faith in our employment of extreme unction at the present day? Who prays over the sick man with such faith as not to doubt of his restoration? Such is the prayer of faith which James here describes; that prayer of which he had said at the beginning of the epistle: "Let him ask in faith, nothing wavering;" and of which Christ says: "What things soever ye desire, when ye pray, believe that ye receive them, and ye shall have them." (Mark xi. 24.)

There is no doubt at all that, if even at the present day such prayer were made over the sick—that is, by grave and holy elders, and with full faith—as many as we would might be healed. For what cannot faith do? We, however, leave out of sight that faith which apostolic authority requires in the very first place; and moreover by elders, that is, men superior to the rest in age and in faith, we understand the common herd of priests. Furthermore, out of a daily or free anointing we make an extreme unction; and lastly, we not only do not ask and obtain that result of healing promised by the Apostle, but we empty the promise of its meaning by an opposite result. Nevertheless we boast that this sacrament, or rather figment, of ours, is founded on and proved by the teaching of the Apostle, from which it is as widely separated as pole from pole. Oh, what theologians!

Therefore, without condemning this our sacrament of extreme unction, I steadily deny that it is that which is enjoined by the Apostle James, of which neither the form, nor the practice, nor the efficacy, nor the purpose, agrees with ours. We will reckon it, however, among those sacraments which are of our own appointing, such as the consecration and sprinkling of salt and water. We cannot deny that, as the Apostle Paul teaches us, every creature is sanctified by the word of God and prayer; and so we do not deny that remission and peace are bestowed through extreme unction; not because it is a sacrament divinely instituted, but because he who receives it believes that he obtains these benefits. For the faith of the receiver does not err, however much the minister may err. For if he who baptizes or absolves in jest—that is, does not absolve at all, as far as the minister's part is concerned—yet does really absolve or baptize, if there be faith on the part of the absolved or baptized person, how much more does he who administers extreme unction bestow peace; even though in reality he bestows no peace, if we look to his ministry, since there is no sacrament. The faith of the person anointed receives that blessing which he who anointed him either could not, or did not intend, to give. It is enough that the person anointed hears and believes the word; for whatever we believe that we shall receive, that we do really receive, whatever the minister may do or not do, whether he play a part, or be in jest. For the saying of Christ holds good: "All things are possible to him that believeth;" and again: "As thou hast believed, so be it done unto thee." Our sophists, however, make no mention of this faith in treating of the sacraments, but give their whole minds to frivolous discussions on the virtues of the sacraments themselves; ever learning, and never able to come to the knowledge of the truth.

It has been of advantage, however, that this unction has been made extreme, for, thanks to this, it has been of all sacraments the least harassed and enslaved by tyranny and thirst for gain; and this one mercy has been left to the dying, that they are free to be anointed, even if they have not confessed or communicated. Whereas if it had continued to be of daily employment, especially if it had also healed the sick, even if it had not taken away sins, of how many worlds would not the pontiffs by this time have been masters—they who, on the strength of the one sacrament of penance, and by the power of the keys, and through the sacrament of orders, have become such mighty emperors and princes? But now it is a fortunate thing that, as they despise the prayer of faith, so they heal no sick, and, out of an old rite, have formed for themselves a new sacrament.

Let it suffice to have said thus much concerning these four sacraments. I know how much it will displease those who think that we are to enquire about the number and use of the sacraments, not from the holy Scriptures, but from the See of Rome; as if the See of Rome had given us those sacraments, and had not rather received them from the schools of the Universities; to which, without controversy, it owes all that it has. The tyranny of the popes would never have stood so high if it had not received so much help from the Universities; for among all the principal sees, there is scarcely any other which has had so few learned bishops. It is by force, fraud, and superstition alone that it has prevailed over the rest; and those who occupied that see a thousand years ago are so widely diverse from those who have grown into power in the interim, that we are compelled to say that either the one or the other were not pontiffs of Rome.

There are besides some other things, which it may seem that we might reckon among sacraments—all those things, namely, to which a divine promise has been made, such as prayer, the word, the cross. For Christ has promised in many places to hear those that pray; especially in the eleventh chapter of the Gospel of St. Luke, where he invites us to prayer by many parables. Of the word he says: "Blessed are they that hear the word of God and keep it." (Luke xi. 28.) And who can reckon up how often he promises succour and glory to those who are in tribulation, suffering, and humiliation? Nay, who can count up all the promises of God? For it is the whole object of all Scripture to lead us to faith; on the one side urging us with commandments and threatenings, on the other side inviting us by promises and consolations. Indeed all Scripture consists of either commandments or promises. Its commandments humble the proud by their requirements; its promises lift up the humble by their remissions of sin.

It has seemed best, however, to consider as sacraments, properly so called, those promises which have signs annexed to them. The rest, as they are not attached to signs, are simple promises. It follows that, if we speak with perfect accuracy, there are only two sacraments in the Church of God, Baptism and the Bread; since it is in these alone that we see both a sign divinely instituted and a promise of remission of sins. The sacrament of penance, which I have reckoned along with these two, is without any visible and divinely appointed sign; and is nothing else, as I have said, than a way and means of return to baptism. Not even the schoolmen can say that penitence agrees with their definition; since they themselves ascribe to every sacrament a visible sign, which enables the senses to apprehend the form of that effect which the sacrament works invisibly. Now penitence or absolution has no such sign; and therefore they will be compelled by their own definition either to say that penitence is not one of the sacraments, and thus to diminish their number, or else to bring forward another definition of a sacrament.

Baptism, however, which we have assigned to the whole of life, will properly suffice for all the sacraments which we are to use in life; while the bread is truly the sacrament of the dying and departing, since in it we commemorate the departure of Christ from this world, that we may imitate Him. Let us then so distribute these two sacraments that baptism may be allotted to the beginning and to the whole course of life, and the bread to its end and to death; and let the Christian, while in this vile body, exercise himself in both, until, being fully baptized and strengthened, he shall pass out of this world, as one born into a new and eternal life, and destined to eat with Christ in the kingdom of his Father, as he promised at the Last Supper, saying: "I say unto you, I will not drink of the fruit of the vine until the kingdom of God shall come." (Luke xxii. 18.) Thus it is evident that Christ instituted the sacrament of the bread that we might receive the life which is to come; and then, when the purpose of each sacrament shall have been fulfilled, both baptism and the bread will cease.

I shall here make an end of this essay, which I readily and joyfully offer to all pious persons, who long to understand Scripture in its sincere meaning, and to learn the genuine use of the sacraments. It is a gift of no slight importance to "know the things that are freely given to us of God," and to know in what manner we ought to use those gifts. For if we are instructed in this judgment of the Spirit, we shall not deceive ourselves by leaning on those things which are opposed to it. Whereas our theologians have not only nowhere given us the knowledge of these two things, but have even darkened them, as if of set purpose, I, if I have not given that knowledge, have at least succeeded in not darkening it, and have given others an inducement to think out something better. It has at least been my endeavour to explain the meaning of both sacraments, but we cannot all do all things. On those impious men, however, who in their obstinate tyranny press on us their own teachings as if they were God's, I thrust these things freely and confidently, caring not at all for their ignorance and violence. And yet even to them I will wish sounder sense, and will not despise their efforts, but will only distinguish them from those which are legitimate and really Christian.

I hear a report that fresh bulls and papal curses are being prepared against me, by which I am to be urged to recant, or else be declared a heretic. If this is true, I wish this little book to be a part of my future recantation, that they may not complain that their tyranny has puffed itself up in vain. The remaining part I shall shortly publish, Christ being my helper, and that of such a sort as the See of Rome has never yet seen or heard, thus abundantly testifying my obedience in the name of our Lord Jesus Christ. Amen.

> Hostis Herodes impie,
> Christum venire quid times?
> Non arripit mortalia
> Qui regna dat cœlestia.

THE END

CPSIA information can be obtained at www.ICGtesting.com
Printed in the USA
LVOW12s1154161214

419093LV00001B/146/P